VIRGIN
Mother
CRONE

The scarves the author uses in performing "The Myth of Hera, the Triple Goddess," whose three Persons are Virgin (top), Mother (middle), Crone (bottom). Batik on raw white silk, 39 x 39 inches, painted by Dolores Amore.

VIRGIN
Mother
CRONE

Myths & Mysteries of the
Triple Goddess

DONNA WILSHIRE

Foreword by Riane Eisler

Artwork by
Jim Ann Howard & June Withington

INNER TRADITIONS
ROCHESTER, VERMONT

Inner Traditions International, Ltd.
One Park Street
Rochester, Vermont 05767

. . . .

Copyright © 1994 by Donna Wilshire

Library of Congress Cataloging-in-Publication Data
Wilshire, Donna, 1933–
Virgin mother crone : myths and mysteries of the triple goddess / Donna Wilshire.
p. cm.
Includes bibliographical references.
ISBN 0-89281-494-2
1. Goddesses—History. 2. Mother goddesses—History. 3. Hera (Greek deity)—
History.
4. Trinities—History. 5. Goddess religion. I. Title
BL473.5.W54 1994
291.2'114—dc20   93-25310
                                  CIP

Printed and bound in the United States

10 9 8 7 6 5 4 3 2 1

Text design by Bonnie Atwater

Distributed to the book trade in the United States by American International
Distribution Corporation (AIDC)

Distributed to the book trade in Canada by Publishers Group West (PGW),
Montreal West, Quebec

Distributed to the book trade in the United Kingdom by Deep Books, London

Distributed to the book trade in Australia by Millennium Books, Newtown, N. S. W.

All artwork, unless otherwise noted, is by Jim Ann Howard

For Bruce, Gilbert, Rebekah

The Artwork

. . . .

Preparing the art for this book was not a matter of copying photographs (although I did work from as many photos as I could get my hands on). Rather, I was looking for what the photographs obscured. The presentation style found in museums and archeology books, typified by object isolation, sterile backgrounds, and harsh lighting, emphasizes an emotional distance on the part of the viewer that is inappropriate for considering images of the Great Mother Goddess. My goal was to reinstate a sense of process to these figures by extending my involvement with the subject of my drawing to the very paper on which I was working.

It was apparent to me that the creators of these images had a connection to their environment and their work that was entirely different from what we are accustomed to. They were not making idols; they were acknowledging relationships, claiming kin—not only with the rocks and clay, but with the wind and rain, the moon and stars, the birds and insects, every living thing in a world where everything was living. To this day, I think of sitting in my studio facing a wall covered floor to ceiling with nothing but female imagery, and I smile.

Jim Ann Howard

The Artists

. . . .

Jim Ann Howard, a mixed-media artist, did eighty black-and-white drawings for this book, using for the most part pastel and charcoal on handmade paper. She resides in Manhattan's Upper West Side and maintains her professional studio downtown in Chelsea.

June Withington, a commercial artist in her youth, painted—in her eighty-ninth and ninetieth years—seventeen black-and-white watercolors for this book. She resides in southern California, where she still paints portraits professionally.

Dolores Amore, an artist from Utica, New York, painted the three scarves (cover and frontispiece) on raw white silk.

CONTENTS

. . . .

FOREWORD

. . . .

When I was a child, the words "once upon a time" were like a magic incantation, a passport to a place where fairy queens and princesses dwelled, where the impossible became possible and the world was full of wonder and awe. It was a world that attracted me enormously, even though I did not then know what I do now: that the fact that so many of our fairy tales have female protagonists and so many women with magical powers reflects an earlier time long before girls had to wait for princes to rescue them, a time when women were themselves still powerful.

This is the time that *Virgin Mother Crone* takes us back to, vividly, dramatically, through the magic that only storytellers, like the bards of old who were often also performers, can evoke. Donna Wilshire is such a storyteller-bard-performer, and *Virgin Mother Crone* has grown from her many years of honing and perfecting this ancient art. Unlike the epic tales of Homer, however, which celebrate men's power to conquer and kill—the power to dominate—Donna Wilshire's poetry celebrates a very different power: the power that in my work I have called the power of the Chalice rather than the Blade, the kind of power appropriate for a partnership rather than dominator world.

It is this world that Donna Wilshire charges us to remember in *Virgin Mother Crone*. To re-member, in the sense of again piecing together, so that we may, together, once again create a modern version of such a world. Because, as she writes, one of the most powerful technologies for personal and cultural transformation is a new mythology—a mythology we urgently need in our time, when the Blade is the nuclear bomb and man's fabled "conquest of Nature" threatens our very survival.

So, unlike Homer's epics of martial demigods and hymns to Olympian Zeus ruling from the skies with his thunderbolt and sword, Wilshire's hymns are to Hera. But I should stress here, as Wilshire does, that hers is not the Hera of the Greek Olympian pantheon—already reduced, during the shift from a partnership to a dominator world, to being Zeus's sub-servient wife. Rather, it is the primeval Hera: the archetypal Virgin, Mother, and Crone; the ancient Triple Goddess once venerated as the symbol of a cyclical, self-renewing world, that like all of Nature is a recycling of life, death, and rebirth.

This is why this book is such a gift to all of us—not only as women so long deprived of our integral connection with that which we call divine, but as women and men and boys and girls so long deprived of stories, symbols, and images that validate our real-life, day-to-day experiences, not as of a lesser or base order, than that which is not of this world, but as in their very essence—including the essence of our own bodies—imbued with the divine. It is also why I take such pleasure in writing the foreword to this book.

I first met Donna Wilshire six years ago, when shortly after the publication of *The Chalice and The Blade* she wrote me a wonderful letter. When we met in person we were like long-lost sisters, as if we had known each other all our lives. Already at our first meeting she told me of her plan to write this book, and over the years I followed Donna's labor, a labor of love but still at times a painful labor, as she crafted and recrafted her hymns and her text. So to now see this book, with its beautiful illustrations and evocative content, reach its final flowering is a pleasure indeed—a pleasure that I think will be shared by all who have the opportunity to read and use it.

Riane Eisler
September 25, 1993

ACKNOWLEDGMENTS

. . . .

*O*f special importance to me has been the scholarship, vision, inspiration, and friendship of certain women who have written extraordinary books on the Goddess, in the main: Marija Gimbutas, Elinor Gadon, Buffie Johnson, Catherine Keller, Monica Sjöö, Riane Eisler, and Barbara Walker. A thank-you seems to be too tame and cold a response, but I do thank them for gifts that will never stop giving. The work of Mary Daly, Sonia Johnson, Carol Christ, and Naomi Goldenberg has also had a profound influence on me. And I have been irrevocably changed since meeting Susun Weed, whose intuitive understanding of the Old Ways now undergirds who I am and what I think in many essential ways. Although the writings of many men (including William James, John Dewey, Gilbert Highet, Haim Ginott) have also been a bountiful source of inspiration and knowledge for me, the above-mentioned women and their work have offered a Model and given me a new sense of being a woman that needs a special accounting and thanking.

I wish to give heartfelt thanks to my gifted mother-in-law, June Withington Wilshire. She deserves a rest, but in her ninetieth year—when she might have been doing just that—she gave many days—weeks!—to creating seventeen watercolors for this book, not allowing the arthritis in her fingers and cataracts in her eyes to diminish the quality of her "washes" (her name for her paintings). It is a wonderful feeling to have this courageous, life-full woman be a part of this special project with me.

Quentin Smith and Glen Mazis have drawn me out, challenged me, given unstintingly of their brilliant minds, generous natures, and their unthreatened, unthreatening maleness. Ed Casey read an early version, listened to me, taught me, shared with me his unique vision of the lived-in, remembering body. Gene Clemens read part of the manuscript and pointed out some errors so that I did not have to see them in print. What remarkable men I have for friends! Their willingness to let me test my notions on them and to give honest feedback is a blessing I wish for everyone. Their encouragement and positive reactions to the

Goddess have often revived me and given me the courage to continue this work.

Susan Bordo has been a beloved sister to me; she gave me the opportunity to give the first performance ever of the "Myth of Creation" and the second of "Hera, Triple Goddess." Susan edited and published an article I wrote that turned out to be the general outline of this book. (At the time, though, I didn't know it would become a book.) Marie Cantlon made invaluable suggestions, the most exciting one being that I give the Crone Her own myth-evocation. Marjorie Graybeal and Jean Graybeal made unique contributions, some clear and succinct, some intimate and unspecifiable, all of which have been essential to me. Carol Raftis and Lynn Peters have unfailingly given me encouragement and nourishment and shared their unquenchable love of life—not only a pleasure for me, but a necessity, enabling me to maintain the presence and buoyancy to work sequestered long days and months on my Goddess Model and still thrive.

I am indebted to the audiences with and for whom I created these myth-scripts. There is a powerful two-way street between a performer and her audience. They often thank me for what I give to them, but I too must thank them. Without my audiences and their encouraging, even critical, responses over the years, I would never have found my way out of the old, defended, fear-full shell I grew up in. My audiences have mothered the blossoming of my Self; they have shown me that I have Goddess powers as well as a supportive community.

My editors, Lee Wood, Jeanie Levitan, Gretchen Gordon, Dana Goss, Anna Chapman; designer Bonnie Atwater; and the entire design and production team of Inner Traditions are a blessing to me. Their creativity, attention to detail, and tireless efforts have made preparing a manuscript for publication the joy and cooperative venture it ought to be.

I thank Gilbert and Rebekah for the occasion to perceive the immanent Mother Goddess in myself. I am one woman who really wanted to become a mother; motherhood has been the occasion, the groping process, through which I nourished and found my own Selfhood. You two are the very fiber of my Being, much more than I am the fiber of yours. You fill me with the wonder and joy one must have to understand what is sacred. You will recognize yourselves all through my myths and stories, for through them I try to honor the mystery of life, birth, love, and the continuity into eternity you embody for me.

And I thank Bruce, a Goddess-loving man and my all-time favorite person. The story-telling tradition works for us—for living and learning. He is a bottomless well of information and love, and he is receptive to hearing even the most outlandish propositions I can think of. It is so wonderful when he gets a point I make. And it is wonderful too when he does not get the point; that gives me the opportunity, need, encouragement, and help to discover and clarify what I am on the verge of thinking. Reading and discovering new things by myself is exciting—I do a fair amount of it. But sharing new and old observations out loud with a special someone at all hours and places, getting valuable critiques and appreciative responses (sometimes in the form of bolstering quotations rendered in a sonorous voice), tossing ideas and insights around until they begin to fall into place, take hold, and give meaning to my life is . . . indescribable. Living with Bruce is surely part of the ecstatic whole-making Self-as-Other experience the Pregnant Goddess of prehistory models for all of us.

INTRODUCTION

. . . .

This book is a hymn to womanhood.
Come sing with me.

At the heart of this text are verse portraits of the Great Mother Goddess Hera in Her three aspects or Persons. These three portraits express an ecstatic joy in being female, an intense respect for life and a determination to savor it fully. The basic ideas for these new-old stories come from the research of scholars in many different fields who have discovered in the last few decades much new information about the Great Goddess of pre-history—an Earth Mother who was the first deity of humankind—and the Old Ways out of which She evolved.

Myth-making and storytelling are as ancient and vital as humanity itself.[1] When thinking about what is special about being human, it is interesting to note that only human beings tell tales to one another, sing songs, and carry memories *over many generations*.[2] To primal peoples the Oral Tradition—song, chant, speech, storying—is sacred.

Storying is how we human beings express ourselves *as human*, how we form our values and gain self-understanding. The members of every clan or group generate their own story about who they are—their own *mythos*. Telling and retelling our mythos is the way we create, re-create, and recreate (enjoy) ourselves, the way we sustain our identities, the way we share our personal lives and what has meaning to our group. Our children learn what they can dream and hope for from the stories we tell *and how we tell them*. A vital, realistic account of what it is to be fully human must state that we are the creatures who engage in joyful—even ecstatic—story and song.

Storytelling—creating our own mythos—is the oldest and best way to inspire women and men to be all they can and want to be.[3] It is also the surest, most advanced "technology" we can employ for bringing about change in the world.[4]

CHANGING OUR STORIES

Our world today is in turmoil. There is a
nearly universal disintegration of societal net-
works as well as of the environment. It is time
we had a look at the story we are telling ourselves about what a human being is and what our
proper relationship is to one another and the
earth. It is time to focus hard on our mythos, fer-
ret out any misinformation, any unwarranted beliefs, any destructive, self-fulfilling prophecies—
and change them.

We have grown up hearing stories that debase
this mundane world and our physical bodies, stories that assume competitive hierarchies are built
into Nature, stories that foster in us hopes of
dominating others before they can dominate us,
hopes of someday transcending our bodies and
the earth. These same narratives praise male deities and idealize masculine heroes for their de-
tachment, brute force, and accomplishments in
battle. Our mythos says men are made in God's
image, so maleness is the favored gender in our
sacred texts as well as in our jokes. Maleness, because it is judged to be the ideal, has become the
norm for *all* human behavior and warrants
honor, opportunity, and rewards for men but not
for females or to female-associated behaviors. It
is no wonder that most men and women prefer
their firstborn to be male.

There is no mystery about why maleness is
preferred. Our stories, the source of our values
and role models, portray females as "the
Other"[5]—in the main as helpless maidens in need
of rescue, as idle decorative ladies, as compliant,
service-giving matrons, as nagging shrews, or as
wicked witches. In these idylls females get their
names and Selves from their relationship to
men—whose wife or daughter they are—and no
female is portrayed as God or even Godlike.

This tilted norm—its ideals and stories—have
molded our lives. And yet this competitive, hierarchical Model is not rich and versatile enough
to satisfy basic human longings. It does not tap

deeply enough into human resources—male or
female—to solve the critical problems facing our
planetary society today.

Merely leaving behind the Model of heroic
men and *their* women, limiting as it is, won't suf-
fice. "Symbol systems cannot simply be rejected,
they must be replaced," thealogian [*sic*] Carol
Christ warns, for when there is no replacement a
vacuum develops into which pointless mischief
and nihilism flow.[6] *We must have a new symbol
system, a story that helps us discover what is
valuable about our humanity, a story and Model
that helps us remember what men and women
can treasure about themselves and what we all
can treasure about being earthlings.*

The mythos of the Goddess Hera, as retrieved
in the myths, evocations, and essays of this book,
tells such a story. Although new to us in our
highly developed separate-from-Nature culture,
the values and Model of human nature described
in this Goddess-based symbol system came into
being as our species came into being. It was successful for our matristic forefathers and foremothers for more than thirty thousand years before it was supplanted by a patristic paradigm—
about five thousand years ago.[7]

MEN AND THE GODDESS

Although this book focuses on women and
the Goddess, there is nothing dismissive or derogatory about males here. Men are women's
sons, lovers, partners, brothers, fathers, uncles—
our beloved ones, essential to our Selves. And
from the beginning men practiced the ways of
the Goddess too. *The Iliad*'s Argonaut *heroes*
from Mycenae literally were "Hera's men," She
their favorite protectress.[8] Many men are honored, quoted, respected in these pages—directly
and indirectly. The myths are offered as insights
into the meanings, joys, and possibilities of
women's lives, but they are meant also to offer
serious implications and Models for men.

Men and women both suffer the deficiencies

of our inadequate patriarchal mythos. In a patriarchy only a few men rise to the top of the pyramid of power and authority; all other men are underlings along with the women and other Others. And the so-called fortunate men on top must ever be on guard, ready to fight, in order to stay there. If we succeed in taking the inequities and war out of our world and our relationships, it will be because men and women will both have felt the need for such a change and both will have worked together in mutual respect and affection—in partnership—for it.

As lawyer-scholar-futurist Riane Eisler has written, "The underlying problem is not men as a sex. . . . The root of the trouble lies in a social system in which . . . both men and women are taught to equate true masculinity with violence and dominance."[9] The problem—and the solution—is in the stories we tell.

INSIGHTS AND PATTERNS, NOT ANSWERS

Literal statements are good for describing objective facts, for how a thing-in-itself is *different from* other things, for minutely pinpointing what is happening here-and-now. But for describing overarching principles, for discovering *what unlike things have in common*, or for focusing on the quality of the relationships between people and things, one needs another kind of looking, a less specific, broader, more inclusive way of speaking. For investigating or celebrating these other, more enduring truths, one needs a more powerful and more expressive linguistic medium: one needs primal myth.

Myths are special kinds of stories whose truths come in the form of parables, time-honored metaphors, and sometimes in the form of fantastic, collective images. The caduceus has lost its power for us today because we no longer understand the non-literal sense of two serpents coiled on a winged staff, but for many millennia this symbol served to identify wholistic healing

and unselfish service to others.[10] When people recognized its symbolism, no one needed to give a detailed, factual explanation of what it meant; one glance told a rich, complicated story, full of personal and cultural significance.

Because myths and metaphors are not literal statements of truth, some people see them as "not true," but their way of presenting reality is very powerful. When Jesus spoke of the lilies of the field and mustard seeds, he was not trying to make literal statements—botanical facts did not interest him. He chose to speak in parables, to speak metaphorically about the world, because that form was best for expressing wonder and mystery, for explaining how small, seemingly insignificant life forms share divine love with human beings. Similarly, when a woman complained once that Mary Daly had *reduced* the Goddess to "just a metaphor," Daly responded, "To the contrary: When I say metaphor, I mean something *tremendous*!"[11] Metaphoric truth speaks to such a deep core of our common humanity and the meaning of life that it can justifiably be said: parables, myth, and art are in some ways *more real than mere factual reality*.

Carl Jung described myth as a source of wis-

Caduceus

dom that poetically posits the inescapable essentials and truths of the human condition. Frederick Turner writes: "Myth, that most basic expression of the human spirit, has nerved all civilizations and when destroyed, has left pathology and death in its stead."[12]

Joseph Campbell liked to say, "Myths come from the heart and from experience, even though the mind may wonder why people believe such [fantastic or illogical things]. . . . Myths are great poems; *they don't represent answers but are, rather, attempts to express insights.*"[13]

Insights emerge in our bodies even before we can formulate questions in our minds, much less answers. Myth alerts us to things we know—have wisdom of—in a very deep place without consciously thinking, without being able to put the knowing into factual statements.[14] Once we are put in touch with our own deepest *in-sights* by means of the associations that come to us from certain tried-and-true symbols and metaphors, what we know pre-consciously has a chance of coming into *sight*, into consciousness, to be thought about, and then acted on, if we so choose.

For these reasons I have confidently chosen myth as the medium best suited for composing a portrait of the Great Mother Goddess Hera to share with contemporary people. She is a metaphor for the Life Force that manifests throughout the universe, and She is a metaphor for Femaleness, representing what it means to be female by symbolizing what all women throughout time *have had in common, our Always-So.* Hera does not celebrate one particular great deified woman of antiquity, nor does Her myth claim to offer literal or specific answers to specific women's problems. Her myths do, however, contain insights our foreparents had about the relatedness of all forms of life, and about their joys and obligations as bearers and sustainers of Life.

The Goddess's myths and Mysteries reflect Her people's lifeway, the PATTERNS that sustained them from time out of memory in nurturing, supportive, closely interrelated, mother-centered clans, *at home* in the wilderness. Hera's myths prime us to become aware and respectful of what goes on in-between things and people, to listen to our own intuition and insight, helping us access what we already know about ourselves and the world we live in, albeit not always consciously. These myths can aid us in becoming midwives to our Selves and help us feel *at home* with the wild, unintended, unplanned aspects of our Selves.

No dogma or final answers will be found in these myths, no fixed body of knowledge about a Goddess religion that must be learned. No techniques or rituals must be mastered—ancient or modern. There are no rules or predetermined *oughts* to conform to. You *will* find here stories about another way of looking at women, Nature, and society, stories that utilize other PATTERNS of thinking and other modes of being-in-the-world than can be found in the western tradition.

Primal myth reports such enduring essentials that it is often in the present tense, as in the myth that says "Demeter gives birth to Kore." This story is a metaphor for a regularly occurring event in Nature that everyone depends on for life: "Mother Earth [Demeter] gives birth to Her daughter the grain-corn Seed [Kore] every year, again and again, time without end." The present tense is often used to tell a myth because its stories are timeless. Myth speaks about the essentials of life that never change, about phenomena that count experientially as *the Always-So.*[15] Myth, therefore, is inherently non-linear; its truths do not "progress" or "go anywhere." That is the great virtue of myth, the source of its ability to put us in touch with enduring truths about ourselves.[16]

THE INNER WISDOM TRADITION

*If you do not find the Wisdom and
Mystery of life within yourself, you surely
will never find it without.*

—"The Charge of the Goddess,"
central premise of the Inner
Wisdom tradition

*The wisdom traditions . . . lead one to an
inner poise that allows vivid awareness
and relational insight into all we may
observe and experience in and around us.
They yield revelation, not on demand but
according to the rhythms and creativity of
the cosmos.*[17]

—Charlene Spretnak

One powerful reason for going back to study
Nature religions, to hear the story of the Inner
Wisdom tradition of primal Goddess peoples, is
that many men and women today discover
wholeness and deep healing in it. Often after I
present these Goddess myths to an audience,
people come up to thank me enthusiastically
and say with relief, "I've always known that's
how things are, I just couldn't put it into words
before!" Repeatedly I hear these same words,
along with expressions of deep satisfaction at
beginning to feel "put together" for the first
time.

Reaching into the past for the Goddess
Model of "how things are" is not going backward in a derogatory sense. For me and for
many others it has been *coming home.*[18]

I want to make much of the fact that all the
different sources and materials that have gone
into this book came together into one cohesive
whole *without any conscious intention or deliberate plan on my part.* I only knew what it was I
was doing after I had finished writing. At times I
worked hard and consciously at the research
and composing. Still the process, impetus, and

direction were *not* directed by my calculating
brain but rather by an unplanned, non-deliberate
Necessity inside. Although I enjoyed doing the
work, as a matter of fact, *I had to do it.* I was
compelled from within. And without planning or
having intended it to be, the result reflects the
authentic center of my Self.

So this Necessity was not a cruel taskmaster.
Just the opposite. All that was required of me
was openness; I needed only to allow the invol-
untary, precognitive part of my nature to respond to the mythic images of the Goddess,
allow my responses to manifest and lead me as
they would—to my Self, sometimes to things I
already knew (but didn't know I knew). Several
times I was visited in the middle of the night—
once with Hebe's sounds. "That's it!" I said out
loud and got up to go to the piano to play and
write down the notes that had sung themselves
to me. I later recognized them as the cuckoo's
call, and much later I learned that the cuckoo
was once revered as Hebe manifesting in Her
role as "harbinger of spring." Of course, since
that nighttime revelation, Hebe's bird sound has
been an essential part of the way I express Her.

The Goddess, Her myths, and Her Mysteries
celebrate Inner Wisdom, an openness to and allowing of the emergence of the Necessity inside
all of us. The Goddess's Old Ways constitute a
philosophy, a practice, and a process—a dance
of life—that reveals and treasures the mystery
and "yolk" of our Self. The *yolk* is the nourishing, rich, regenerative core of our Being that
sometimes defies cognitive description but that
we recognize, call on, rely on—not always for
final answers, but always for insights and clues
about what is true and good for us.

This ageless primal way of knowing and
living is wholistic, that is, it is deliberately non-
dualistic. This is the major difference it has with
our tradition. It is the cause of much puzzlement
to those who have accepted that dualisms describe the universe and reality "as it is."

DUALISMS

Let me describe a very clear example of dualistic thinking. In a 1993 television interview, a woman with a shaved head proudly described herself as a "Christian, neo-nazi skinhead." She spoke passionately of her devotion to Jesus and yet defended teaching her child hate and violence against Jews and dark-skinned peoples, claiming this to be God's law. "You can't have love without hate—that's the way God created the world," she insisted. The belief that polar opposites are not resolvable, that they are interdependent, that neither can exist without the other, comes from assuming the universe is constructed out of dualisms, that is, out of inseparable pairs of opposites. This theory claims that struggle and opposition are built into reality, that warring opposites are "just the way things are." The worldview of the Goddess does not make these assumptions. In the Goddess's Way, there is no imperative for evil or for opposition; love requires nothing but itself to exist.

One living example of the wholistic (non-dualistic) philosophy of most primal peoples is an Apache ritual in which one person does a dance of Self-expression inside a circle drawn on the ground with a stick. (I saw a man do it.) Any Other that enters the circle is regarded as a gift of enrichment to the dancer's Self. Be it a bug, the wind, rain, a bird, snake, or person that comes into the dancer's Self-circle, he dances the essence of that Other into himSelf, dances until he has enlarged his own Being by becoming that Other in some essential way.

Many Amerinds experience everything in the universe (literally, "one thing turning") as being related or kin to everything else, and therefore they believe themselves interconnected in some physical, embodied way to all else. In this wholistic philosophy of life, extreme differences are not seen as opposed to each other (as when light and dark are assumed to be opposites and therefore in competition for possession of the sky). Rather, differences complement and enlarge each other in positive ways (as when light and dark are both seen to be necessary for life, taking turns giving their gifts to us, both beautiful and full of special significance and importance to life). In the wholistic paradigm, it is possible to leave out any reference to contrariness (from *contra,* meaning "against" or antagonistic to). It becomes possible for everything to come into perfect balance and harmony all at once, for a person to have it all together, for one to "walk the Beauty Path" and to experience life with no oppositions or evils or contrariness lurking anywhere.

It is written that Siddhartha, the young Buddha, had the great gift of becoming—not merely *like* a stone, a crane, or a tree, but of truly *becoming* those entities. Sharing the lived essence of other Beings is the core shamanic experience that undergirds the Goddess tradition too.

In the dualistic worldview hate is inescapable, said to permeate all basic relationships. In the non-dualistic worldview love resolves all Otherness, turns it into Self.

In a dualistic culture, Self and Other are perceived as forever and irreconcilably in opposition to each other as with the skinheads who consider themselves eternally in battle with all Others, naturally at odds with all who are different from them. This mythos, this belief system, gives social, even theological, permission to any group to prescribe what a normal, natural Self is and then to exclude Others, any who are different from the norm they have decreed, labeling and ostracizing Others as unnatural, as inferior, as polluting. Dualistic thinking is the rationalization behind any group's claiming—or even seeking—purity in themselves or in their philosophy. It is the justification for religious intolerance and for racism and for sexism. If God and all other males are the norm, anything that is not male is Other and inferior.

Of course, Self and Other need not be in perpetual opposition to each other. Positing dualisms as inherent to the universe is a false belief system. Any schism between people and the earth that has been caused by this ideology can be healed by just pointing out examples that demonstrate how the idea of dualisms is incorrect.

Let's have a look at some dyads that are considered dualisms in the patriarchal tradition. When one knows what the problem is, it becomes easy to fix.

GOOD / BAD (or Less Good)
positive / negative
knowledge / ignorance (the occult, taboo)
higher, up / lower, down
spirit / world, nature, earth
mind / body, flesh, womb, blood
light / darkness
reason, the rational / emotion and feelings, the irrational
order, control / chaos, out of control, allowing
objective / subjective
public sphere, outside / private sphere, inside
hard / soft
independent / dependent
individual, isolated / social, interconnected, shared
self / other
MALE / FEMALE

You will recognize that the dyad in each of these dualisms is hierarchical—one automatically and supposedly by its nature has higher value than the other—and these hierarchies and innate values are thought to be in fixed, eternal opposition to one another. I have put the side of each pair that has the "higher" value—the one associated with GOOD—in the left column, and the one that has less worth, in the right column under BAD or Less Good. It surprised me when I first noticed that the words in the GOOD column are typically associated with males in our

culture, and the words in the BAD (or Less Good) column are more typical of or more often identified with females.[19]

Aristotle explained that because the two sides of a dualism are innately unequal, one side naturally "rules over" the other. For example, mind supposedly rules over body, reason rules over emotion, men rule over women, and so forth. Since the lesser entity keeps raising its inferior, lowly self into our affairs, one must exert constant force to keep it down. Struggle, therefore, is experienced as ubiquitous to all of life.

UP/DOWN are not simple direction words in our language; they are loaded with metaphysical implications. As philosopher Mary Midgley observes, "One of the lasting nightmares caused by Copernicus was the fear that *up* and *down* could not function properly.[20] God, after all, was supposed to be *up* in the sky. To worship meant to look up. The devil was *down;* the underworld was his evil domain. Today, *up* is still good and *down* is still bad in our language; values and moral implications about right and wrong are built into the words themselves.

So, despite our scientific advances, this dualism still functions as an eternal *linear* verity at the heart of our thought and value system, eliminating from our consideration the blessings of the Goddess's Underworld *and all of its positive associations,* prejudicing us against—and giving us no positive Model from which to live and speculate about—the *cyclical* in our lives.

This automatic assumption that higher is good gets us into trouble when we least expect it. Influenced by what our group accepts as good or trains us to regard as unattractive or sinful, some label the parts of our indivisible Self as "higher" or "lower." But in doing this, we oblige ourselves to experience part of our Self as unacceptable and to avoid and repress not just anti-social behaviors but the font of spontaneous, sincere feelings at the core of our Self—our truth detector!—that should always be kept open for our own edification and pleasure. (See the discussion of "Hera's Anger" as Divine Wisdom beginning on page 36.) Who has the authority to label anger as negative and "low" when it can inform us so well about injustice? Or to label lust as evil and "low" when it can inform us about the ecstatic possibilities in our bodies for union with one another and The All? These feelings should be treasured as a source of Inner Wisdom. How can we possibly benefit by denying something at the core of our Self, or labeling it "lower," meaning negative and unacceptable? The Goddess Model refuses any attempt to divide a Self against itself into two opposing "sides" or "selves." She is the One-and-the-Many, ultimately the Oneness—the One sacred Self—in Whom all differences are complementary and unified. *In her image,* I am only *one* unified self!

The prejudices in the dualistic mid-set—like the moral values automatically attributed to *up* and *down*—seem harmless to us because we have innocently believed them since we first heard our language, but this mind-set robs us of our wholeness in countless subtle ways. We can easily take the negativity out of *down,* because "low down" means close to our Mother Earth and the nourishing underearth, Her Womb of Creation. The Goddess is a model of seeing all extremes, not as struggling opposites but as many different, complementary moments—all potentially wonderful—in one cycling, changing continuum of experiences. This Model opens to us possibilities that our dualistic thinking has arbitrarily put a lid on and that our traditional use of language has not even let us imagine!

Male/female is a dualism when men are assumed to be superior to women, the natural rulers of women. The dualistic belief system describes the normal, natural relationship between men and women as the "battle between the sexes." The ideology of eternal opposition gave rise to experiencing the penis as a weapon, as a means for man to dominate women. The dualism is dissolved when the penis becomes a

means of connecting the sexes, when it is used as a non-hierarchical joining device for bringing differences of equal value together in cooperation for mutual satisfaction. When men and women each are valued for their special gifts, neither duplicating the other, neither higher than the other, both cooperating, sharing with the other, then the PATTERN of reality between MALE and FEMALE cannot be described as dualistic or in ubiquitous opposition. The battle will not be won; it will, however, have dissolved into non-existence.

The Charge of the Goddess, the basic premise of the Inner Wisdom tradition, contains some key words that usually appear as one half of a dualism, but in this book these words do not carry that meaning. The *inside* of the Self (*within*) is not in opposition to the *outside* (*without*). *Self* is not the opposite of *other*, and *knowledge* is not the opposite of *ignorance*. We need not think, for example, of our body-Self as having an *inside* that is isolated from the *outside* and separated from Others by a boundary of skin. It is possible to conceive of the Self as whole (not finished but not fragmented), as infused with enriching Otherness, as serene, as an ecstatic growing Being something like a vibrant web of incalculable interconnections spinning itself, connecting inside and outside. This Self is not clearly defined, not easily quantifiable, not pre-determined, but is instead open-ended and ever-changing. Such a body-Self is experienced as a *mind-body interacting fully in the environment-universe.* This non-dualistic sense of Self is inclusive of Other; it is at minimum a Self-in-the-world with no clear boundary between inside and outside. In the wholistic tradition, Self-and-Other is perceived as one unit, wired together with the All, however imprecisely.[21]

Thinking of our skin as that part of our Self that serves as an envelope to keep our *inside* Self separate from the *outside* world—as the boundary that distinguishes our Self from every Other—is a limited understanding of human

Self. Our skin is an essential receiving part of our inside Self that cannot be separated from the outside. Our skin—including eyes, ears, tongue, fingertips—automatically records at all times the temperature and any and all other conditions, emotional and atmospheric, that are going on outside but that instantly become part of our inside because of our skin's receiving and transforming functions. Our brain—inside—could not exist or develop, could not do its organizing work, would not be a fully well-functioning, necessary part of our already-Self, if it did not keep working, sorting, sifting the stuff our skin brings in from outside to become additional Self by being processed through the brain inside. The brain is not an entity separate from the world, with the skull serving as the boundary. The brain would not be a brain if it didn't have the outside to process.[22]

As this example shows, trying to establish a fixed boundary between *inside* and *outside* creates at best a blurred distinction. These are good, useful words. We can use them profitably. We need only remember that these areas work *together*—not *in opposition to* each other—and we have to accept that sometimes any difference disappears. Thinking of these as fixed opposites, with one ruling over the other (the objective world outside taking priority over the subjective world inside, or vice versa) blinds us to the harmony and cooperation that play constantly inside, outside, and all around us. Thinking and perceiving dualistically distorts the experience of living. Setting such artificially clear divisions and oppositions does not help us understand ourselves, the world, or our experience of Being-in-the-world. An educated person applies exactitude only to subject matter that requires it.[23]

The non-dualistic concepts inherent in the Inner Wisdom tradition take a while for many westerners to comprehend. In this tradition, *knowing* is wholistic. Western science has prided itself on isolating the things studied from their meaning-giving contexts, but if one is to

know the whole, one must refuse to see things stripped of their environments or contexts. Wholistic *knowing* always integrates *forms* (the separate things in the world) with their *formless implications* (their relationships and meanings). Wholism blends Self with Other and has an innate reverence for life; moreover, the sacred is experienced as ubiquitous in All-That-Is.

Mircea Eliade can help to dissolve the dualism perceived to exist between objective and subjective, between the real and the sacred. In his research Eliade found that for primal peoples basic archetypes or PATTERNS are both real *and* sacred: "For the primitive [person], *symbols are always religious* because they point to something *real* or to a basic *structure of the world*. For on the archaic levels of culture, the *real*—that is, the powerful, the meaningful, the living—is equivalent to the sacred."[24]

An ancient observation by Plotinus also helps us eliminate dualistic thinking. He wrote, "All perceptible things are but signs and symbols of the imperceptible," a succinct way of saying that *forms*—measurable things perceived in the world—can reveal *formless*, unmeasurable "things" like values, meaning, and mystery. Relationships are *formless* but are vital to life. And the meanings that relationships have for us do not exist by themselves; meaning and relationship are *not* clear entities that exist apart from the things related. Relationship and meaning always happen in-between quantifiable forms, in-between things in the present world. So the search for meaning and for what is sacred does not lead us to a separate "disembodied soul," not to "another world," nor to "the hereafter," but back into the life-teeming world itself.[25]

Any of us who want to search for meaning in our lives can let our myth-making, symbol-making ancestors teach us through their myths and metaphors how to look for unseen, basic relationships by using age-old archetypes and PATTERNS. Perhaps we will learn eventually how to devise some symbols, metaphors, and meaningful images of our own. But when we discover meaning, it will have been found right where we might have predicted: in our Selves, our surroundings, and the relationships in-between things in the world.

The core of the Inner Wisdom tradition, as I understand it, is that there is an essential but unmeasurable interdependence between all the forms (things) of the world. And experiencing the way all *forms* work together in the Web of Life—that is, experiencing their *formless* relationships—is what produces meaning, mystery, and the Self-knowing called Inner Wisdom.

THE GODDESS ANANKE

Psychologist and mythologist James Hillman goes into great detail about the Goddess Ananke (pronounced: ahn-AHN-kay) and the sense the word *ananke* (which means "necessity") had in classical Greece—how it meant Fate, doom, burden, that-to-which-one-must-submit, one's "yoke." But he also shows that in pre-classical times the word had a different sense—the one I give it here: inner fulfillment, coming from the core of the Self, "yolk," a close tie or bond, or *a female relative*.[26]

Heroes with angst and other dualists—those who see opposition, confrontation, sin, and suffering everywhere and in everything—have long said that Necessity—rather than being a *yolk*—is a "yoke," a burden, a pre-determined cruel fate imposed from outside one's Self by adversarial forces in nature. Should this "yoke" story be true in some sense—if suffering does exist, imposed from the outside—we need not dutifully reconcile ourselves to it by calling it necessary or letting our total reality be governed by it. The "yoke" philosophy has increased human oppression by encouraging us to accept without protest sexism, racism, class distinctions, violence against people and Nature as "just the way things are," as our karma or fate.

We must finally begin to tell each other the

other truth of our existence. We must begin to emphasize the part about that remarkable, life-loving, caring, wise *yolk* inside each woman and man that is connected to All-That-Is, and do what we can to see that *that* story becomes "just the way things are," that *that* story becomes the mythos that informs our lives and future.

The subject matter of all Goddess's myths—the core of the Inner Wisdom tradition throughout millennia—is that everyone's personal Necessity comes from *within* the Self-in-the-world, from the Goddess (a metaphor for the authentic human Self) at the core of our Being, from life-giving, gift-giving, bounteous Nature within that has a yeasty intimacy with the outside world through one's skin—which is both Self and Other because of its bacteria, microbes, all that it breathes, picks up, transmits, transforms. This philosophy says: our *yolk Necessity* is that part of our Self that desires and insists on growth and becoming. This kind of Necessity tells us who we truly are, what we need, and is the only path to love, ecstasy, and ongoing renewal in life. Respect for the Necessity inside ourselves and others promotes harmony within oneself and between peoples, makes us partners with Nature in the creation of ourselves. The myths of the Goddess merely access this Wisdom of the Self and world—this Wisdom of Being—that each of us already has.

I have named my own Inner Wisdom after the archaic Greek Goddess Ananke. She—my necessity-inside—sends me Becoming into the world. Ananke sometimes manifests when called, although more often She comes unbidden, bringing me gifts of greater value than I would have dared ask for: ideas, music, movements, connections, a sense of what is good and true for me. When I am open to Her, Ananke becomes a lie detector and truth detector, indicating to me what my needs are, what my right relationship to others and the world is, when someone is trying to use me or deceive me, and so forth.

Ananke—my Inner Wisdom—manifests in mysterious ways. Often, when I listen, She lets me know specifically what I must do or say, even what I must avoid or stop doing. Sometimes I find myself knowing that "I must sing!" or "I must go live where the earth is red" or "I must be about my Mother's business now" or "I must be with my daughter more often this month" or "Today I am Eagle!"

Socrates advised that everyone listen attentively to her or his own Inner Voice. This famous teacher, "the wisest man of antiquity," gives credit to his own teachers, two midwives, both practitioners of the Old Ways: his mother and the venerable priestess Diotima. Listening to their Inner Voice has always been the way that midwives, artists, and other creative people live and work.[27] Listening to an Inner Voice is the way all myths began—in the collective thinking and dreaming of a tribe or a clan about their place in the world, about their lives and joy, about their yolk, Necessity.

Ananke—a timelessly old shamanic Goddess—offers the only reliable source of advice for contemporary women and men to discover new paths, models, and ideas as we shuck off the old restricting ones and struggle and seek to find out who we are, who we might be, and how we can best relate to one another. I often repeat Her name to affirm and confirm Her presence and acknowledge my received, as well as my as-yet-unknown, possibilities and joys.

Ananke.

WISE WOMAN WAYS

My methods and basic philosophy about the Goddess closely resemble those of herbalist Susun Weed. Susun looks at everything that comes into her life as an opportunity or, using our favorite metaphor, as if everything brings some form of blessing from the Goddess. In *Wise Woman Herbal* she writes that even our worst problems carry gifts from Mother Nature

if we learn to recognize them. "Ask yourself these Wise Woman questions: How is this problem my ally? What gifts or insights does this problem or illness bring? If I accepted my problem as a gift, how would this make me, and the world, more whole?"[28]

For Susun this ally can be some very specific information about one's lifestyle and values or a more general opportunity for self-knowledge and self-empowerment. It can be a chance to become less isolated, a chance to give and receive support that helps one contribute to making a stronger community and world for oneself and others.

Susun uses the following mantra to help her focus her daily actions so that she will stay attuned to her blessings and always remain in harmony with the timeless values of the Wise Woman Ways of the Goddess: "May what I do now be pleasing to my grandmothers, the ancient ones. And may it be of benefit to all beings." This echoes the saying common in the Oral Tradition of many Amerinds, including the Wolf Clan of the Seneca Nation: "In our every deliberation we must consider the impact of our decision on the next seven generations."

Susun's questions and deceptively simple mantra help me in my search for something more *primal* than I have known before. By primal I mean something basic and essential at the core of being alive and being human, something whole-making and generous to myself and others, something sensual about bonding with others. The primal is something that our western patriarchal culture systematically represses and considers wild, uncivilized, unacceptable, attributing baseness to it and sensing it as competing with traditional values for our "higher Self and soul."

This primal way of living focuses on our being earthlings, on the gifts of Nature, on togetherness, on the ecstatic possibilities in being alive. Heroic patriarchy, on the other hand, tends to emphasize isolated individualism, stoic suffering, angst, obligatory lessons to be learned. This masculinist tradition tends to seek knowledge and truth from authorities *out there* (revelations from sky deities, from any rules or orderings determined from above, handed down from the heavens or from a throne) rather than from one's innate *Wisdom within*. Heroes like to adopt a fearful, hostile, defensive warrior stance toward Nature, deeming the world full of deceit, illusion, or evil, trying to conquer it by force or to transcend or withdraw from it, rather than trying to discover Nature's principles in the world and in one's own center through wonder, respect, empathy, engulfment, and gratitude. (Significant differences between the masculinists and matristic traditions and the different social PATTERNS they exemplify are discussed in Chapter 6, "Mother Consciousness," and charted in Chapter 11, "Male and Female Deities Who Create the Universe.")

Modeling ourselves on solitary heroes and the masculinist myth that places highest value on opportunistic individualism and transcendence (for example, spiritual, unsexed, out-of-body experiences and knowledge from the heavens) has turned our culture into *the Lonely Crowd,* an alienated society priding itself on its objective facts, into greedy, goal-oriented seekers vainly asking "What does it all mean?" But we will not find meaning or wholeness in a solitary, heroic quest; paradise—a rich life full of meaning—can only be found in intimate relationship with our embodied Selves, with Others, and with our home, the Earth.[29]

The Goddess's Inner Wisdom tradition promotes awareness that all life is of and in this material world-universe (not some immaterial otherworld "out there"), that all life is sacred (not fallen, illusory, or evil), and that life is meant to be lived and shared ecstatically (not dutifully). In this Old Way one can fearlessly embrace All-That-Is and passionately accept one's full Self, one's whole body, all emotions and dreams. The Goddess Way is a leap into life.

The sacred stories of the Goddess Hera's three Persons and Her Mysteries tell about this leap. For when one becomes most aware and full of life, rather than certainty, the mystery appears. And then, even the telling is dangerous, for then myth-making, the singing, the leap into life all become a leap into the unknown. Both the Virgin and the Crone model uncertainty and mystery as paths to Inner Wisdom—each in their own consciousness, in their own way of knowing and being.

USE OF SOURCES

The primary sources for the material and critiques in this book are the *experiences of women*, past and present. The Tao advises: Be empty of ego and dogma and *full of experience*. This approach constitutes the underlying mode for this book. For a book about women and the Goddess, it is entirely appropriate that the primary sources for the information and Model be the experiences of women. One of my tutors in this practice has been Mary Daly, who points out that any text authored by a man, living or dead, is of necessity a secondary source for women, although Daly uses them as important "springboards,"[30] as do I.

Experience is a difficult source to propose or use, for its validity is belittled in our dogma-bound western tradition. We are told by our religions and by science to suspect our own experience, which supposedly leads only to sin and error, to unreliable "subjectivity," and to the deceptions of a worldview demeaned as *naive realism*. Any brief examination of the history of religious and political dictatorships, however, shows that familial, cult, and mob tyrannies occur when people are deprived of trust in the validity of their own experiences, emotions, and powers of observation by parents, priests, or other benevolent despots who claim the authority to think, feel, and decree for others. I have found that abandoning my own experience as a guide leaves me without a sense of truth, with no basis for making decisions in any area, and prey to abuse and subjugation. Learning to focus on one's experience gives a person a strong center for living, for making choices, for evaluating the opinions and advice of others as well as for choosing one's own sacred mythos.

Our lived experiences as women will help us ask and answer the all-important questions that will determine our lives, mythos, and futures. We should especially question the sacred patriarchal stories, asking, Does that Model or metaphor correspond with my experience? For example, when our own experience tells us that only women give birth, that only females create life out of their own bodies, how can the so-called sacred story about First Man's creating life (in effect, giving birth) out of his body provide us with an affirming, truthful metaphor to live by? Or does this reversal of roles—this stealing of a female prerogative, an archaic patriarchal practice that Samuel Noah Kramer called "priestly piracy"[31]—foster insecurity in us by male authority figures? Does it float us in neediness by teaching us to believe without question ideas that defy Nature and contradict our own experience about the origin of human life?

Learning to trust the experience of living in our own bodies can help us ask and answer the question: Is the spiritual practice being proposed right for me? Does it honor and sustain me as I am, or must I submit myself to unnatural changes, to hard lessons and esoteric disciplines, before I am good enough to receive its promised state of bliss? In following this Way can I have blessings, peace, and love just as I am, or must I, in order to receive the proffered sanctity, imagine my insides—which are naturally full of close-and-holy darkness—flooded unnaturally with light that enters through a make-believe hole in the top of my head? Do the suggested mythos and imagery confirm me as I am as part of sacred Creation? Do they help me acquire confidence in myself and love for myself as I am?

Only the habit of weighing a mythos against one's own experience and insights can provide one with an authentic Self and protection against violation or from becoming a mindless, Self-abnegating follower. This book has been compiled by me using my experience as my lie-and-truth detector and as my one inviolable source and standard for what is desirable and good.

I wish my efforts here to serve as recognition of the intelligence of our foreparents and of the basic human PATTERN and Way they lived throughout pre-history. Even though their technologies were not very advanced by our standards, their values and societal structures that were based on the life-giving and life-sustaining values of women's bodies and lives were emotionally and spiritually sophisticated, by any standards. The lifeway of our matristic ancestors has been a powerful source of information and insight, opening up a whole new life for me, as well as some astonishing new ways of learning. It is impossible to discover the primal wholistic Way, its values, and point of view by studying more thoroughly the great men and Great Books of the linear, dualistic western tradition. So if we are to imagine and story ourselves whole (not aiming to be finished, just not fragmented), and if we are to envision and bring about a future in which earth and earthlings thrive together, we must consult non-traditional sources, most especially the experiences of women throughout the ages—even though not all of these sources come to us in writing.

I have studied the written work of many creative, courageous, contemporary scholars and artists—both men and women—who have been recently (in the main only for the past twenty-five years) rediscovering and redescribing the Old Ways as virtuous, as non-dualistic, and as containing wisdom we today might consult. I have incorporated many of their viewpoints into my Self and owe all of them a great debt, although I can no longer always remember from whom I learned what I know or whom I copied to become who I am. The exciting work of Model building is a collaborative effort; it does not progress and accumulate along a straight, sure path. Each of us makes our contribution using the work of others, so I cannot claim that any of the insights and visions in this book are uniquely my own. Each of us does bring her or his own judgment and values to the task, though, and I have constantly made my own judgments, selections, and choices as to what I deem important in the research on the matristic Model, what fits it, and what does not.

When specific credit can be given, I have provided detailed notes. But in the final analysis, any book about matristic traditions is only a step in the right direction. All any book can do is serve as a clue toward understanding. Women's lives and experiences—as well as the Old Ways—are a process, not a collection of facts, and the world and life itself are the primary sources for learning about such things. Although one can definitely learn much and be guided and prompted by written (that is, "secondary") sources, the point is to refocus our attention to the immediate, primal, primary material web of our embodied, worldly experiences and to reap the profit of that Way. I have learned to listen for and to things I had never heard before a decade ago. I have begun to study Nature as my guide-Self. I have learned to dance my Power Animals so that I can receive their strength, guidance, and information. I have learned how to learn from birds, greens, stones, from my drums and my dijeridu. I here honor and credit these and other sources, unspecifiable as they have been essential. They have brought me unwritten but vital knowledge about female-associated things like non-linear time, process, non-goal-oriented and Earth-based values.

In composing these myths I have looked for the basic Always-So PATTERNS that have been characteristic of women's lives and of the All-Mother wherever and whenever She has been found: in the Middle East, China, Old Europe,

the Americas, Africa, Australia. I have tried to preserve accurately the general essence of the sacred Female, while selecting specific images from different places to emphasize. I have sorted through the ancient symbols, documents, and rituals, leaving out some things and modifying and embellishing other things that spoke to me as being important and helpful, combining information from many different places into the three myths I tell here.

I have with particular care researched archaic (pre-patriarchal) Hera, and I believe these three portraits of Her Persons are reliable reconstructions of what is known about Her at this time.[32] Still, I can point to no one culture as having a Goddess exactly like the one described here as Hera. For example, in the song the priestess sings on Hera's sacred Coupling Couch (in Chapter 8, "The Myth of the Triple Goddess") the words "my sweet honey man" and "he will adorn me with agates" are taken from a hymn written more than four thousand years ago to celebrate the wedding of the Goddess Inanna,[33] a Sumerian cognate of the Semite Goddess Ishtar and similar to Hera with respect to Her sacred Couch. I cannot cite a written source that proves these words about Inanna are perfect for Hera, but my studies of comparative mythology and my experience as a woman lead me to judge that they are. The Hera you find here is a composite; that does not make Her inauthentic.[34]

I have selected from the artifacts, drawings, footprints, carvings—the relics of our foreparents' lives and outlooks—to shape these stories with two things in mind. I hope, first, that they help a contemporary woman or man understand the core of primal people's experience and how it parallels our own, the strengths of mother-centered kinship groupings with their wholistic worldview, and how such things might enrich our own groupings and worldview. And second, I hope to share through the Goddess's myths and Mysteries the meaning womanhood has for me.

You will find here different kinds of recountings. Often I tell some part of an archaic story as authentically and simply as possible. Sometimes I dramatically develop an ancient theme or plot in order to explain more fully for a contemporary reader the meaning it had for the original tellers —as best as I can with the evidence I could find.

Scholars can tell us a great deal about the religions and practices of some early Goddess-revering peoples, but there can be no extant myth, *per se*, of preliterate peoples. They left us only as much of their stories as can be "read" from their relics, symbols, images, and architectural ruins. Therefore, in re-creating a prehistoric mythos or belief system, of necessity I constructed a skeletal story-form on which to display poetically and dramatically the factual information scholars have gleaned from the extant artifacts. For example, in writing "The Myth of Creation" I carefully selected and arranged many Goddess symbols and images that illustrate the concept of Her divine immanence. The images are authentic—neither I nor the artists have doctored them in any intentional way. But in general the form and words of the story are mine.

SOME TECHNICALITIES

1. I *capitalize* words that represent what I hold in awe and kinship, images or ideas that point to the basic structure and meaning of life for me. Since I am trying in this book to point out a different way of looking at the world than can be found in our tradition, capitalizing certain words helps me show clearly what is special to me or what is considered sacred in the myths, especially things demeaned by our western culture. The device serves its purpose when capitalized words—like Goddess, Nature, Her Body, the Earth, Becoming—slow down the pace and help readers look at these things in a new way or context.

   Consistency, however, will be found only in the meanings of the words. For example, I use a capital *N* when Nature means the Oneness of All-That-Is, but I use a small *n* when I speak of human nature or the nature of life in general. I capitalize the Goddess who is my divine Model of wholeness but not the classical goddesses—and I write "model" with a small *m* when it is a verb or is not my ideal standard. "She" means the Goddess, while "she" is an ordinary woman; "Virgin" is the Goddess or the Sacred Maiden archetype while "virgin" is an ordinary maiden. And so forth. This rule for capitalizing words is a good one, but sometimes I let the device serve me without sticking precisely to the rule, for occasionally, randomly, I use a capital letter simply to draw attention to the Possibilities that accrue from looking in a more sacred way at one particular word or concept. Rules and answers are not the subject matter here; insight is. So I use any and every device that can provoke insight.

2. The abbreviation B.C.E. means "before the common era"; it indicates the same date that B.C. does. The abbreviation C.E., "of the common era," corresponds to A.D. Many scholars now use these abbreviations, since they do not require non-Christians to use words that imply religious devotion every time they put a date to a historical occurrence. B.P. means "before the present."

3. Endnotes document the sources of some of my information and often contain additional information or books for further reading. Still, it seems important to me that the book can be read satisfactorily without once consulting an endnote.

4. I emphasize looking at and for PATTERNS, processes, and things in contexts rather than at individual things observed in isolation. I put the word PATTERNS in capital letters to make an important point about the Goddess Model and Way of Seeing. Western science has traditionally sought knowledge by study-

ing things in isolation—in laboratories, under microscopes, free from the uncontrollable variables in the natural environment. It has been the pride of such scientists to try to describe each thing studied as a thing-in-itself. Many critics of this method see the deliberate stripping away of the contexts and relationships in which things originated and have their *raison d'être* as an unacceptable limitation on what can be learned—perhaps a distortion of reality. Many think that a fuller, truer understanding of Nature can be acquired by looking for the overall PATTERNS and processes that swirl together and overlap in Nature, influencing one another. Of course, observing things-in-contexts, things interacting with and impacting on other things and with their whole environment, is far more difficult than observing isolated things and behaviors in a laboratory.[35]

Looking for PATTERNS and relationships in Nature is at the heart of the Old Ways, another instance in which we can learn from our ancestors and go home to find out more about our Selves and our world. Looking for PATTERNS, relationships, and natural contexts or environments is also the starting point of the new science of ecology. This environmental science tries to account for things and phenomena as they actually exist and function in their never fully predictable normal surroundings, no artificial controls being placed on what is studied. The methods and goals of such scientific endeavors sacrifice the extreme accuracy that the scientists in laboratories can aspire to. But context-oriented investigators are willing to sacrifice highly precise measurements in order to gain a broader, more comprehensive understanding of the larger PATTERNS at work in Nature.

Some physicists today deny that things can be precisely located, and many describe some aspects of reality as indeterminable.[36] Some have abandoned the search for any "pure" thing-in-itself, proposing instead "chaos theory" and "complexity theory" to explain the workings of the universe.[37] Many—like ecologists—pursue the contextual way of looking at the world and of analyzing data; they often follow an out-of-the-laboratory methodology appropriate to a "systems" or "field" theory. And many insist that "fuzzy logic" or the "fuzzy systems theory" is a truer way of explaining natural phenomena and of making predictions than "hard" western science can offer.[38]

The contextual way of perceiving Reality is central to understanding the Goddess, for She is never quantifiable, never "one thing in Herself." Rather She always represents many special things *and* at the same time represents their relatedness to one another, "the Way" they are interrelated, the PATTERN they reveal, and what that PATTERN means for our lives. She is the Much-At-Once, the Web that reveals the basic PATTERNS and connections of Nature—the in-betweens.

The tendency of western speakers and readers is to search for purity. We all tend to try to identify one single decontextualized thing or individual in every example. By keeping the word PATTERN in capital letters, we can maintain the focus on seeing each thing mentioned, not for itself alone, but as it fits into a web of interrelated entities.

May storytelling and song be for you all—for all men and women—a manifestation of Ananke, the Goddess who personifies Self-creation and Inner Wisdom as our Necessity and Ecstasy. May reading the myths of Hera and exploring Her Mysteries evoke a way of knowing and being that excites your Wise Woman and nourishes your love of life.

Ananke.

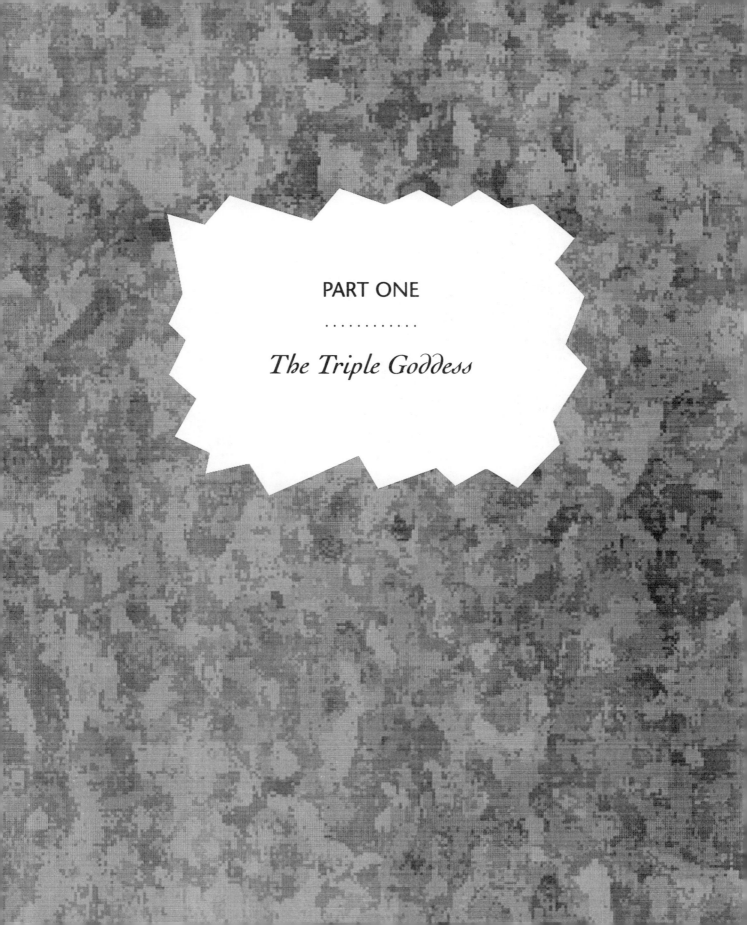

PART ONE

. . . .

The Triple Goddess

The Great Mother Goddess from Laussel. France, c. 25,000 B.C.E.

One

· · · ·

THE TRIPLE GODDESS

Virgin-Mother-Crone

> *Let it be understood from the start that we are not dealing with one goddess [who is the female equivalent of God]; we are discussing diverse realizations of a single magico-religious idea. This idea is embodied in figures that are not identical, but equivalent, having evolved from the same generative impulses among disparate . . . peoples. . . . Such a figure cannot be cataloged in detail. Goddesses merge into one another with the ease of the three shape-shifting Celtic Morrigan, who transforms from eel [symbol of Virgin][1] into heifer [Mother] into crow [Crone] while we impatiently insist that they [She] stand still to be described.[2]*
>
> —Pamela Berger

*T*hirty thousand years ago, people who were genetically like us made images celebrating their primordial deity, the Great Goddess, an awe-filling, if somewhat amorphous, Nature and Earth Mother they revered as Source of Life and Great Mystery of Life.[3] Those who inhabited a hillside shelter under a natural stone overhang (near what is now the town of Laussel in the Dordogne of France) noticed "hovering" above them on a stele at the end of a long protected terrace some natural curves and bulges that resembled the body of a woman with pregnant belly and pendulous milk-full breasts.[4] Someone chiseled around the edges, enhancing the outline of this Female Presence that had manifested naturally in the limestone. And then the numinous figure was painted with red ochre, emphasizing the people's perception of Earth-Rock as wondrous Mainstay, Source, and Life-giving Nurturer.[5]

The left hand of this limestone icon points matter-of-factly to Her pregnant belly and pubic area, while the right arm holds up an ibex horn resembling a moon crescent with thirteen lines cut into it, each mark made by a different instrument, presumably at different times.[6] It is impossible to say precisely what the incised horn meant, but Alexander Marshack, who has done extensive work on Paleolithic symbols, considers it a time-factoring device: a lunar calendar. He writes, "There was a tradition of lunar notation as early as the Aurignacian-Perigordian," that is as early as 32,000 B.C.E.[7] He proposes the possibility that the faceless head is also meant to represent the moon.

Marshack hypothesizes that the "'goddess' with the horn" from Laussel is "a forerunner of later Neolithic, agricultural variants. . . . The Goddess who was called 'Mistress of the Animals' had a lunar mythology, . . . was associated with . . . the lunar crescent, the crescent horns of the bull, the fish, the angle-signs of water, the vulva, the naked breasts, the plant, flower, bird, tree, and snake."[8]

Lest anyone surmise that the great age of the Laussel image indicates primitive simplicity, Marshack writes, "My study of the 'female' im-

ages indicates a mythology and use of the image more complex and diverse than [including but not limited to] that of goddess of hearth and hunt and ancestress of the clan." He notes that the images "played a number of specialized and generalized roles across the complex, integrated, time-factor[ing] culture . . . [including] a complex animal mythology associated with symbol and notation."[9]

A growing number of researchers in various fields see a high probability that for more than thirty millennia reverence for this cosmic "'goddess' with the horn" continued unbroken in its essential nature—that is, in the perception that femaleness, cyclicalness, and the Sacred are ubiquitous and immanent in Nature—with any changes in symbology reflecting cultural modifications necessitated by a change of homeland or a change of land use, such as after the invention of agro-technology.[10] This makes the Great Moon–Animal Mother Goddess of pre-history not only the forerunner of the Neolithic Goddess who frequently bore the titles Mother of All and Mother of the Gods but also the ancestress of Christianity's Mother of God, whose litany of titles is much like the Mother Goddess's titles and who is often pictured and other-

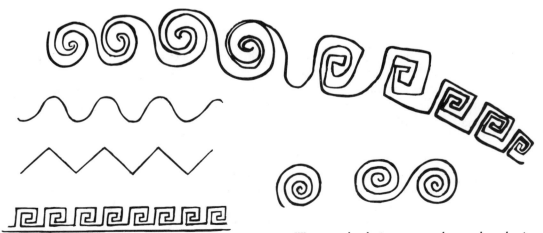

Water-snake designs; meanders and angle-signs of water; growth-stimulating motifs

Double triple-spiral. Stone carving representing numinous cycle of Birth-Death-ReBirth, found in the middle niche (one of three) at the rear of the womb chamber inside Newgrange mound, a sacred site that overlooks Ireland's Boyne River. The river was named for Goddess Bøand, a Celestial Cow Mother Goddess whose "milk" was received by Her people as rain and rivers. There are three different double triple-spirals carved at this site, c. 3200 B.C.E.

wise associated with the moon.[11] Her pregnancy, too, is sanctified, as in "Blessed art thou . . . and the fruit of thy womb."

The archaeological record shows that during that long unbroken period—for thirty thousand years—animals with crescent or spiraling horns (like rams, cows, and bulls) remained sacred to the Goddess.[12] And although the pair of crescent horns sometimes belonged to male animals, they had female calendric associations symbolizing the lunar-month cycle (from waxing crescent through waning crescent) that coincided synchronously with the cycle of women's menstrual bleeding. Moon-horn crescents and spirals also symbolized the year's cycling through its seasons, and by extension they were metaphors or reminders of all the Birth-Death-ReBirth cycles of the cosmos. It is therefore not farfetched to hypothesize, as Marshack and many other scholars do today, that the Great Mother of Laussel[13] holds in Her hand humankind's oldest preserved calendar, recording one year as thirteen lunar-menses cycles. Always the Great Goddess embodied the cycles and attributes of Nature, as She simultaneously depicted the cycles and attributes of Everywoman.

THE THREEFOLD

The relics and symbols that remain of our oldest deity reveal that She—while ever experienced as Oneness, as the whole of many interrelated parts—was often perceived to manifest in three general aspects, each a cosmic reflection of the functions and roles of an ordinary woman—of a virgin-maiden, a mother, or a crone. The Goddess's title *Virgin* stood for Her cosmic Life-Giving aspect; She was the Pregnant One, the Source, who created by giving birth. (It must be noted here that historically "virgin" does not mean "celibate" but rather refers to "an autonomous female who belongs to herself.") The *Mother* or Nurturer is the One who nourishes and sustains Life from the abundance of Her own Body's flesh and fluids. And the *Crone* or Death-Bringer is known as "Changing Woman," She who reclaims all spent forms back into Her cauldron-womb where She ever remixes them, reshapes them, transforming them into new possibilities which She then gives birth to. Obviously, the Death-bringing Crone does not represent a final ending. The Triple Goddess continues always to flow and shift; after bringing death She once more brings life, becoming the Creatrix, Regenetrix, the Life-Giving Virgin again.

Her shape-shifting follows the cycle of the year, each season having a distinct character, yet each flowing without clear boundary into the others: the Virgin is the springtime—*the Blossoming One*; the Mother is the summer—*the Fruiting One*; the Crone is the fall-winter—*the One who goes to Seed*, dies, and falls back into the Earth's dark womb from which She is ReBorn as *the Blossoming One* again. Thus the shape-shifting, all-encompassing Goddess is the personification of the unending, unbroken sacred cycle of Birth-Death-ReBirth found throughout the cosmos. Nature is experienced as the Goddess's ever-changing, cycling, divine Body-Self-Wisdom.[14] Or as described by Marija Gimbutas:

> The process of seasonal awakening, growing, fattening, and dying was seen as connecting humans, animals, and plants: The pregnancy of a woman, the fattening of a sow, the ripening of fruits and crops were interrelated, influencing each other. . . . The rising and growing powers of earth dwell in all living things. Each protuberance in nature, be it a mound, a hill, on a menhir or on a female body—belly, buttocks, breasts, knees—was sacred.[15]

THE TRIPLE GODDESS HERA

One form of this threefold Goddess, which survived into recorded history sufficiently intact that some distinctive highlights of Her pre-patriarchal religion remain decipherable, is archaic Hera. Extant temples, artifacts, tablets, and other relics give us enough rich details and vivid pictures to make a satisfying reconstruction of Her. What is known about Hera is augmented in the myths in this book by many of the core attitudes and cultural values inherent in the earliest instances of the Great Goddess, who was known variously as the Life-Giving All-Mother; Mother Earth; the Triple, Triune, or Threefold Goddess; the Great Mystery of Life; the Goddess of Ten Thousand Names and Guises; the Goddess of Death and Regeneration; and so forth.

Hera's three sacred aspects or Persons represent the same archetypes as does Morrigan: Virgin, Mother (or Woman-in-Her-Fullness), and Wise Old Crone. These three divine Persons, metaphorically representing the natural cycle of the year and all women's lives, are found in widely separated places and millennia from early human times.[16] This Triple Goddess mythos with its rich symbolism and network of meanings is, therefore, the closest thing we have to a pan-human archetypal system, mythos, or PATTERN.[17]

Archaic Hera and the Great Goddess of prehistory are not identical. Hera's people were primarily Neolithic farmers, while the Great Goddess was first fashioned by Paleolithic foraging clans. Although widely separated in time, the two Goddesses are cognates in important ways and reflect the cultural, philosophical, and religious attitudes their different peoples had in common.

The peoples of both ages felt great awe and reverence for the Mystery of Birth and Death and the Renewal of Life, not just in humans but in the entire cosmos. Divinity and the cycle of Birth-Death-ReBirth were experienced as immanent in Nature, and Nature's life-giving, nurturing PATTERNS were observed as being basically female. Female PATTERNS in fact were perceived as the core and Source of Being, giving human Life its meaning. Inheritance and descent —for individuals as well as for whole clans— was matrilineal, meaning kinship was determined by and through one's mother. For obvious reasons this is often termed the "blood kin," "blood relations," or "mother-rights" PATTERN.[18] Yet, although these societies were mother-*centered*, they were not mother-*ruled*.

Mothers could persuade, then as now, but they did not command, since no one played such a role. Cultural historian William Irwin Thompson explains that "there may have been a mother's brother [that is, caring uncles] in 8000 B.C., but I doubt if there was any such animal as a 'husband' [or 'father'] and certainly not a 'lord and master.'"[19]

Flexible, peacefully alternating, shared leadership PATTERNS included both sexes in important work-rituals, but there were no rulers or paramount chiefs.[20] Riane Eisler has coined the word "gylany" to describe this cooperative, non-hierarchical societal PATTERN.[21] No one could wield effective power over others in foraging groups that were constantly changing and fluctuating in their makeup. Rather, according to Dolores LaChapelle, men and women took turns being chiefs (or more aptly, "project leaders") as everyone shared the commune's responsibilities by taking turns taking the lead in different group activities. "There was a chief in charge of hunting deer, a chief in charge of hunting rabbits ('the rabbit boss'), a chief in charge of gathering camas or gathering huckleberries," and so forth, and any of these leaders could be female or male, depending on the circumstances.[22] Furthermore, women-only and men-only rituals in places-set-apart offered men and women opportunities for gender esteem and gender solidarity in addition to the opportunity for marital pair-bonding.

Because of these and other real and important similarities between their peoples, archaic Hera is a descendent of, and an authentic form of, the Great Goddess of pre-history. The similarities between these two beloved, awesome, immanent Goddesses (and the wholistic PATTERNS they represented and modeled) reveal the essence and continuity of our species over countless millennia. The immanent Goddess and a non-hierarchical matristic societal PATTERN prevailed from the earliest days of humankind until the third millennium B.C.E., when hierarchical patriarchy with its transcendent deities (patriarchy came as a package, bringing us rulers in the sky as well as rulers on earth) began to take hold in the Middle East and eventually became our dominant social PATTERN.[23]

In the worldview and social PATTERN that these two Goddesses epitomize lie some clues to the innate potential we human beings have for living peacefully together, for nurturing and sustaining ourselves and our habitat. The Goddess Model and PATTERN are worth close scrutiny today, a pivotal time when the survival of the environmental conditions and societal attitudes that are necessary for animal and human life to flourish are at risk of disappearing.

HER IMMANENCE

The title Virgin-Mother-Crone reflects the Goddess's origin in the natural stages of ordinary women's lives. Rather than being a deification of an exceptional woman ancestor or an impossible, other-worldly ideal, the Goddess (Who was often faceless, without particularity) depicts Everywoman, a personification of characteristics and potentials shared by every woman who has ever lived.

There was nothing *super*-Natural about Her. This Goddess was wholly of and in ordinary Nature, an immanent deity, manifest in All-That-Is.[24] She transcended nothing, for She was The All. Her divine attributes are, therefore, an effective, practical reflection of reality, of this world, each of Her Persons a Model for specific, natural, highly valued behaviors and ways of being, including being closely related to one's Self, other people, and all other life forms. Her people used Her—Her images, symbols, cycles, characteristics—as a convenient, powerful impetus, as a device for stimulating their awareness of the cycles and characteristics of their own lives and for maintaining a dynamic relationship with Nature.

NO WORSHIP, NO PRAYERS

The act of worship involves an acknowledgment of the worshiper as the lowly subject of a deity that is a separate, superior being. So *worship* does not describe the kind of reverence primal peoples held for their immanent deities. How can one *worship* the essence of divinity within the forest or within animals when those entities are a part of one's very Self? How can one *worship* the divinity that is immanent within one's Self and defines one's own essence? Revere, yes, but worship, no. Huston Smith writes that primal religion "turns not on worship but on identification with, a 'participation in,' and acting out of, archetypal paradigms." He adds that a primal person's entire life is ritual: "Mythic beings are not addressed, propitiated, or beseeched. . . . There are no priests, no congregations, no mediating officiants, no spectators"[25]—only reverently made observations of and ritual participations in the PATTERNS and cycles observed.

No prayers. She is called Pandora and Anesidora, the Giver of All Good Things. She gives what is needed willingly out of Her ever-giving Nature in regular, recurring, predictable times (Nature's cycles and PATTERNS). So one need not beseech Her for anything, merely study Her with reverence in order to learn about, and therefore have the ability to predict and maximize, Her gifts.

No churches. One needs no special place to honor what is sacred, for All-That-Is reveals Her uncontainable Self in all Her vastness, *especially out in the open*. Nevertheless, many features of the Earth, ordinary ones as well as special ones—caves, mountains, trees, rock formations—reminded people of the Goddess's attributes with some particular immediacy and relevance, and they were pointed out and honored as being "The Goddess right there." There were special "places-set-apart"—often for gender-specific gatherings—but these were re-

garded, behaved in, and used in a different way than worshipers of transcendent deities use or behave in their shrines, chapels, and churches.

In *the Old Ways*—an age-less kind of knowing and being—there is no place to which one can (nor would one want to) retreat or stand back to get a look at The Sacred. There is no getting out of or away from The Sacred. The Sacred is *the real*, the place and source of the power and joy in living, the source of meaning. And the nature of *the real* includes sacred Me, sacred You, sacred All—all interrelated and inseparable from one another.

The immanent Triple Goddess embodied the way in which the cycles of women's lives and bodies are inextricably interwoven with all cycles and forms of Nature. Her cycling, spiraling rituals kept valuable non-hierarchical PATTERNS and truths about life and meaning in the forefront of Her people's routines and attention. Her shape-shifting—and people's own varied, rich identities, their empathic engulfment in the All—implied egalitarianism within the All. Primal Amerinds felt that "only a fool would imagine himself as somehow exclusively a *human* being."[26] And today some of these native peoples complain that the presence of prayers—a beseeching behavior that disavows that one is a part of the All—has made their Nature spirits, their once ubiquitous presence of immanent divinity, their all-pervading sense of the Sacred and of non-hierarchical participation in Nature, "go away."[27]

Although the immanent Goddess of prehistory would not have been prayed to nor beseeched for favors, She was acknowledged, revered, honored, and participated in, Her many manifestations meditatively studied in order to enhance one's knowledge of one's extended Self. The Goddess religion was a shamanic practice in which Her Wisdom was daily imparted through communication and identification with Her various shapes and forms through trance and ecstatic ritual.

THE THREE PERSONS

There are no boundaries between the Goddess's three Persons; they do indeed "merge into one another with the ease of the three shape-shifting Celtic Morrigan."[28] None is meant to be perceived as having a fixed identity that keeps it from sharing to some extent, the identity of the other two. Nevertheless, *each of Her sacred Persons can be identified by a particular consciousness* and a signifying female image: either a young girl, a mature woman, or an old woman.

Since these three consciousnesses or ways of Being are non-linear, they have no goals associated with them, no progress; the rituals and Models practiced in their signifying Goddess's names do not *advance us* in any way. Rather they are meant to put us in touch with the unchanging core (*Kore*) of our Being, with what we treasure about life and about being human, with what we share with all other human beings, with the Always-So. The three images or Models depict females of different ages but are not meant to be used exclusively by women and men of that Model's age.

The Triple Goddess celebrates something wonderful and ubiquitous about being *human*. Each of the three divine consciousnesses or Persons can be an effective, healing, nurturing Presence and Model for every woman and man at any and every age or stage of life. Many men went through the Women's Mystery School rituals at Eleusis to identify not with a god, but with the Goddess Demeter and Her Daughter-Self, Kore. After participating in the Goddess's Mysteries one Roman emperor was so transported, so transformed—he had "become Her" so completely—that he thenceforth signed his name with a feminine ending.[29]

Why are the divine images female if they can apply equally to men's lives? Because the qualities and consciousnesses being represented are easier to see in women's lives and bodies. In ev-

ery case the Female Model makes a stronger, more powerful metaphor for what human nature is at its best. The concept of Self-as-Other, for example, can be seen in the Pregnant Woman more clearly and emphatically than in any possible male characteristic or image. The interrelatedness—the sameness—of males and females can immediately be seen and *experienced* in the image-metaphor of Mother-with-Her-SonSelf-inside, while males are never such literal containers of the Other. It goes without saying that individual women are neither automatically nor necessarily better human beings than men; but women's bodies and the PATTERNS of women's lives are better metaphors and symbols of basic, shared, sustaining, pan-human characteristics.

Developing one's alertness to and awareness of life's flowings, subtleties, and changes is essential to all three consciousnesses. People who practice the Goddess religion spend vital, acutely *aware* lives.

By archaic times Triple Hera often had three temples in each of Her cities or locations; initiations took place there celebrating the major transitions and changes in women's lives. Each phase-Person—the Blossoming One, the Fruiting One, and the Dying One (the one going-to-seed-with-new-life-inside)—was honored, regarded as sacred and important, in Her own temple. But each initiation marked both the birth of a new phase and the death of an old phase, so the rituals and concerns of one temple were inherently intertwined with the rituals and concerns of the other two, each flowing non-linearly into the others.

Many women today feel no identification with any of the Triple Goddess's three Persons, not with the sacred Virgin, Mother, or Crone. But then none of the phases of patriarchal women's lives have anything sacred about them. There is nothing in these English words that we recognize as essential to women or to men, no symbolic significance or cosmic importance.

Mother Goddess with son on lap, in gold. Perhaps Kybele, for Her throne has feline (lioness) paws. Hittite, 1400 B.C.E.

None of these three words, as we understand or use them, represent important archetypes that play a role in Nature or in things that matter most in our lives or culture.

Therefore, in this book before each verse portrait there is an essay discussing what it was about matristic peoples' perceptions of that Person—that stage in women's lives—that is remarkable. Early women were not basically different from us—every basic description of them can also be a basic description of us. But the attitudinal difference, the difference in consciousness, is extreme. We do not describe women's bodies and unique perceptions as being important sacred Necessities of human life, while our foreparents did.

To become as revered and Self-esteemed as matristic women have been, patriarchal women must *look at ourselves* differently. *We must learn to see remarkableness where we have been trained to see "nothing special."* The myths and rituals of the Triple Goddess Hera offer processes and concepts to help us look at ourselves more fully and richly so that we may become all we can or want to be.

Why do we find ourselves having to *re*-discover that women's lives and bodies are important—even sacred—and can be experienced as important indicators of and clues to the grand scheme of the cosmos? How were such perceptions ever lost, when they are so all im-portant, deeply satisfying, and nourishing to men as well as to women?

Our understanding of this loss—and its magnitude—will come only after we accept that the loss occurred. And then only gradually, and to a great extent intuitively, can we come to any satisfactory explanation, because it took place over a very long time with no written record that identifies the loss as loss. To confound us and discourage a look-back, the loss oftentimes is labeled "progress" or even "civilization."[30]

For some clues to what happened, in the next chapter I will briefly review what is known of Great Mother Hera, how She lost Her sublime Immanence, Her divine Virginity, and became the despised shrew of classical times, the Wife of Zeus. This will help us locate ourselves in history, help us see better the essence and PATTERN of the patriarchy that has shaped all of us—all men and all women. Then later, in Part 2—in the myths and Mysteries themselves—one can begin to experience with one's own Truth Detector something of what was lost by experiencing what might be. We will have something we can compare our own lives and focus to when we enter into the specific *consciousnesses* and *Mysteries* of immanent Hera's three Persons: the Virgin, the Mother (Woman-in-Her-Fullness), and the Crone.

Two

. . . . .

THE DEMOTION OF HERA

From Sublime Triple Goddess to Shrew-Wife

*The Hera of the Homeric and post-Homeric world is, of course, Hera
as viewed by [patriarchal] men. . . . We must go in search of an earlier
Hera belonging to the period dominated by female divinities. . . . The
Hera of cult, the Hera celebrated by women, is viewed in terms of . . .
her beauty, envisioned as quietly content, filled with a secret smiling
knowledge, . . . 'without [whom] there is neither life nor growth.'*[1]

—Christine Downing

*At first sight [Hera] seems all wife . . . but a moment's reflection on
the facts of the local cults and myth shows that this marriage [to Zeus]
was not there from the beginning. In Olympia, where Zeus in historical days ruled . . . supreme, the ancient Heraion, where Hera was
worshiped alone, long predates the temple of Zeus. At Argos . . . the
very name of the sanctuary, the Heraion, marks her supremacy.*[2]

—Jane Ellen Harrison

When I first stood in the ruins of Hera's temple at Olympia, I was deeply
moved, caught up in the elegance and beauty that still remained of a sanctuary
built to honor a most beloved Great Goddess. All the relics of Hera that I
saw—from Rome and Paestum in Italy across mainland Greece and onto the
island of Samos off the coast of Turkey—testified to Her being revered as a
magnificent, inspiring Presence. Qualities of composure, inner peace, and wis-

dom are evident in Hera's stone likenesses— deliberate, intended.

There must have been something wonderful and edifying in Hera's nature to have deserved the devotion and offerings given to Her in those impressive temples. So I was puzzled by a clear contradiction: nothing in the remains reflected the ruthless character or the conflicts, strife, and perpetual distress that ubiquitously accompany Hera, the Wife of Zeus, in classical Greek myth. If the evidence in stone attested to Her majesty, serenity, and holiness, why did the stories I had thus far read about Her tell only of a jealous, hateful, vindictive shrew, full of vanity and implacable anger, in constant conflict with Zeus and Hercules? I became very curious to know: "Why would they build such glorious sanctuaries to honor a bitch goddess?" or else "Why had I heard only terribly negative stories about an exquisite Goddess?" The blatant discrepancies motivated me to research Her, and I was greatly surprised and delighted by what I found.[3]

And who was Hera, the obviously un-Hellenic goddess of the ancient Greeks [the Hellenes]? . . . Although Hera married Zeus (the Indo-European Thunder God) during the Bronze Age (probably before the thirteenth century), . . . [in Her] sanctuaries and pictorial representations, Hera is shown in the central position; she occupies the throne, not Zeus who stands at her side. . . . She, "the Noble One" and "Giver of All," was sculpted and described as tall and beautiful Hera. . . . According to Herodotus, Hera was taken over by the Greeks from the Pelagians, the indigenous people in northern Greece. Her name, e-ra, . . . not of Indo-European origin . . . [is] connected with the air . . . [and] sky.[4]

—Marija Gimbutas

Hera seems to have been one of the Ten Thousand Names of the Great Mother Goddess, the Creatrix, who was revered over vast areas in pre-history. It is likely that originally *Hera* translated as "air" and "sky," indicating *essential life-giving, over-arching Presence* much like Mother Nut in Egypt. Perhaps this name even meant "breathe" or "psyche." Eventually *Hera* was used as a title for the Goddess, meaning something like Great Lady, Protectress, Esteemed Beloved One. In matristic times Her name, like the Sumerian Goddess Inanna's, was incorporated into Her peoples' lives and Selves and was used as if it were synonymous with the words "womb," "woman," "temple," "house," "vessel."

The lands of Hera's people were those areas in southern Europe, the Middle East, and Asia Minor that we now know as Greece, Italy, Turkey, including neighboring islands in the Mediterranean and Aegean seas, especially Samos, as well as the archaic lands of Ionia, Phrygia, Anatolia (Ana-dolu in the Turkish language literally means "land full of mothers" or "land of Grandmother Goddess Ana"). In Hera's earliest appearances, Her name, typical aspects, and statue were interchangeable with those of Demeter, Rhea, Divia, Athena, Kybele (also spelled Cybele), and other prototypes of the Great Mother found in roughly those same areas.

Now that I understand that Hera was for matristic pre-Greek peoples the Great Mother Goddess, revered as Air (generous Life-Giver and Life-Sustainer), as the All-Embracing Sky, and as bountiful Earth, the later myths in which She is depicted as unstable and subservient to Zeus seem to me to be examples of how mean-spirited misogyny transformed history and ourselves by selecting prejudicially what would be recorded in writing, therefore what would likely be "known" of our progenitors. Now that I have felt the inspiring effects of Her temples, when I come upon myths that describe Hera as unrelentingly cruel, vicious, and vindictive, my

Great Mother Cybele with Her drum and lion. Bas relief, third century B.C.E. [JWW]

feelings are the same as Carl Kerenyi's: "Hera cannot originally have been like this!"[5]

Historically, Hera is a much older deity than Zeus. Many of Hera's temples predate Zeus's at the same site by hundreds of years. And since the positive attributes of the early Hera were Hers long before Zeus was invented, She did not come to importance through him as one would suspect from the unflattering stories in which her only claim to fame is shallow physical beauty and the "luck" of being his wife. It should be remembered that in the beginning Hera was not *anyone's* wife. Jane Ellen Harrison reminds us, "Long before her connection with Zeus . . . Hera had three sanctuaries and three surnames," none of which implies "patriarchal marriage."[6]

But the sublimation and reduction of things associated with women and women's culture are not unique to the story of Hera. Goddess demotion is a PATTERN found all across Europe as well as on all other continents in the world. Archaeologist Marija Gimbutas has dug down through the remains of Bronze Age civilizations in Old Europe, including northern Greece, revealing that on those sites matristic Neolithic settlements once thrived but that their Goddess and their mother-centered Old Ways were usually violently overthrown, always devalued and replaced as patriarchy advanced.[7] Catherine Keller, theologian and historian of religion, shows that triune Mother Goddesses and divine Creatrixes like Tiamat were once at the heart of culture in places like Babylon and Mesopotamia, the "cradle of civilization," but that these female deities eventually were demonized, desecrated, turned into monsters—into the Three Furies, the Gorgon, Medusa, or the likes—as sky-god worship replaced the old reverence of Earth and Mothers, transposing sacred matristic rites and worldviews into forbidden heresy.[8] Pamela Berger documents the same demotion and demonization of the Goddess, Her symbols, and women in the Christianizing of western Europe.[9] Mary Condren traces the identical phenomenon in Ireland from pre-historic times into Christian times.[10] It is no wonder Mary Daly has called patriarchy "the Religion of Reversals."[11]

The mythological demotion and humiliation applied also to Hera's children. Hebe, who was once Hera's numinous Daughter-Self or Virgin Persona (see Chapter 4, "Virgin Consciousness"), had by classical times become merely the prototype of an insignificant handmaiden. Hera's son, Hephaestus—once the dramatic Lord of the Smithy, esteemed artist-craftsman, sacred fashioner of gold, and powerful male archetype of creativity—was reduced to being a weak, lame, unmasculine whiner. As Jean Markale writes in *Women of the Celts*, he was "banished to the bowels of the earth . . . replaced in heaven by Zeus."[12]

HERA AND HERACLES—SACRED SEX

For centuries before Zeus had a temple in Olympia, Hera sat alone on the throne of her magnificent temple there. Her young lover and partner, "Herakles Dactyl Parastates," stood behind Her, ready to serve the universe by serving Her. Heracles (or the earlier form, Herakles), whose very name means "the Glory of Hera" or "He whose fame comes from Hera," was not Hera's husband, he did not possess Hera as "his" wife, it was not through him that Her status in life was defined, nor was he entitled to be Her exclusive sex partner. While he was none of these things, Heracles *was* Hera's mate, lover, and *partner in Creation*. Their relationship was based on what they had in common—beginning with *a mutual capacity for ecstasy and power to generate life*—not who had *power over* the other.

It is interesting to note that the period of the archetypal reversals affected Herakles as much as Hera.[13] He whose very name was tied to Hera as Her loving cosmic partner in creation, Her Glory, had by classical times become Her nemesis, Her archenemy, Hercules. But the earlier intimate connection between them remains in an inverted symbol, for Hercules is ever identified in his statues and myths by a club and the skin of a lion, the animal *daimon* that in previous millennia had identified Hera and other cognates of the Great Goddess as Mother of the Animals and of All Creation. In earlier depictions when Herakles was Dactyl Parastates, the fertility *daimon*, he often carried a bough from the Tree of Life (one of Hera's epiphanies—see the illustration of Hera as Tree in Chapter 5, "The Myth of Creation"), but this gentle symbol of Renewing Life transmogrified over time— as did he—into a Taker of Life; as Herakles changed into the violent, "half-barbarian" hero Hercules, the twig became the famous club.[14]

The early relationship between Hera and Herakles modeled sexual love as a blessed, divine aspect of human being, necessary to wholeness and fulfillment. Hera sang ecstatic songs of self-adornment, of desire, and of the delights of lovemaking. "She wanted to be fully met, matched, mated—sexually, yes, but more importantly, psychologically." She sought a partner who could be as fully Male as she was fully Female.[15]

Hera's Sacred Coupling Couch—called her Sacred Marriage Bed only after she became Zeus's wife—was central to Her cult practices and Her *mana*, that is, to Her sacred powers (see Chapters 6 and 7 on Hera as *Woman-in-Her-Fullness*). Throughout the ancient and archaic world the High Priestess of the Goddess managed Her temples. Often it was her duty to choose the king, just as it was her obligation and privilege to authorize his rule (the equivalent of crowning him) by bedding him on the Sacred Couch in a ritual ceremony called *hieros gamos*, or "high marriage."

In the myths, Hera eventually married Zeus, but this marriage never contained Her. She was never the dutiful, subservient wife a patriarch expects and feels entitled to. Before Hera met Zeus, She was not helpless or empty, not in need of being filled up by Her male partner, as is the Wife in the archetype She later models for us.

THE MATRISTIC UNDERCURRENT

Carl Kerenyi points out that the perfect patriarchal family is husband, wife, and their children—their oldest son being his father's heir. One would expect the pantheon of classical Greece to reflect the ideal patriarchal family, but it doesn't. Hera gave Zeus no children, no heir. His crown prince was Apollo, the son of Leto.

Some classical stories say Zeus fathered some of Hera's children because as Greece became more patriarchal, many early Goddesses, like Hera, Demeter, Ge, and Hestia, lost their former influence and their Power to Create on their own. As their earlier hegemonies slipped out of

the memory of many, the stories about them—including those about Hera and her children's parentage—changed. In hellenistic times Herodotus wrote that Hera's children called Zeus "father" or "sire." But Kerenyi cautions that we must not attribute fatherhood to that term, since all members of a court address the king as "father" or "sire." *And in earlier versions of the stories, Hera is specifically said to have conceived Her children parthenogenically.* "Parthenia" is one of Her titles that translates as "Virgin," meaning "belonging to Herself," although it sometimes can also mean "self-fertilizing." In *The Cult of the Mother Goddess*, E. O. James quotes Plato, Pausanias, and Aeschylus's *Eumenides* to show that well into classical times Hera was still regarded as "perpetual virgin."[16] Hera Parthenia's children would by definition have been "Virgin born."

Zeus's children—including his favorite son, Apollo the Light—were born by females, none of whom were his wife. While husband to Hera, Zeus seduced or raped mortal women and Mother Goddesses in every corner of Greece. By classical times only anthropomorphic deities like Zeus, his brothers, and his out-of-wedlock children were in the pantheon that ruled from Mount Olympus.[17] By then these deified personifications of patriarchal values—gods of Rationality, Light, Willpower—and a patriarch's female appendages—his Wife, Daughter, Muse, and so forth—had completely replaced the animal *daimons* of the old pantheon. Also having disappeared from the lineup of approved divine Models were the old dark, immanent female earth deities revered in earlier times, along with the wilderness values they represented (for a discussion of *wil-der-ness* see "A *Wild* Woman is not Feminine" in Chapter 3).

As classicist John C. Wilson reminds us about Zeus and his pantheon, "The Olympians are very late and are literature rather than religion." He writes that Jane Ellen Harrison's work made it clear that not the classical Olympian gods but "the Mysteries . . . *are* Greek religion."[18]

The myth of the birth of Athena celebrated the turning point from matristic times and the centrality of the Mysteries of the Mother Goddesses to patriarchy and the ascendancy of the Olympians. According to the ancient Greek historian Pindar, Zeus raped archaic Mother Metis, the Titan Goddess of Dark Earth and Inner Wisdom, causing Her to conceive a child. Although Zeus later had Mother Metis incinerated (some versions of the story say he swallowed Her), he rescued their embryo and placed it in his head where he brought it to term himself. Proud of having given birth to Athena, Zeus claimed sole parentage—as the Virgin Mother Goddess had of old—and Athena thereafter was known as Goddess of "head" Knowledge and Military Strategy. (Her temple, the Parthenon, dominates the high hill fort in Athens, the city named after her that is renowned for its militancy as well as for its art and philosophy.)

With the mythic destruction of Mother Metis, the age-old chain of daughters inheriting from their mothers was broken. Also broken was the tradition of esteeming Dark Inner Wisdom: intuition and the knowing that comes from Nature's Mysteries, from emotional involvement, from an awareness of one's own Body-Self—and from sharing that knowledge with others orally, intimately, while mutually engaged in the daily process of life. The deities Apollo and Athena, both conceived by Zeus "out of wedlock," modeled mental intelligence, enlightenment, written records, and dispassioned, objective, factual knowledge as the most esteemed ways of knowing.

Classical Greeks gave great honor to Aeschylus's *Oresteia*, a mythic drama that forgave matricide in a father's cause, that debased kinship through one's mother's blood, and that celebrated the patriarch-god's power to give birth to Knowledge while justice was meted by Athena in the name of the fathers rather than in the name of the mothers, as had traditionally been the case before. By then the values the Great Mother Goddess had stood for—the core of the matristic heritage—were mortally wounded or nearly obliterated at the written surface level of Greek culture. The Greek mood at that time was one of eagerness to proclaim the authority of the fathers and the Light, and in order to forge and align themselves with those powers, the literati set about re-creating, transforming, eliminating, and debunking the dark, musty Old Ways that had centered on mother-rights and mother's-blood kinship PATTERNS. So now only subtle clues remain in the artifacts and written records to enable those who are familiar with matristic values to recognize and remember them.[19]

The structure of the Greek pantheon—in which the king-god does not father his wife's children and she does not give birth to his—is clear evidence that an earlier, unsubduable, non-patriarchal influence survived in the myths as an undercurrent or counter-current to classical Greek life. Notice the contradiction between the male-authored myths about Hera and the Mysteries of Hera as practiced by women, both versions existing for a while at the same time. Arthur Evans points out that the "two-tiered nature of Greek history . . . was reflected in a two-tiered religion."[20] The matri-focal tradition of pre-Greek society had been so strong and well-loved that it could not be overthrown entirely, not by conquest, not by propaganda. E. O. James writes: "That Hera's matrimonial affairs were not always running smoothly may be an indication that her cult and that of Zeus had separate origins and were in opposition to each other."[21]

NO ORTHODOX VERSION OF MYTH

Occasionally someone tells me, "That's not the way I heard Hera's story," suggesting that there must exist somewhere one official, ortho-

"*. . . in Her lap.*" Demeter, Mother Earth.
[JWW]

dox version of Hera's or any other deity's myth-story. This is an unreasonable expectation. As a rule ancient myths changed frequently, so there is no one official version of any Greek deity's story; each myth, each divinity, can have countless variations. Consider that Demeter, like Hera, can be Zeus's wife, while in the archaic city of Paestum Hera's mate was Poseidon, although *posei-Don* literally means "husband of Don" (or of De, Da, or Dea), that is, "mate of *De-Meter*" (literally, "mate of Mother De," for *meter* is "mother" in Greek).[22]

Readers need not keep track of these variations to enjoy this book. I mention them so that no one will be thrown by inconsistencies they find in the countless versions of the myths of antiquity.

On the other hand, one also finds striking similarities between different Mother Goddesses. Archaic Hera, for instance, closely resembles Kybele, Demeter, Divia, and Rhea in many crucial ways. These Goddesses all embody the same general Great Goddess archetype and their statues are often interchangeable, although their religions were practiced in different, even distant, locales. Parallel deities like these are called "cognates."

The Hera-Zeus story—the Husband-Wife idyll or myth—as told on the Greek island of Samos (near Ephesus, Turkey) says that She and Zeus enjoyed an idyllic courtship and wedding night—no rape.[23] But Hera's story by and large follows a PATTERN of constant battle with Zeus and Hercules—and a constant demotion, which tells us something about Greek history, Greek art, and the fate of women in Greek culture.[24]

From receiving the homage of all men and women as the Virgin Mother Goddess, Creatrix, and Source of All Life in archaic times, Hera was by 450 B.C.E. reduced in the myths to being the spiteful, deeply frustrated Wife of Zeus, powerless to make things right for herself. From once being synonymous with Great Mother Rhea, the Creatrix of All, She was reduced in the stories of Homer and Hesiod to being Rhea's daughter, the *older* sister and wife of a more recently invented deity, Zeus. Four hundred years later She was reduced further to a hysterical shrew and Zeus's insignificant *younger* sister in the stories written by Herodotus. From being known as Most Compassionate One before Her marriage, She was reduced to being Most Spiteful One afterward. And so forth. But in spite of the prevalence of the negative stories about Her, Hera, the threefold Goddess, survived and thrived as a major influence in the lives of classical Greek women.

HERA AND HER HEROES

From archaic times Hera was the beloved Mother Goddess of the people of the plains of Argos, long centuries before the famed Argonauts began their expedition across the Aegean Sea to fight the Trojans in the bloody war described in *The Iliad*. Around 1100 B.C.E. two brothers, Agamemnon, the king of Mycenae (a fortress town in Argos) and Menaleus, the king of Sparta, led a large army to Troy—with Hera, the traditional Protectress of Argivians, as their divine sponsor—to bring back Menaleus's wife, the Spartans' Queen Helen, from the arms of Paris, her young Trojan lover.[25] The Argive *heroes*—literally, *Hera's men*[26]—won that Trojan War, even though Zeus was the divine patron of the Trojans. The myth says She outsmarted Her husband. But it was a hollow victory in the long run. This and other territorial wars led eventually to the destruction of the powers and traditions of the mother-right clans and decimated the authority of the Mother Goddess religion and traditions in the plains of Troy as well as in the plains of Argos.

The lion or lioness had been the most sacred epiphany of many Mother Goddesses, including

*Hera as Pillar-Column-Tree.
Flanked by two lionesses, over
gate to city of Mycenae in
province of Argos, Greece.* [JWW]

35

Hera, Kybele, Rhea, and Astarte. The stone entrance to Mycenae, Agamemnon's home city in Argos, is called the Lion Gate, because over the entrance is a carving of two lionesses.[27] Their front paws rest on the base of a stone tree-column exactly like those that were used over millennia to represent the Great Goddess in Her pillar cults that thrived throughout eastern Mediterranean lands.[28] Many scholars feel that the lioness-pillar carving over the gate at Mycenae pictures Hera Herself, identifying that city of *heroes* as one of Her strongholds.

MYTH AND HISTORY

Myths cannot always be read as history, but the deities in Greek myths often are metaphors for the people whose experiences the myths record. When the myth says that Zeus finally raped and married Hera after three hundred years of courtship, Kerenyi speculates that this story about these two divinities is actually recording metaphorically the historical event of Hera's peoples' finally being brought into submission after enduring many centuries of war and invasions from the north by horse-riding tribes, mainly Dorians, Hellenes, and Ionians. The fact that Earth Mother Hera finally joined the pantheon of the enemy in a subservient role to the sky-father Zeus signals that Her agrarian followers and their culture were, over the centuries, greatly subverted by Zeus's warrior-led followers. By classical times all the Goddesses of Earth and Female Wisdom—Goddesses like Hestia, Metis, Themis, Demeter, Gaia—had lost their former status and held no position of authority in Greece's Olympian, male-dominated pantheon. These Wise Old Crone Goddesses had become monsters of various kinds. Such "mythological defamation" comes down to us, Catherine Keller writes, as "history from the vantage point of the victor."[29]

Hera's people did not give in easily to the victors. Since the religions of Mother Goddesses survived in some form—although severely diminished—far into classical times, we can surmise that it was a long time before the arms-loving tribes of sky-father Zeus achieved a total psychological victory over the Earth Mother's peoples.

Hera in the myths—as stand-in or symbol for Her people—did not give in easily either. For more than a thousand years after the mythical wedding, the story keeps telling that Hera—conquered but not subdued, married and in a subservient role but not subservient in demeanor—continued to fight Zeus like a wounded, cornered animal, Her power to rule gone, but Her anger a vital clue to Her sense of justice denied, as well as to Her nature—and to mine.

HERA'S ANGER

The wrath of the lion is the wisdom of God.
—William Blake

Hera's anger once seemed an unattractive, indefensible characteristic to me. I have come to understand, however, that the anger of Hera-the-Wife was not merely the pettiness of an insubstantial mate. I now experience Hera's anger, at least in its initial form, as divine Wisdom in the form of a primal rage against injustice. The early hymns to Hera praise Her for Her compassion and for bequeathing just laws to Her people, so when the later myths picture Hera as full of fury, I interpret this as reflecting metaphorically Her people's fitting rage at their loss of justice, at having their laws and traditions, their Goddess, and matrifocal Old Ways overthrown, of being conquered and belittled. Hera's anger comes out of a fierce opposition to the brutalities that Zeus and his sword-wielding, horse-mounted followers engaged in against the settled, simple agrarian communities who revered Her.

One courtship myth tells how, after centuries of pursuing Hera unsuccessfully, Zeus finally won Her hand in marriage through deception and force. Because Hera was known as Most Compassionate One, Zeus knew he could count on Her sympathy when, disguised as a little cuckoo (one of Hera's favorite birds, the harbinger of spring that epitomized Her Hebe Persona) he flew into Her presence on Her mountaintop temple at Stymphalos, tossed and drenched by a violent storm. Hera, of course, tenderly reached out and picked up the wind-bashed drowning creature and put it in Her lap to dry and comfort it in the folds of Her skirt. Having gained access to Hera's lap, Zeus immediately revealed himself and threatened to rape Her unless She married him. Trapped and humiliated, Hera lost Her will to continue fighting Zeus's aggressive advances. By marrying him, She lost to a significant extent Her psychological status as *Parthenia*, the archetype of a-woman-who-belongs-to-herself, and thereafter was storied as the archetype of *Wife*, a woman whose primary identity comes from belonging to a husband.

Harrison, Kerenyi, and others familiar with Hera's archaic nature and stature, as well as with the later male-authored myths about Her, describe Her fierce, erratic wifely behavior as being like that of a "captured native princess" whose people have been conquered, she herself forcibly taken as the bride of the victors' king. Such kings—whether Zeus or Helen's husband Menaleus, both being the same mythical archetype to some extent—desired and would fight for the sexual pleasures of the native princess's body—for Hera's body or Helen's or the high priestess's—but more significantly, such kings coveted the prestige of the authenticating *hieros gamos*, the Coupling Couch ritual that legitimized their kingship. Of course, neither "native princess Hera" nor Helen (who ran away!) nor any of the Goddess's loyal high priestesses would have willingly legitimized their enemy's patriarchal, hierarchical rule. They must have been taken fiercely screaming, the way Hera

screams in the later myths, the same fierce way the Amazons are fighting the Greeks for their lives in the famous marble frieze on the Mausoleum of Halicarnassus.[30]

In the myths Hera was seized, Her people and land were seized, Her titles and prerogatives were seized. And when She complained, She was denounced as "shrew." She could not win, but She was not silenced either.

Rage seems an entirely appropriate response for Hera the Wife. Contemporary therapists Jean Shinoda Bolen[31] and Sylvia Perera[32] point out that the ancient, raging Wife archetype remains strong in the lives of contemporary women who are angry at secondary status, angry at having their identity come from belonging to someone else, angry at the wife abuse that is all too common. Psychiatrist Jean Baker Miller asserts that in marriages, when the power balance is skewed in favor of the husband, a wife who does not repress her feelings entirely will eventually become like Hera the Wife, nagging, bitching, perpetually carrying anger, resentment, and bitterness in her heart and on her tongue. This is indeed the ubiquitous archetype for wives in patriarchy.[33]

Rather than looking down on and urging the repression of modern women's rage, I am coming to think of this anger as an appropriate response to injustice, as embodied pre-verbal Wisdom, as a valuable inheritance from Hera, a redeeming, sacred Model of a woman who will not submit totally to losing her Virginity but instead to some extent tries to retain her own identity, her own Self—*at least her own authentic emotional responses.* I feel that Hera's anger and Her story put my anger—all women's expressed or subdued anger—into a perspective from which we can derive much understanding and compassion—for our mothers, ourselves, and one another—and eventually relief and renewal. "The wrath of the Lioness is Her divine Wisdom."

VIRGIN

Mother . . . .

CRONE

HERA—BRIDGE TO PAST AND FUTURE

Re-membering

*1: Re-calling the Original intuition of
integrity; healing the dismembered Self—
the Goddess within women; Re-calling the
Primordial connections/conversations
among women, animals, and Other
Elemental beings*

*2: Realizing the power to See and to Spell
out connections among apparently dispar-
ate phenomena: Spinning, Creating*[34]

— *Webster's First New Intergalactic
Wickedary,* Conjured by Mary Daly
in Cahoots with Jane Caputi

I have chosen to tell the story of the Great
Mother of pre-history as Hera because Hera's
specific story and Mysteries endured for two
thousand years, had roots before that, and echoes still into the future. Hera's connections and
longevity make Her an ideal bridge between me
and the far distant past when women were
strong and capable and enjoyed the power of
animal *daimons.* She is, as well, a bridge between me and classical times when patriarchy
was establishing the limiting roles and PAT-
TERNS that have determined my life so far.
And when I am telling Hera's myths, I also feel
a way bridged ahead for me into a future in
which I and all women can again become Self-
authorizing.

The story of classical Hera comes out of our
impoverished European heritage that values
light and enlightenment above all, equating
darkness with ignorance and evil. But Hera—
who was in the beginning a prototype of the
Great Mother whose sacred province was the
close-and-holy *Darkness,* She whose lightless Inner Sanctum was Her Womb, the underEarth—
models *Darkness* as a source of Wisdom and
Creativity. I experience the demotion of the
Great Goddess, Her images, symbols, and values

as a reflection of the sexism of the west; and I
consider any demeaning of the Dark while privileging the Light as sole source of Life and
Knowledge to be unjustified, a reflection of
deep-seated racism.[35] After all, Dark and Light
could be seen as taking equal turns in Nature,
rather than as banishing each other. And remarkable new underwater technologies now reveal strange but strong forms of life thriving in
total darkness at the bottom of the seas, emerging from and feeding on mineral-rich volcanic
seepages down there—completely without light.

The Great Mother—of whom Hera is a
form—was Black.[36] She is therefore a vital kinship link and bond between a light-skinned person like me and the dark-skinned people of the
world. It is the Great Mother who looks out
from the hundred-some-odd statues called Black
Virgins that grace Roman Catholic churches
throughout Europe; some centuries back these
Pagan renderings of fertile Black Mother Earth
were subsumed into Ecclesia, the Mother as
Church.[37] Hera as Great Mother is a direct link
from me to:

- the peoples of Africa whose Yoruban
  Goddesses Oya and Oshun can be traced to
  show a direct relationship to the Great
  Mother of Old Europe, a direct connection
  between the early cultures and peoples of
  both continents[38]

- the dark Dravidian peoples of India and the
  hundreds of Goddesses who are still revered
  there, including Black Kali[39]

- those Native Americans who have enjoyed a
  matristic heritage and Creating Mothers
  (like Changing Woman) from time before
  memory[40]

- the peoples of the Middle East where the
  black meteorite Mother Goddess Kybele
  and the Milk Mother Goddess Ah-Lat (and
  Alli-Kubaba) modeled human values for
  their people long before They became

Islam's Kaaba and Allah in the archetypal reversals that resulted from the "priestly piracy" of patriarchal Arabia[41]

Through All-Mother Hera I am related to the dark Aboriginals of Australia who revere All-Mother Rainbow Snake Who embodies the dynamic Mystery of the Great Flow that periodically comes washing over Her people, symbolizing the awe, wonder, and power in the tides, monsoons, and women's synchronous menstrual bleeding.[42] Through Earth Mother Hera I am related to the Aboriginal peoples who say, "There

She is, right there" as they point with pride to Creating Mother Warramurrungundji Who still stands protectively on and of the earth—a tall formation of red stone in the northern flood plains, a presence that constantly reminds Her people what is important.[43]

Through Hera I feel connected to all women alive and to all people who have ever lived. She helps me re-member mySelf, both as whole and as Spider Woman exuding an ever-unfinished web into every direction . . . never stopping the *Spinning, Creating.*

"That rock is our Mother Warramurrungundji . . . that rock right there." An Aboriginal Dreamtime story about their Creatrix, the First Ancestor Mother, now said to be this vigilant, ever-present red sandstone column in the flood-plains of Arnhemland, Australia.
[JWW]

Three
· · · · · ·

ALWAYS FEMALE,
NEVER FEMININE

*The Great Goddess [is] too large a concept for the Jungian constructs
of "the feminine." Jungian analysts speak of the Goddess as being
synonymous with "the feminine principle, Eros" or with "feminine
nature." True, the Goddess was the ultimate expression of female
being, but her nature was all-encompassing (e.g., giver of divine law,
fierce protector, gentle nurturer). If she were a pure expression of . . .
"the feminine consciousness," these traits . . . would have to be
explained via "animus [male] energies," which would be impossible
in an embodiment of pure "femininity." The Great Goddess
was supreme power and was all.[1]*

—Charlene Spretnak

*M*any use the words "feminine" and "female" as if they are interchangeable, but they actually have significantly different meanings.[2] The Great Goddess and archaic Hera both represent the Divine *Female*, but neither can be described as the Divine *Feminine*. Women and men who are interested in more
satisfying roles for themselves and an improved relationship between sexes
must make this essential distinction.

Not all women are *feminine*, nor do all want to be, so this cannot be the
word that describes the perennial, unchanging PATTERN of women's lives.
Femininity describes the values that have been constructed by our society to
determine a woman's social goodness; being unfeminine often means a woman
is socially unfit. The highest accolade we confer on a woman who has attained
true femininity is to call her a "Lady," a title that originally differentiated "the
female of the favoured social class" from her inferiors.[3] But the standards of
femininity and the title of Lady do not reflect the typical behaviors or appearance of women in lower classes. The word "feminine" certainly does not de-

scribe the dynamic, self-sufficient, influential, empowered, menstruating-all-at-the-same-time, culture-creating women foragers and hunters of pre-history.

Everyone recognizes a *feminine* woman, knows what she looks like, how she behaves, how she sits, runs, walks, throws a ball. Our traditional standard for what is feminine involves submissiveness, dependency, passivity, non-assertiveness, selflessness, living only for others, weakness ("Please open this jar or car door for me"), vulnerability, immobility on a pedestal. Being dainty and wearing small shoes has been essential to being *feminine*.[4]

Because of these traditional limitations, at this moment we do not know the extent of what the average *female* person can do or think, or even how she might choose to look if society placed no artificial judgmental standards on her and did not stress *femininity* or being seductive as the highest indicators of beauty. But things are changing. A big, strong self-sufficient woman who takes up lots of space can now in some places be considered beautiful. Notice what has happened to women's bodies and female athletic records—and to footwear!—in the last two decades since the restrictions of femininity have begun to be challenged and lifted. See what has happened since women have been allowed to play seriously and work outside the home. Notice trousered, booted women using heavy tools easily and well atop telephone poles. Notice women doing scientific experiments in space capsules, piloting fighter jets, carrying briefcases into their own corporate offices while shod in running shoes!

Urging a woman to be *feminine* restricts her possibilities, limits her dreams, keeps her poised precariously and daintily on high heels or a pedestal (or the psychological equivalent), keeps her dependent on a man, limits her expertise, denies her intellectual, physical, and character strength. Some of us remember that a woman used to feel she had to ask her husband what her opinion ought to be on slavery, religion, and politics!

On the other hand, allowing women to be fully *female* gives them open-ended possibilities, unknown potential. If a woman wants to be dainty and weak, if that is her desire and nature, she is to be respected and still honored as being fully *female*. Strong, assertive women who want to drive earth-moving equipment are fully *female* too. Any type and any possibility is acceptable as fully and wonderfully *female*. The only test or criterion for what counts as being female or womanly is that it be authentic or necessary for a particular woman.

GENDER IS CONSTRUCTED

Just as female and feminine are not synonyms, "male" and "masculine" do not mean the same thing either. All boys and men are not inclined toward being masculine. It does not automatically happen that when a malechild grows up he enters Manhood—the home of the warrior, of the "real" masculine man. Masculine manhood is being constructed by society when its members tell a young boy that he can't cry without being sissy, that he can't play in nurturing ways with dolls without being unattractively feminine . . . I need not go on. We all know the gendered, masculine behaviors, values, and prejudices we instill in our little boys without noticing their preferences, without asking for their consent.

A child is born being *male* or *female*.[5] That is a child's sex; society does not construct the sex of its children. Society does exert pressure to construct its children's gender, its people's *masculinity* and *femininity*, according to its prejudices and learned preferences for certain looks and behaviors. In the western tradition men and women must struggle to learn behaviors that will earn them the right to be called ladies and gentlemen, the right to wear the gender labels of masculine and feminine. Many men and women forget their early sacrifices, but their gender achievement has often cost them dearly, has inflicted great pain while denying some dear part of their very beings. Especially does the earning of manhood come through struggle and angst. Masculinity does not "come about spontaneously through biological maturation, but rather is a precarious or artificial state that boys must win against powerful odds."[7]

Culture provides strong Models of what is acceptable and praise-worthy, showing how difficult becoming a man is: Hercules had twelve impossible labors. Knights had armor to wear, prescribed foes to battle, required trophies to be won. The corps of masculine men is something of an elite club for the high achievers. Sadly *not all males make it.*

The Great Goddess of pre-history was not the Model for membership in the exclusive club of women who watched and fashioned themselves carefully until they achieved standards of behavior and appearance that would earn them status as members of "the Feminine" elite. The Goddess is not a Model for women who must pride themselves on their niceness, grace, deference, and cleanliness. She was Everywoman: the Divine *Female*, made out of Earth and Blood, wearing Her ingredients with pride, as signs that She births and nurtures all Life in the cosmos. As Charlene Spretnak writes, She "was supreme power and was all."

JUNG AND "THE FEMININE"

Carl Jung's insights into the universality of myth and archetype have made a great contribution to humankind. We are all indebted to him for his revolutionary work on the power of symbol, metaphor, and the preconscious. He was far ahead of his time in many respects.

But Jung was also a product of his time. His description of the basic gender archetypes as "the feminine" *(anima)* and the "masculine" *(animus)* does not advance our understanding of

ourselves. These concepts are merely formal descriptions of the sexist stereotypes and prejudices that permeated the Caucasian, European culture in which Jung was raised. Hear the fixed categories and judgmental tone: man should be *active,* woman should be *passive; Mind* is a function of the animus, while sensuality of the *body*—Eros—belongs to the anima and is synonymous with "the feminine"; and so forth down the list of dualisms.[7] We must honor Jung for his wonderful contributions while understanding that his special wisdom did not permeate all aspects of his writings or thought. As Charlene Spretnak states in the quotation at the beginning of this chapter, "The Great Goddess [is] too large a concept for the Jungian constructs of 'the feminine.'" Likewise, women—*in Her image*—can aspire to a larger Model of Self than "the feminine" can offer.

Spretnak attached a note to the above passage: "For a discussion of the patriarchal biases involved in the Jungian theory of the anima/animus, see Naomi Goldenberg's work, *Changing of the Gods.*"[8] Actually, many feminists, like Goldenberg, call themselves Jungians in honor of the vital, important work he did, and yet they write critically about his blatant sexism, which stems from the dualistic framework in which he cased his gender archetypes.[9]

Jung brought our attention to the Goddess, for which I am ever grateful, but he divided Her and all women—as patriarchy always has—into two separate opposing archetypes: the Good Mother and the Terrible Mother. His notion of anima and animus again describes us as having two sides that struggle against each other for dominance of our Self. Many sensitive therapists have now made it poignantly clear that when we divide ourselves into two personae, one acceptable and one unacceptable, we automatically repress a real, vital part of our Selves. We thus become fragmented and live in constant subliminal distress, forced to maintain a facade and avoid emotions that could actually be sources of Self-knowledge. The notion that we become whole by integrating our animus side with our anima side begins with the premise that we have two sides, two natures, which *need* to be reconciled. That is an unhealthy premise. Wholeness requires that we refuse to see our Self as having sides in the first place. Happily, much of the help we need to think and feel our way out—even out of Jungian dualisms—will come to us from Jung himself in his writings about mythos as the authentic core of ourSelves and the way the stories we tell—and the images we adopt as real and good—determine who we are.

DIVIDED WE FALL

The goddesses in the patriarchal pantheons of ancient Sumer, Greece, Rome, and so forth played narrower, more *feminine* roles than the earlier Great Goddess did. Those goddesses—like the women of those times and ours—were not Female Models of the All; they were slivers of the great cut-down Tree of Life. Reduced from being "the All," they were divided into parts, fitted into limiting categories, subjugated, objectified, restricted to less powerful feminine hegemonies (Goddess *only* of Sexual Love, Goddess *only* of Music, and so forth). Further*less*, each of these goddesses' purpose and reason for being was defined primarily by her relationship and service to a male—*his* wife, *his* mother, *his* daughter, *his* Muse and inspiration, and so forth.

Women are sexual beings, but Eros has never been "synonymous with" women, as Jung and other western theorists have so often described us. Women are not primarily nor inevitably sex objects for the use of men. Nevertheless, as the western mythic system reflects, many men and women have grown accustomed to—have accepted—the Rape of Persephone (the archetype of the Ravished Maiden) as a sacred metaphor for women's lives. This story presents the defile-

ment of maidens as normal, in some sense and to some degree a necessary aspect or phase of being *feminine*, as if this were an unavoidable ingredient of a woman's growing up, our Always-So, rather than merely what too often happens to women in patriarchy, wherein the anima Model prescribes that a "real" woman be passive and submissive to men. In the matristic myths of the Great Mother Goddess as I have reclaimed them here, neither sexual reification nor rape is a part of the mythos. There is always a "Descent into the Underworld": *the Seed—Earth Mother Demeter's daughter Kore—goes there, into the close-and-holy Darkness, every year—without any trauma—to gestate and be reborn!* Notice that there is no ritual defilement to be overcome in the basic story, no automatic sexual violence. In this mythos, rape is not essential for a girl's initiation or transformation into womanhood; violent subjugation is not needed for women's renewal, not essential to being *female*, not an Always-So for women.

In the earlier Great Goddess mythos of matristic times I have found no evidence of a god—no divine Male Model—who proves his masculinity and power by raping young girls or queens. Herakles was Hera's Glory, Her Dactyl Parastates, Her erect, fully sharing, participating partner in sexual congress—but not Her ravisher. He is the Phallos, the "standing tree," the Herm.[10] In his arm he carried respectfully, reverentially, a gently arching leafed bough from the Tree of Life, his face happy, mellow, his stance firm and strong as the oak but nothing harsh or aggressive in the position or lines of his body.

In *Goddesses in Everywoman* Jean Shinoda Bolen describes the ways in which the classical goddesses represent the archetypes of women in patriarchy, how women in our culture live their lives within the narrow confines of the categories those deities personify. She notes that "the attributes, symbols, and power that once were invested in one Great Goddess were [later] divided among many goddesses," whose diminished divine natures and compartmentalization reflect non-divine women also as diminished and fragmented, as only part of what we might be. Bolen reminds us that only the Great Goddess of earlier pre-history was a Model of female wholeness.[11] Jean Bolen, Christine Downing, Sylvia Perera, and Ginette Paris are four scholars today who combine extraordinary intelligence, intuition, and inner awareness with a gift for healing to discover and point out clues in the classical goddesses that can help women begin to recover the wholeness that the earlier Great Goddess modeled. The virtues these therapists find in the patriarchal goddesses harken back to the Great Mother and matristic values; these writers are reclaiming perspectives that are not obvious to every reader of the classical myths; they laud some female attributes that have not been a part of typical patriarchal women's lives for a long time.[12] But the classical goddesses remain stripped-down versions of Woman.

Samuel Noah Kramer writes that in the patriarchy of Sumer the Goddesses who "held top rank . . . were gradually forced down the ladder by male theologians" and "their powers turned over to male deities."[13] Jungian Sylvia Perera writes, "Even in the tales of Inanna and other early Sumerian, Semitic, and Egyptian writings there is evidence that the original potencies of the feminine [sic] have been 'demoted.'"[14] Inanna's sister Erishkegal, before She was imprisoned as the "Lady of the Great Place Below," was Ninlil, the Grain itself, manifesting both in Her *full bloom* state—growing and fruiting in the light and air above—and in Her *seed* state—dead, lying in the dark earth below, gestating, about to sprout again. Ninlil was Self-authorized; She contained the entire cycle of Birth-Death-ReBirth in HerSelf, needing no help from outside HerSelf to effect Her continuous, unending transformations; she went naturally—

without trauma—into the underworld as all seeds do, and came up out of the underworld, reborn, all under Her own powers. In *The Hymn to Inanna* of patriarchal Sumerian times, Inanna, although invested with many powers, is not able to return from the underworld using her own powers. She must call on Enki, the god of waters and wisdom, to retrieve some remnants of dirt from under his fingernails to bring her back to life. Erishkegal, the former Ninlil, had lost all of her Self-authority by the time that hymn was sung to her sister Inanna, even the power to petition. By then She would remain un-reborn forever.

In the oft-told story of how Demeter rescues Her daughter from Hades for part of the year, the Earth Mother has likewise lost Her authority over the Earth's seasons. She has lost Her earlier nature, which was Self-authorizing and whole. She is forced by Zeus, the god who allowed Her daughter to be raped by his brother Hades, to make concessions about Nature's cycles, although formerly Nature's cycles were simply the unmanipulated cycles and phases of Her woman's Body. (See the discussion of the year as Virgin-Mother-Crone in Chapter 1.)

The limiting categories and assigned characteristics of the classical Greek and Sumerian goddesses remain reduced stereotypes. I find them destructive, dependent, insulting models for women. Absent from the nature or concerns of any patriarchal goddess is Self-knowledge as Wisdom; absent is any desire to be whole and well-rounded, much less an effective, fully developed Model for women. Lost is the Self-authorizing aspect of the Self-fertilizing Virgin Mother that had been associated with the Great Goddess of pre-history and that no woman or man can be whole without.

It is essential to look outside of classical myths to find an inclusive female archetype about which a woman can ecstatically claim, "This is a Model for my unadorned, unmodified

Self, who I am and want to be just for myself without reservation." It should be stated unambiguously that the partitioned classical feminine goddesses—including Hera the Wife—are not celebrated in this book. Only the whole Divine Female is treasured as a Model here.

Examining how women and the Divine *Female* functioned in prehistory, before patriarchy invented *femininity* as a standard of behavior control for women, opens up exciting possibilities for women's lives. Hera's three Persons—the *Virgin* (meaning belonging-to-Herself, *not* meaning celibate!), the *Mother* (Woman-in-Her-Fullness), and *Crone* (Wise Old Healing Woman)—expand our concepts about women, about what being female means or might yet mean in every stage of our lives—and therefore also what being male and human can mean.

A *WILD* WOMAN IS NOT FEMININE

The metaphor of the garden is perfect for a Lady.[15] A lady is domesticated and well behaved—as is the clematis that is trained to climb her garden trellis. A lady likes having someone take care of her. Just so, in a proper garden everything is taken care of by the gardener, everything is under his control, and nothing wild is allowed. Weeds and unattractive or unplanned growths are removed. Everything is cultivated, cultured, is in order, in its place. The garden's aspects—from roses to espaliered pear trees—are the most domesticated, decorative, and bountiful that civilization can devise or force.

The garden metaphor glorifies a feminine woman. But it will not do for the Goddess. The metaphor of a virgin forest or the wilds of Nature is more suitable for the Goddess. The wilderness was not a forbidding place for people who practiced the Old Ways; the wilderness was their home, their provident Mother. The literal sense of the word "wilderness" (*wil-der-ness*) is that the "will of the place" governs what

happens there, not an outside force.[16] And the will of wild Nature is mother-like, it provides a nurturing environment, sufficient for all who live there. Nothing in the wilds is cultivated to be other than it is, nothing is trained, rushed, or otherwise forced or domesticated to produce more or be more beautiful than it already is. Everything in the wilds is *allowed to be* as it is.

We have been conditioned to think of wild Nature as a place rife with brutal struggle and ruthless competition—opposites struggling for power over one another—something akin to ubiquitous warfare. But that notion of wilderness must be rethought, for many scholars and observers of Nature now see that metaphor as grossly inaccurate. Microbiologists Lynn Margulis and Dorion Sagan write that

the view of evolution as chronic bloody competition among individuals and species, a popular distortion of Darwin's notion of "survival of the fittest," dissolves before a new view of continual cooperation, strong interaction, and mutual dependence among life forms. Life did not take over the globe by combat, but by networking.[17]

Philosopher Robert Augros and theoretical physicist George Stanciu challenge the Darwin-Spenser theory of "the survival of the fittest" as it is generally understood: the fallacy that nature-in-the-wilds is a cruel and indifferent hunting ground. They suggest instead that the data properly interpreted show Nature—wilderness—to be a harmonious "cooperative alliance" of interrelationships.[18]

Biologist Lewis Thomas writes that in the organic world "the urge to form partnerships, to link up in collaborative arrangements, is perhaps the oldest, strongest, and most fundamental force in nature. There are no solitary, free-living creatures, every form of life is dependent on other forms."[19]

Organic life seems to be so . . . *organic.* Augros and Stanciu elaborate: "Life works with the environment, not against it. . . . Every living thing is beautifully attuned to its environment. Effort is . . . minimal because each animal and plant is so well designed . . . in its use of the least material to produce structures to accomplish what is needed with the least work."[20] Anyone can see the profound cooperation that takes place in any herd, flock, school.

So each individual life form in the forest, in the wilds, in organic Nature relates intimately to every other form, and "populations are self-regulating."[21] Observing this as the uninterfered-with PATTERN of All-That-Is argues well for adopting the Model of the Wild Woman for ourselves—or for just *allowing* it in ourselves. This archetype can be seen manifest in the Great Goddess of pre-history, She who was the bounteous Life Force of the Plants and Animals of the wilds back in the times when people foraged and gathered from Nature's uncoerced, freely given plenty. That was the PATTERN of life many millennia before anyone felt a need to plant crops, long before there was such a thing as a garden where roses were cultured, pruned, and staked and statues of

beautiful feminine women stood poised, immobile, on gleaming pedestals, where the only non-human animals were leashed and closely monitored—and all was fenced in for its own protection (at least, so it was said).

What would it mean or feel like to be a Wild Woman, untrained, free, and full of Possibility? From extant artifacts it is clear that at some time in the past the Old Ones looked at Woman as full of wild Mystery and Potential, as always Becoming, as reliable, giving, and capable . . . but unpredictable—something like the forest, something like the wilderness itself.

Everywoman, living in the wilds, expressed herSelf in, cooperated with, and adapted to the will-of-the-place and the will-of-her-body. These overlapping, unfenced, self-regulating wills constituted her home and inspired and nurtured her creative, intuitive Self; they guided, formed, allowed, without a fixed Plan but with much Self-interest in the harmonious workings of All-That-Is. From this will-full Wild Woman came the idea and Model of *the Divine Female*, the Triple Goddess.

PART TWO

. . . .

Her Myths & Her Mysteries

Goddess ritual, in-sofar as it generates reverence for and celebrates that which is female . . . is fiercely empowering, . . . [with] possibilities as limitless as the sunshine and the wind.

—Sonia Johnson

Four
......

VIRGIN CONSCIOUSNESS

Hera as Maiden or Virgin is called Hebe Parthenia
(HEE-bee pahr-THIN-ee-yah).

*F*or early cultures the word "virgin" did not mean "one who has never had sex."[1] For a female it meant one who is neither the dependent child nor wife of a man, but rather *one who belongs to herself.* It seems to have been assumed in matristic societies that sexuality is a natural ingredient of Everywoman's and Everyman's being, because directly or indirectly, it is a sacred attribute of all three Persons of the Triple Goddess. A sexless category was either inconceivable or held no concern for Her followers.

In its primal sense the word "virgin" describes a maiden, a very young woman who is leaving girlhood, just beginning to explore and taste her grown-up Self. She is in bud—full of potential, unfinished, entering the unknown in a state of joyous uncertainty. Such a one is full of wonder and Becoming, curious about all the possibilities in herself and the world—open to the Mysteries and dangers that lie ahead.

Clarity does not apply to her, for She is in process, in-between. Anticipation, freedom, and spontaneity do describe her. She is highly susceptible to falling in love—with the dawn, with the changing seasons, with any and all creatures in their miraculous diversity, with people, their eyes and stories. For whatever the risks, the virgin experiences Nature as full of good things and gifts, full of Possibility.

GIFTS COME UNBIDDEN

The visible signs of a maiden's physical maturation—her first show of menstrual blood and swelling breasts—come in their own time. A girl can do nothing to earn them; they come not as the result of prayers, not as the outcome of her will, nor are they due to any practiced skill. She can only wait, for they always come unbidden in a mysterious process of unfolding.

So this is not a goal-oriented consciousness. Unlike her brothers, a maiden cannot achieve her adulthood, she does not have to go on a quest for it, it is not the result of any effort, not a reward for some arduous accomplishment. In early societies the visible signs that identified a girl as having reached womanhood were eagerly anticipated, and their coming was celebrated with momentous rituals of transformation and initiation.[2] Many mothers today are also arranging celebrations for their Budding, newly Bleeding daughters, honoring their menarche with gifts and rituals of Promise.[3]

The virgin, the girl-woman, is one who is pregnant with uncertain but miraculous Possibility. The essence of maidenhood can thus be understood as the state of being receptive to the unknown, to Great Mystery, to gifts. Her defining attitude is one of—simply but fully—allowing, Being, and Becoming.

Receptivity is at the core (*Kore*) of this consciousness, but passivity is not present. Although the expectant maiden may do no particular or prescribed thing, she waits and is keenly alert, developing an ability to respond authentically to Self and Other, and that is not the same as doing "nothing"! Great courage and confidence are required for her to remain receptive while letting be, while not knowing. She is in a blessed state of ignorance, for one who knows has nothing to learn and therefore cannot grow and Become. Thus, aware of not knowing, but extremely alert and on the lookout for treasures (after all, they come unbidden—she won't know ahead of time what they are or where they will be found), she allows herself to flow in the waters of life without control, letting the current take and bring her Self—whatever that might be or become—in its own time.

Being virgin is risky. Wildness lurks as a definite Possibility when one allows . . . whatever . . . in the face of uncertainty and Great Mystery. This consciousness is a state of readiness, of excitement about being at home in the unknown, expecting gifts, of being in love. It is typical of a virgin, of a girl-becoming-woman,

but obviously, this consciousness belongs to all men and women and happily can last throughout a lifetime.

The sweet, smiling, quiet knowledge of the Mona Lisa typifies the virgin: poised, ready for whatever comes, carrying within herself tremendous reserves, strength, potential—and secrets. Secrets. She is alert, aware, ready for love. And pregnant with unknown Possibilities.[4]

SELFHOOD

In the Goddess idyll a virgin is one who is her own person, one who allows herself fully to be and become without limiting herself to what a man desires from her nor to any predetermined societal plan or purpose. There is a feeling of open-endedness to her. She belongs primarily to herself—not primarily to her parents or lovers. She is receptive to random gifts from others and from Nature, but she is not passive and not a victim. As she matures, she grows in being responsible for herself; she is developing courage, good sense, and physical strength, becoming capable of taking care of herself, knowledgeable in how to avoid displeasure or harm to herself. The maiden also grows in her awareness of how vital and nourishing her family, community, and home-place are to her Self.

In a wholistic view of the world Selfhood implies a long-range view of Self-interest. Wholism means that all forms of life and matter are experienced as related to every other form in a great non-hierarchical interdependent web of being, so the interests of Nature and society-at-large are simultaneously one's own Self-interests. The Virgin archetype represents the highest virtue in a social system that urges one to allow, nurture, and sustain one's Self while simultaneously honoring the Other-as-Self.

THE GODDESS AS VIRGIN

Hebe, the Virgin as Goddess, is the Self-

Responsible, Self-Fertilizing, Self-Creating One. As the Birth-Giving aspect of the Goddess, She is said to be Pregnant with All Possibility, containing Other-within-Self, the Fountain of All Being, the Most Dynamic and Fertile Life Force.

The name Hebe is the Greek version of Eve. The Bible's Yahwist author links Eve's Hebrew name *Hawwah* to the Goddess of Creation by calling her "Mother of All Living."[5] Some scholars regard Hebe (Eve) as the eponymous ancestress of the Hebrews.[6]

The Goddess *Hebe Parthenia* stands for—is a metaphor for—youth, springtime, the beginning and renewing of life and love. This aspect of the Goddess represents that part of every woman, young or old, who recognizes the start of each day and phase of her life as a new birth; each new cycle or moment means being at the edge of something unknown, offers something to discover—perhaps some new behavior or attitude to love and admire about herself. A Hebe

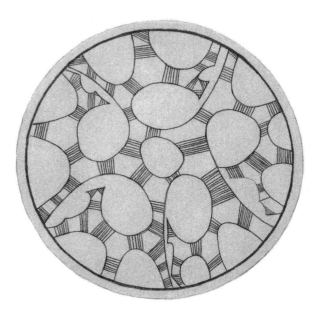

"Becoming!" Egg and swirling waters design in clay dish. Malta, 3000 B.C.E.

woman anticipates the unknown—the Great Mystery—for its blessings, and treats each new start as a gift with its own rewards and wisdom about the world and oneSelf. Even the start of a final illness for a Hebe woman can be celebrated as a New Beginning. It is Hebe's gift that every day—even one's last—can be a profound new experience.

Hebe is the Model of the Virgin's consciousness. We are *in Her image* when we too are expectant, full of life, becoming, budding, pregnant with possibility, Self-responsible, Self-motivating, Self-creating—ever giving birth to our Self, ever finding something new to love about Life. The Virgin—the Maiden Goddess—models these things for men of all ages as well as for women of all ages.

VIRGIN WATERS

The highest good is like water. Water gives life to the ten thousand things and does not strive.[7]

—Tao-te Ching

Water plays a big role in the rituals of Hebe. The flow of any life-bringing liquids—water, blood, milk, vaginal honey—announces and represents the blessing of a new beginning and brings Hebe's *mana*—Her innate, inner, renewing powers—to the event. Hera Parthenia's statue was bathed in a fast-flowing stream every spring as women sang in celebration. And without fail Hera emerged from those renewing waters reborn. Her hymn says, "Hera, like the April bough, is drenched in dew and water that She may burgeon and blossom anew." Hebe Parthenia personifies the ever-returning springtime and the life-giving properties of flowing waters. Her ritual immersion and rebirth was a natural event in Nature, enacted and reenacted annually from time out-of-memory, hence Her title: Ever-Virgin.

The Virgin Mother—*Hebe* and often *Mari* (our word "marine" comes from Her name)—is the Sea, the Rains, the River, the Waters from which life flows and receives sustenance. The Virgin models *the Way of Water* as a PATTERN of life: waters flow where they will, nourishing as they go; so, the Virgin models letting be, flowing with the current of life, expecting to give and receive nourishment and gifts as one goes. Waters follow the line of least resistance and are themselves irresistible. Waters have no clear or fixed boundaries. When entered slowly and gently, waters will part and allow penetration without resistance, yet when entered disrespectfully with solid force, they resist with an equally solid force. The waters nourish everything they touch and roll effortlessly over obstacles, yet they wear away the hardest granite in their paths. Water strives not to rule over or even to *be* over anything, but rather always flows downward to be close to and mix with the supporting earth, a Model of sacred lowliness-oneness to be appreciated and emulated.

As the Sea, the Virgin models the oneness and cohesion of the human Self even though it is ever-changing and ever-unfinished. We can see that different unbounded streams become one cohesive entity when they flow together to form the sea; but the sea, although it is one entity, is also a vibrant, containing but ultimately uncontainable, unfinished, ever-changing body of water with undulating boundaries. As Heraclitus wrote, "One can never step in the same river twice." That applies to all bodies of water; they are all constantly changing. As is Hebe. As is our Self.

The ancients thought of Hebe-the-Waters as a mirror in which they could recognize their divine unbounded nature. Waters represent the Virgin's freedom, joy, and spontaneity. Through watching and imitating the Way of Water, we can emulate Her to find, effortlessly, our own path and Self.

VIRGIN CONSCIOUSNESS

The Goddess is Changing Woman in all three of Her Persons. The aspect of the Goddess whose attributes are experienced in ever-changing *ever-new beginnings* is the Virgin. She models the ubiquitous expectation of being able to start over, of not being stuck in habits of behavior or thought.

We are in Her Image when we remain receptive to the goodness of life and the universe, when we *allow* ourselves and the sacred PATTERN of All-That-Is just to *be* without manipulation, allow ourselves, our dreams, and our talents to exist just as we are, when we allow the All to be just as it is, with honor, without trying to control or resist What Is.

The Virgin is not a garden. The Virgin's consciousness, rather, provokes one to feel one's Self a virgin forest where myriad life forms proliferate. The more a virgin forest is left alone to be what it is, the more varied and rich and interdependent are its components. When we think of ourSelves as a virgin forest, every wild, wonderful, and unpretentious aspect of our Self is welcome and allowed to manifest, mingle, and thrive with all the other unbidden aspects of our Self. In a wild virgin-forest Self no need and no outcropping is judged or deleted.

No, the Virgin is not a garden. A garden must be weeded; only certain forms of life are allowed to stay and receive nourishment there. In a garden the worth of each permitted life form is determined, prejudged, controlled by some authority outside the garden. A proper gardener keeps out the deer, rabbits, and birds with scarecrows, nets, and poison, for only certain creatures are qualified or allowed to feed there. In a garden all of Nature's potential components and gifts are not allowed to come into being, and all of its allowed life forms are not found growing in their naturally interdependent PATTERNS of relationship. When we are expe-

*Young Spring Goddess rising from Earth as Tree-Column. She is holding hands up
in "drawing down the moon" position, wearing cone-shaped omphalos headpiece
decorated in front with poppy heads (possibly indicating ecstatic trance rituals).
Terra cotta, Crete, 1350 B.C.E.*

riencing the Virgin's consciousness, we will not think of our Self as a garden, for there only certain aspects of our Self-crop would be allowed to come up, only those budding aspects of our Self that are prejudged to be worthy and proper would be allowed to receive care and thrive.

We follow in the Virgin's Way when we make a primordial *leap of faith* into life, when we get into the flow of things without planning, without holding the flow in check, without fear of the unknown, without fear of not knowing, appreciating our ignorance as the gift of innocence. A virgin, eager for life, understands that she cannot learn from what she already knows. She therefore walks right into uncertainty, into the Mystery, alert and aware, expecting unbidden gifts that she knows nothing of and cannot predict.

Again, *allowing* in the Hebe mode is not passivity. A Hebe woman allows natural PATTERNS and flow; she does not allow the dysfunctional PATTERNS of a concocted, unjust society. One allows earthquakes and cyclones, but one resists war and brutality as solidly and instantly as water resists blows. In Hebe's Image one falls against rape and murder; one resists all *violations* of Nature's renewing PATTERNS and the sanctity of Selfhood with the full force of an unstoppable waterfall.

Hebe is Nature's child; She personifies Nature's sacred creative, re-creative, life-giving PATTERNS. When we try to contradict or fight Nature's PATTERNS, we are not acting in Hebe's Image. In Hebe's Image, one can use the PATTERNS of Nature to create technology, like using flowing water or wind to move a fan for cooling. In this consciousness one can utilize technology—something not found as it is in Nature—to enhance life as long as the techniques and technical devices follow and respect Nature's PATTERNS, but do not try to conquer or subvert them.[8]

It is said that Confucius esteemed manners, courtesy, and "correct forms" as "the way" for people to be in control of their actions, to get along, and to live the best lives. On the other hand, the Virgin is like the Tao; this Way of Life abhors artificial manners, this Way refuses to prescribe controls and proprieties, for prescribed behaviors and prohibitions repress sincere feelings and one's ability to know and honor one's authentic Self and every Other's authentic Self too. What is the need for *cultivating* manners (the garden PATTERN), when in the Virgin's Image one fully honors and *allows* one's own position and the position of all Others (the Virgin forest PATTERN) with integrity, honesty, and love, without needing to weed out parts of one's Self or parts of Others, without needing to inflict pain or rudeness to maintain or acquire some advantage?

The Virgin Goddess is the Creatrix: strong, pliable, resilient, the Source of all Potential, of all Becoming. She conceives and creates life, carries, gestates, and nurtures it inside Her own Body. Thus She models giving birth to oneSelf, allowing the Self to emerge from one's Necessity inside, as a gift that comes unbidden from one's own body and experience. The Virgin Goddess thus models courage and openness to change. She is the perfect example of being one's own person, of belonging to oneSelf. Hebe demonstrates Self-centeredness—but without egotism or conceit.

CREATRIX—BIRTH-GIVER

The Creativity of the Virgin inspires resourcefulness in us. Getting into ruts and staying there reflects a failure of our creativity, a failure to access our innate resourcefulness, a failure to invent a New Beginning, failure to follow in Her Image, failure to allow Rebirth, a failure to love or trust enough in Possibility. As changes come, our creativity is challenged; as changes come, new responses are often called for or must be invented, opportunities created or allowed so that our Becoming can continue to flow.

Those who are in their Virgin consciousness are always regenerating their Self, because they are always pregnant with Possibility and always alert to Life and what its flow might bring. They are always falling in love with some part of themselves, some part of the All.

In our culture birth-giving is valued to some extent, but there is no divine Model of the physical creation of life and its processes, no reverence or sacred celebration for gestation, labor, "the Crowning" (the first show of the top of an infant's head at the mother's vulva), and birth. We have no divine Model that sanctifies vulvas and raises *Giving Birth* to the level of Most Holy Sacrament as the Virgin Mother Goddess Model did for our matristic ancestors. Goddess people revere vulvas and wombs as the place of creation and source of life; they treat yonis with awe and esteem, draw them, sculpt them, honor them as sacred icons and portents when they find them in natural formations.[9]

CIVILIZATION AND CULTURE

Ancient myths tell us that the Virgin Mother gave many gifts to women for the use of humankind: seed culture, musical instruments, weaving, holding devices (such as slings for carrying young children, pots for water, baskets for foodstuffs), nets, processes for extracting oil from olives for use as food and fuel—the list recorded in extant myths is very long. History too records that it was primarily women who were instrumental in creating civilization, initiating the arts of getting along together, healing, ceramics, spinning, decorating, writing, meting justice,

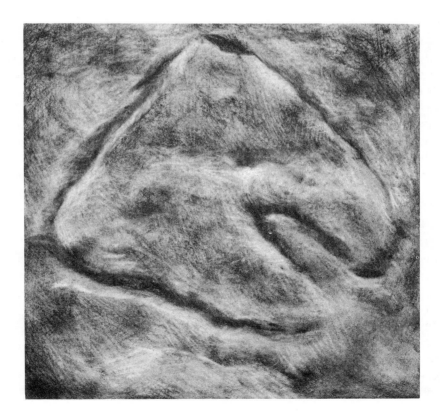

Vulva in stone,
c. 15,000 B.C.E.

agriculture, pharmacology—inventing technologies and culture.[10]

Anthropologist Evelyn Reed has observed that "the households [early women] managed were not merely kitchens and nurseries; they were the first factories, laboratories, clinics, schools, and social centers."[11] In earliest times there was a clear gendered division of labor—no hierarchical valuing of one kind of work over another, some things were just obviously *women's work*. Women therefore invented the means for carrying children, water, foodstuffs. Women devised multiple uses for gourds and found many uses for fire and clay. It was women who discovered that one could make threads from plant fibers and fabrics from threads. Women—the gatherers—first conceived the idea of sowing and harvesting seeds and figured out how to do it successfully where they wanted to.[12] Home-makers and nest-builders from the beginning, women were the first architects, devising many different ways for making shelters.

In the beginning of our kind there were women, creating *in the image of the Virgin* extended families and long-lasting coalitions that transformed opportunistic male and female primates into social, caring people. *In the beginning* there were women, turning footloose individuals who acted primarily in their own interest into cooperative clans who lived in helpful concert together, not absconding to eat alone the meat they had caught and nuts they had gathered, but sharing what they had with each other, feeding one another, living by *mothering* each other, devising and perpetuating the altruistic, cooperative philosophy of share-and-share-alike, sometimes called the Potlatch or Give-Away society. *In the beginning* there were women, creating the cohesive, committed groups of people that made language possible, that made song, verbal nuance, and mental agility our inheritance, that made moral responsibil-

ity to others our nature. *In the beginning* there were women—creative *virgins* all—bringing into being many of the good things that have happened.[13]

SOME VIRGIN GODDESSES

The Anglo-Saxon Goddess Easter is a familiar example of a divine Virgin Creatrix. She personifies spring and dawn.[14] All new beginnings are sacred to Her: spring-green leaves, budding bulbs and flowers, chicks and lambs in barnyards, fawns and baby rabbits in the renewing forests. The Egg—the Cosmic Egg, Source of Creation—is one of Easter's primary symbols.

Birds—especially those associated with life-giving waters, waterfowl like geese and swans—are egg-layers and therefore are Nature-signs that put people in mind of Creation. The Egyptian Goddess Hathor was the three-toed, triune, creating deity "Mother Goose" who laid the Golden Egg, or Cosmic Egg, the Source-of-All. Birds in general symbolize Source or the Creating Mother. Bird-associated signs include the *V*, which resembles a goose or other waterfowl in flight, and chevrons (two or more *V*s layered).

Greek Artemis and Roman Diana are both Virgin Goddesses. Neither is married, neither a mother, both belong to Themselves. Both are self-sufficient huntresses, at home in the wilds of Nature, at home with Their *own* wildness, pregnant with Possibility, comfortable with danger and the unknown. In Their image, we can find our own wildness and oneness with Nature; we can also learn to be comfortable with danger, risk, and Mystery. Although neither has given birth, both are midwives who watch over the births of animals and humans, over all emerging life: emerging vegetation, emerging Selves.

The Goddess Ananke, who personifies Self-realization or the "Necessity inside that produces ecstasy," falls into the Virgin's consciousness. In some ways She is like the pre-Greek Maiden Goddess Kore, who personifies the Seed

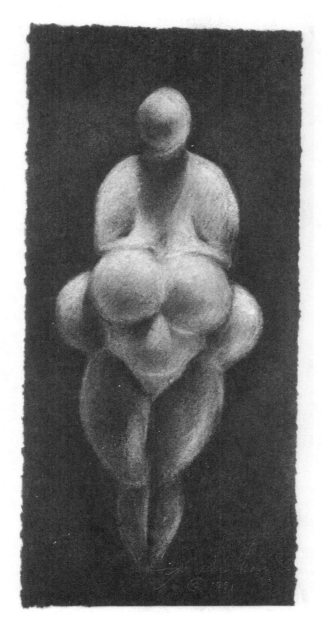

*Great Virgin Mother of Lespugue. Bird Goddess
with nest of eggs inside (and tail feathers in back,
not legs), She the Source, the Great Becoming,
pregnant with Possibility. France, 21,000 B.C.E.*

*Nippled ewers representing the Creatrix as Singing Bird Goddess, She the
Bountiful Container and Vessel of Creation, She the Waters and Cosmic Egg.
Terra cotta, Thera, Greece, 1500 B.C.E.*

or essential Germ of the grain, and whose name
gives us our words "core" and "coronary,"
meaning the center or heart of things.

Symbols of the Virgin Goddess. The Virgin is
the patroness of all New Beginnings: dawn,
springtime, birth, new relationships, striking out
in new directions, starting over. Her symbols include: eggs, newborn creatures, vulvas, flowing
waters, *vessels of creation*—such as wombs,

caves, woven baskets, water jugs, and chalices—
buds, April showers, and sea fish—such as
salmon—returning to the rivers to spawn. All
signs of spring show Her at work.

The Snake Goddess is as a rule associated
with Creation, that is, with cosmic Birth-Giving.
It is common to find the features of water, creation, and serpents combined into one symbol-
image. The Goddess who personifies heavenly

(cosmic) waters or the sea as (cosmic) amniotic fluids is simultaneously the watery Womb of Creation and is simultaneously visualized as a Cosmic Serpent. It is easy to understand the pairing: the wavy line that stands for water is identical with the shape of a snake, so sacred water and snake medicine or magic are found indissolubly mixed conceptually as well as in ritual practices around the world. The snake's coil is the symbol for the spiraling cycle of Birth-Death-ReBirth, and waters are the amniotic fluids that always accompany birth. Water nourishes life and snakes are symbols of body and earth Wisdom; even Moses, the biblical patriarch, urged his people: "Be wise as a serpent." The water-snake-creation combination is found from Paleolithic Europe to contemporary North American Amerind mythology. Great Mother Tiamat was the Cosmic Serpent Creatrix of the Babylonians,[15] and archaic Hera was portrayed both as the Waters (dew, rain, river, flood) and as a Snake Goddess Creatrix, Her hair hanging in reptilian coils.[16] The Aboriginal Rainbow Snake ("rainbow" for New Beginnings) is also a primordial Creating Mother who manifests in the form of the flooding, spiraling waters of the monsoon and women's menstrual periods.[17]

PURIFICATION

Our tradition primes us to think of baptism or any ritual use of water as a cleansing or purifying act. In the religious traditions of the west, the body is thought of as "fallen" and sinful, therefore—before we are good enough for an encounter with the transcendent deity—we feel we must cleanse and purify ourselves.

In Hera's tradition, however, each person is assumed to be created in the Image of the Goddess, each creation—animal, vegetable, or mineral—a worthy, sacred manifestation of Her limitless divine Possibilities. (This assumption is mirrored in the Buddhist saying: "Even at birth there is nothing lacking in you, and you yourself

are no different from the Buddha.") Therefore, there is no reason to purify or cleanse the ordinary human body to please Hera. We are already in Her Image, already *perfect* earthlings just as we are—even though unfinished or hesitant or groping. That is, after all, the way a perfect human is, unfinished, always changing, always Becoming—as She is, as our Virgin Mother Marie the Sea is.

A show of menstrual blood on women's thighs is not dirty or in need of being cleansed off; it is sacred stuff—the creative Blood of Life. And although Hera's followers in Argos washed it away in ceremonies at the Brook of the Free-flowing Waters, the purpose of that ritual was to finish a cycle, to honor the end of the month—the simultaneous end of one cycle of the moon and one cycle of women's bodies—and to celebrate the beginning of another.

Through women's womb blood and its cycle humankind perpetuates the creation of life and participates in the enduring cosmic cycle of Birth-Death-ReBirth. Therefore, the ritual in the Virgin Waters is not a ritual purification so much as a ritual marker of the clear end of one good and holy period-cycle in a woman's life and the clear beginning of another good and holy period-cycle. The special significance of water—of all ritual washing or bathing—is that it honors and celebrates transitions and transformations—simultaneous endings and beginnings—both essential, treasured ingredients in flowing life.

By trying to clarify the use of the Waters, I am not suggesting that there should never be purification rituals in the Goddess's lifeway. If there is a crime, a cleansing may be called for, as in Deena Metzger's novel about Goddess priestesses in pre-history, *The Woman Who Slept with Men to Take the War out of Them.*[18] My concern is that women not routinely practice cleansing. Purification should not be a matter of course for us. I am concerned about what is good for women to do and think about themselves every day, about how women use water in rituals that observe the normal course of daily events. If divinity is immanent within human beings, then women and men are not basically sinful and do not need to be regularly ritually cleansed. There needs to be a specific, appropriate cause for a cleansing, and that cause must not be presumed to be a general state of unworthiness.

In the Old Ways the free-flowing, non-judging wild Waters nourish, bless, and confirm human nature. By observing the PATTERN of Virgin Waters, one can train oneself to emulate better the Virgin's consciousness. But habitually thinking of water, not primarily as nurturing and transforming but first of all as a cleansing agent, presupposes a reason for guilt or shame or a sense of not measuring up. Doing purification rituals as a matter of course, for no particular reason except an *assumed* need for them, keeps unworthiness, lowliness, and dirtiness on our minds and undermines the qualities of sensuous authenticity, wildness, freedom, the Wisdom-within, the divinity, Self-love, and Selfhood we yearn for and deserve.

Women and men must do nothing that habitually promotes or continues a routine feeling of guilt or shame about their bodies. In my head I can still hear a hymn from my childhood in the convent school, a negative mantra endlessly repeating, "Oh, Lord, I am not worthy." I used to hear it night and day. Goddess rituals must do nothing to aid and abet such Self-hatred—nor do anything to trigger even a *suspicion* of innate inadequacy.

Water rituals can flow over us, letting us be, confirming the Life-flow in us and the divinity immanent in us. A water-associated mantra should confirm: "We are all good and worthy—just as we are, *without striving* for a higher or different Self. You and I are Goddess—Ever-Virgin, sister and divine child of holy,

nourishing, Life-giving Waters—just as we are."

The Virgin's consciousness maintains a readiness to receive gifts, always admits to goodness in one's Self, always bears an expectation of good in the offing. When accidents or ill luck befall one, the Wise Woman question—the Virgin's attitude—is: "How is this problem my ally, or a gift?" (See my discussion of Susun Weed's Wise Woman Ways in the Introduction; see Chapter 9, "Crone Consciousness," for an examination of primal attitudes toward decay, death, and good riddance.)

VIRGIN WARRIOR GODDESSES

The Great Mother Goddess personifies the entire spectrum of human experience, and Her influence is thus felt throughout peoples' lives. The influence of patriarchal goddesses is always limited to specific categories of experience or hegemony. Naturally, Indo-European goddesses serve the needs of the patriarchal societies that created them, usually by modifying the persona of deities that were already a part of peoples' lives. The Great Mother Goddess who had represented the entire unending cycle of Birth-Life-Death-ReBirth was typically reduced to either one or both of these: The Good (nurturing) Mother who brings life and joy, or the Terrible (destructive) Mother who brings death and disaster and often loses her temper. Warrior goddesses spring from the Mother Goddess as Death-Wielder who has been reduced and militarized.

It has been explained that Indo-European societies function at three levels or castes (the priestly class, the warrior class, and the artisan-worker class) and that their mythologies were designed to nurture those who worked in those castes, to ease and abet their functioning.[19] It is very important for women today to feel that we have some power over our lives, and that if any of us want to create warrior goddesses to help us fight for our rights, we can do it. But the warrior goddesses of ancient patriarchal societies were not fighting for women; they were not models meant to inspire women or show them what they could do. *The goddesses of wisdom nurtured and gave wisdom to the men in the priestly caste; the warrior goddesses nurtured and gave energy to male warriors.* The Muses did not show women how females could be great artists, actors, or writers; the Muses were devised to inspire men (artisans in the third castes) to do those things.[20] The Goddess Metis of pre-classical times personified Earth Wisdom and the Wisdom of women's knowing bodies; the wisdom of Her daughter Athena was military knowledge, and to dispense it Athena was installed in a fortress temple wearing helmet and carrying shield and weapon and was "best known for being the *inspiration* of male warriors."[21] Some warrior goddesses retain some vestiges of their former self-sufficiency by exerting rage, but "most of the Classical-Age Indo-European goddesses . . . become strategic warriors"[22] instead, having lost any sign that they were once models of *women being the agents of their own lives.*

The early gathering-hunting people who revered the Goddess were egalitarian and non-hierarchical, living according to a cooperative Give-Away and share-alike philosophy that had no place for war or warriors. "The concept of an enemy, an unfriendly Other, is a Neolithic invention," says cultural historian Morris Berman, author of *The Reenchantment of the World* and *Coming to Our Senses.*[23]

It is likely that human beings in pre-history had temper tantrums and that tribal scores had to be settled, but there were other kinds of controls in place in Paleolithic societies that made such events rare and sporadic at most. Without doubt, the profession of warrior was not a part of the human experience before five thousand years ago.[24] The Warrior, therefore, is not a uni-

versal human archetype, not our fate, not unavoidable, not a Necessity in our human nature, not an essential PATTERN, not written in the stars. The god Mars is a very recent mythological invention, and the red planet we have named after him—giving honor to his predilection to shed blood violently, bestowing glory on his compulsive need to dominate others—was once named for our Mother, the Crone, its color said to symbolize the red Blood of Life. So war has not long been integral to our lifeway, nor eternally ensconced in our stars. It seems that even constellations and astrology underwent an archetypal reversal!

Athena, Amazons, Durga, and other female warriors in Europe, India, and elsewhere are recent mythological creations. Let us not lose sight of the fact that first and foremost their function was to inspire male warriors and to help keep real women in their places. Warrior goddesses are personality deities, not immanent deities. No matter how worthy their wars seem to be, these female warriors are not aspects of the immanent Goddess of pre-history. A warrior deity—male or female—models violence as an authentic, sacred way of being-in-the-world. I cannot accept that as an enduring truth about human life or as an aspect of the Model the Goddess embodies.

To a great extent we create a Model for ourselves and others by the stories we tell. By our stories we CREATE OURSELVES! Since we determine who we are and what kind of world we and our children live in through the stories and images we promote, I cannot in good conscience tell any story in this book about the Goddess as a warrior. We need a new Ideal Image for ourselves, a new Model, a new story.

THE CREATRIX AND HER MYTH

The Creatrix proceeds out of wonder and claims the Mystery, claims not-knowing, as an essential part of Self. She is Changing Woman, modeling Becoming, personifying an evolving universe made up of ever-emerging new PATTERNS. Pre-judgments or societal prescriptions about who we are or should be make no appearance in Her myth. Rather, new life, and unplanned, unbidden Possibilities come out of Her, are allowed, welcomed, delighted in.

This myth mirrors the version of reality that is coming out of the new physics, out of chaos theory and complexity theory. These new ways of doing science—these new ways of looking at the world—are revealing that new PATTERNS are constantly emerging, randomly, without adhering to any plan, that cause-and-effect explanations are inadequate for doing science because they do not describe all that is happening or manifesting in Nature's complexity; they miss the wider Much-at-Once.

This myth is intended to be a ritual dance that reconnects ordinary life with the numinous. Ritual is a device that reverses the isolating process in which we westerners have trained ourselves to narrow our focus down to see all entities as things-in-themselves. Rituals help us reconnect the cycles of the water, stars, moon, stones, vegetation, and all animate beings including ourselves—revealing the symbolic relatedness of All-That-Is.

May the telling of this myth help us celebrate the wonder and Mystery of being earthlings. May it encourage us to play. May it remind us to expect and appreciate our own goodness, to look for relatives everywhere, new Potentials, new PATTERNS, New Beginnings.

Blessed be.

Ananke.

Five

· · · · ·

THE MYTH OF CREATION

The Story of Hebe, the Virgin

[*Storyteller stands upstage center, legs wide apart, knees bent to outside, eyes closed, head down, perfectly still. She gradually makes audible, deep, breathing sounds—like the surf. She slowly raises her head and becomes fully alert, arms reaching out to each side and up, "drawing down the moon." She rings one pair of the finger cymbals she wears once—RING!—and listens to the sound as it fills up the entire space in the room. Like the Goddess Vak, the Hindu Creatrix who sings the cosmos into being, the storyteller sings on one long, sustained high note:*]

. . . A l p h a ! . . .

[*Another single RING! of finger cymbal. Then, speaking:*]

Alpha! The beginning!

In the beginning
        NOTHING
                that is was.

                        No.   Not yet !

Bird Goddess as Source of All, rising from Vessel of Creation.
Clay, Romania, 4500 B.C.E.

In the beginning
       everything that is was mere Possibility,
       everything that is was merely Becoming,
       for everything was gestating
              in the womb of the Great Goddess,
                gestating
              in the close-and-holy Darkness
                   of Her great womb.

For in the beginning SHE WAS!
In the very beginning SHE is ALL that was.

            SHE, The Source.
            SHE, our VIRGIN MOTHER !

[Both pairs of finger cymbals dance!]

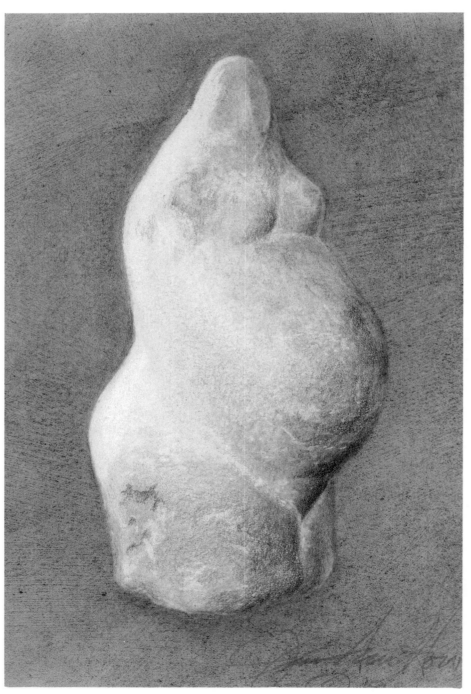

Virgin Mother, pregnant with Possibility

VIRGIN, our Mother,

> For in the beginning
> > She—being All-That-Is—
> > > conceived by Herself!

VIRGIN!   not meaning celibate.
VIRGIN!   meaning She who is sufficient-unto-Herself.
VIRGIN!   not meaning celibate.
VIRGIN!   meaning belonging-to-Herself-alone.

The VIRGIN MOTHER!
> Primordial Oneness.
> > Pregnant with Possibility!
> > Pregnant with untold POSSIBILITY ! !

Ohhmmm!   Ohhmmm!   Ohhmmm![1]

[*Finger cymbals dance.*]

VIRGIN
Mother . . . .
CRONE

From the beginning
She could feel the Becoming inside.
She could feel Her
      lissome, lithesome, limitless body
            growing ROUND . . .

And
She rolled and rolled,
      loving Her roundness.
She rocked and rocked,
      treasuring Her growing fullness.

What ecstacy to have a divine womb!
    And it so round and
        so full of potential!

Oh . . .   Ohh ! . . .   Ohhmmmmmm ! !

Becoming! Swirling egg-water motif, painted in clay dish. Bulgaria, 4500 B.C.E.

VIRGIN
Mother . . . .
CRONE

But
When the Becoming had filled Her, . . .
When the Becoming had filled Her to overflowing!
    the fullness gave way,
        and the great body heaved, . . .

            OMM . . . OMM . . . OMM . . .

And the Virgin brought forth . . .

            OOOOOOOOOOOOOOOOOOHM ! ! ! !

                . . . the EARTH ! !

Earth Mother in white chalk. England, c. 2850 B.C.E.

VIRGIN
Mother . . . .
CRONE

Blessed Earth!
        Her own flesh and blood!
        divine as she is divine!

Earth's hills and
        valleys and
        round mounds Her Body!

The majestic mountains,
        the great snow-covered breasts of nourishment
                all Her BODY!
                alive with Her Life!

Earth's nature and fiery center unsubduable,
    as
Her nature and fiery center are unsubduable!

"The Paps of Anu." The breasts of Ireland's Earth Mother Goddess Anu
(sometimes called Danu or Anann).

VIRGIN
Mother . . . .
CRONE

To celebrate the joy of creating
She promised that:
New land would forever be forthcoming
    from Her volcano,
    from Her cauldron's wide mouth,
    from Her vulva,
    from Her endlessly giving vulva.

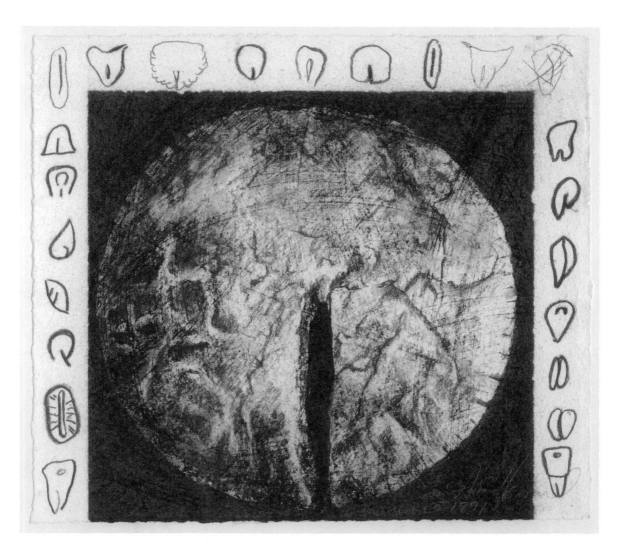

Carved and engraved vulvas, c. 30,000–9000 B.C.E.

*"The waters." Detail on gold door, decorating egg-shaped
libation vessel. Crete, 1500 B.C.E.*

[*Storyteller swirls her long blue skirt like waves:*]

Just then . . . there poured forth from Her womb
The Waters!

Waves!
          of primeval Waters!
Rivers of washing, birthing fluids
          collecting in the Sea.
She, the flooding, nourishing Rivers!
She, the deep-dark solacing Sea!

Our Mother, the Sea!
Maa-Maa! Ma-re!
Marine Mother, Marie, the Sea!
Our Virgin Mother Marie, the Sea!

[*Deep, loud breathing in . . . out—like the surf:*]

And She breathed
    all round
      the Earth.

She breathed round all of Her creation,
      exhaling stars,
        creating the heavens, galaxies.
She breathed far out—
      even beyond our imaginings!

And as She witnessed Her manifesting Self,
    She exclaimed,
        "I am Alpha! I am All-That-Is!"

And still She felt the Becoming!
She, the Source!
She, Primordial Oneness!
    in a burst of creativity
        became a plethora of many-ness!

          As out of Her Body came . . .

Becoming! Rain and water lines enclose eggs marked with Xs, representing their inherent regenerative energy. Ukraine, 3900 B.C.E.

STONES!

She gave birth to STONES!

STONES,

Divine, for they are of and from Her Body.

STONES—in Her own image,
of Her own essence.

STONES are the Mother Herself,

She the ever-enduring
ROCKS,

She the firm foundation of
GRANITE.

She the MOUNTAINS that heave

as She brings forth . . .

Earth Mother of Laussel. Enhanced natural formation found on limestone stele.
France, 25,000 B.C.E.

Goddess Isis as Tree, suckling King Thutmosis III. Thebes, Egypt, 1490 B.C.E.

TREES!

She gave birth to TREES!

rooted in Her breath the air

[*Mime, reaching high with both hands.*]

and rooted in the earth Her body.

[*Mime, reaching down, arms close to sides.*]

VIRGIN
Mother ....
CRONE

She, the TREE,

        COLUMN of divinity,

        PILLAR of strength,

        the TREE, our Mother,

        connecting, linking, holding together
            all three realms:
            air, earth, and the underworld,

                    that is Her bountiful womb,
                    the overflowing Sea

                    out of which She brought forth . . .

Hera as Tree-Column. From Heraion, Samos, 560 B.C.E.

Fishes, water, and net-womb symbols on storage jar.
Greece, eighteenth century B.C.E.

FISHES !

She gave birth to FISHES ! !

[*Hands mime swimming fishes.*]

VIRGIN
Mother . . . .
CRONE

And all manner of SEA CREATURES!

[*Hands mime crabs, lobsters.*]

All divine as She is divine.
All in Her own image.

And DOLPHINS.

[*Leap around.*]

And WHALES!

[*Mime and make sounds:*]

PPLLOOO-OOOOOMMM . . . PLAH! . . . Pssshhhh . . .

all at home in the deep,
in Her dark womb

out of which came . . .

Jug with octopus. Greece, fourteenth century B.C.E.

*Owl-headed Madonna and hieroglyph of owl. Terra cotta, Cyprus, 1450 B.C.E.;
drawing on stone, Egypt, 1300 B.C.E.*

BIRDS!

She gave birth to BIRDS!

Divine feathered creatures of spirit
At home in Her breath, the heavens!

BIRDS !

Wise as the Mother is wise.

Do BIRDS not tell the seasons
with their goings and
comings?

Do BIRDS not lay EGGS?

EGGS of
eternal
regeneration,

Models of Her own Cosmic EGG,
The Source of *all* life,

out of which She brought forth . . .

Athena Nike, Goddess of Victory.
Samothrace, 190 B.C.E. [JWW]

Snake Madonna. Terra cotta, Greece, sixth century B.C.E.

SsssSNAKESsss!

[*Dancing slowly and sensuously,*
body moving in various S-shapes,
arms entwining up and down
and around.]

She gave birth to SsssSERPENTSsssssssss.

In   Her own image,
Of   Her own essence,
        Her own flesh and blood, the

                SsssSNAKESsss.

Subtle, flowing, winding . . .
Wise as She is wise!

Do they not shed their skins in acts of
                                eternal
                                regeneration?

                        perpetual
                        renewal?

                SsssSNAKESssss . . .

Who cycle as She cycles!

                SsssSNAKESssss . . .

At home in the Garden of Paradise,
At home in Her womb the Earth

                        out of which She brought forth . . .

Great Mother Goddess Kybele. Enthroned and flanked by
Her leopards, giving birth (to bull?).
Çatal Hüyük, Anatolia, Turkey, c. 7100 B.C.E.

ANIMALS!

She gave birth to ANIMALS!

[*Mime stag.*]

So many kinds of ANIMALS!

[*Mime bear, elephant,*]

All in Her own image!
All of Her own flesh and blood.

[. . . *rat, cat,*]

Life Force as Bull. Knossos, Crete, 1550 B.C.E.

ANIMALS!

[... *giraffe.*]

All divine as She is divine.

For She is our loving Mother . . .

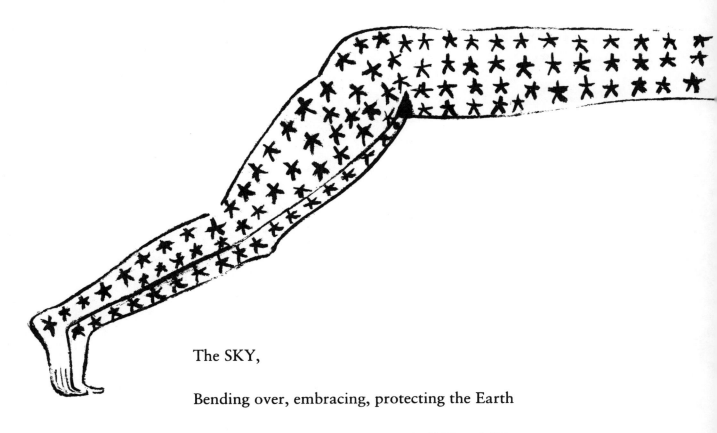

The SKY,

Bending over, embracing, protecting the Earth

and all Her children.

At night one can see
the milk of Her cosmic breast
spilling across the heavens,
a milky spill across Her dark, soft,
bending-over belly.

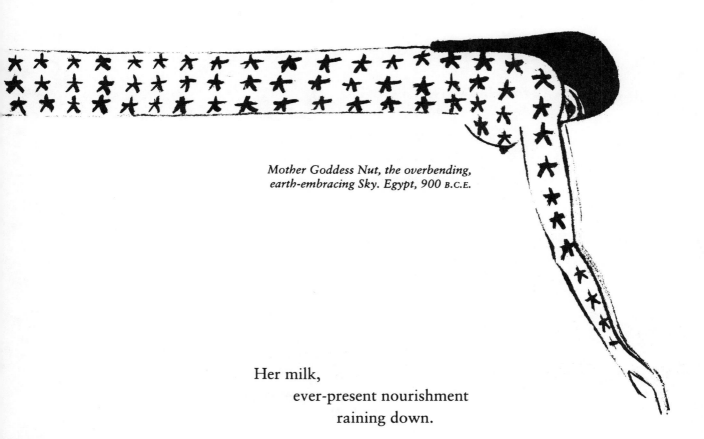

*Mother Goddess Nut, the overbending,
earth-embracing Sky. Egypt, 900 B.C.E.*

Her milk,
    ever-present nourishment
        raining down.

For She is our Succor,
            our Source,

Who brought forth . . .

VIRGIN
Mother . . . .
CRONE

All the HEAVENLY BODIES

and set them to cycling,
round and round—
round like Her body.

All divine as She is divine!
All cycling, spiraling, changing,
All She cycles, spirals, changes!

She—ever-renewing,
ever-lasting Life!
She—ever-regenerating:

Mother-Daughter
Mother-Daughter
Mother-Daughter

And She gave birth to . . .

*Mother-Daughter, the Power of two, unboundaried,
melding, interpenetrating . . . White marble Goddess,
Çatal Hüyük, seventh millennium* B.C.E.

Demeter, Mother Earth, holding, nurturing Her Daughter, Kore, the Seed.
Stone, archaic Thebes, Greece. [JWW]

DAUGHTERS!

Divine as She is divine.
See? See!

[*Indicating women in audience.*]

DAUGHTERS!

In Her own image!
Of Her own essence

DAUGHTERS!

Of Her own flesh and blood!

And She gave birth to . . .

Virgin Mother Goddess Isis-Meri, suckling Horus, Her son the sun, born on Winter Solstice (December 25, Roman calendar). Copper, Egypt, 2040 B.C.E.

SONS!

Divine as She is divine.

SONS

In Her own Image.
See? See!

Of course Her SONS are
In Her own Image,
Of Her own flesh and blood!
Is She not the Source and Model of ALL life?

*"Fully female and fully male. . . ." Bird Mother Goddess with testes-
breasts and phallus for neck-head. She has beaked face and almond-
vulva eyes, and she wears omphalos-shaped head covering.
Thessaly, Greece, 5900 B.C.E.*

Does She not conceive by Herself?
        . . . fertilize Herself?
Then She is as fully MALE,
        as She is fully FEMALE,

and out of Her sacred birthing Body
        She brings forth All-That-Is

        in Her own Image.

[Begin Women's Sacred Birthing Dance:]

AND HER SEXUALITY—AND OURS—
IS A DIVINE, HOLY ENERGY!
HER SEXUALITY—
THE ONE, TRULY CREATIVE FORCE
IN THE UNIVERSE!

In the beginning
The Great Mother discovered
Her rhythms! Her energies! Her power!

And She danced Her exultation!
And She passed on Her dance of exultation
to us, Her children,
And it became our dance—
A sacred dance of Becoming and creating,
Our Holy Sacrament for remembering Her joy,
for celebrating Her Oneness.

Ohmmm . . . Ohmmm . . . Ohmmm . . .

For She is the Life Force of the universe—
spiraling and ever-lasting,

And in Her own Image
She brought forth . . .

Female singers-dancers and flutist. Egypt, c. 1420 B.C.E.

VIRGIN
Mother ....
CRONE

The EVER-GREEN
The TREE that does not die,

EVER-green to remind us that
She is EVER-lasting Life!

She: the spiraling,
       EVER-renewing Life Force.

[*Sung:*]

"O Tanna-baum, O Tanna-baum,[2]
How lovely are thy branches."

[*Spoken:*]

She: the pine, the yew, the fir—
        EVER-GREEN and SPIRALING.

[*Sung:*]

"How faithfully evergreen are thy branches."

[*Spoken:*]

Oo! See?
The ivy—EVER-GREEN and spiraling . . .
And the holly!
The holy holly, is She too!

Whorls, spirals, and cones. In myth these are associated with magical women's rites, with transformation, with the cycle of Birth-Death-ReBirth. They are often cyclones, tornadoes, or monsoons, spinning out rain, rivers, and other amniotic, life-giving fluids like milk or menses blood.

[*Sung:*]

"THE HOLLY AND THE IVY."

"The Holly tree bears berries
Red like the Mother's blood.
Of all the trees that are in the wood
The Holly wears the crown."

[*Spoken:*]

A round wreath of evergreens
   to remind us of Life everlasting.
      There's no beginning and no end to Her.
      She is the undying Source of Life:
         Our Virgin Mother

Who eternally brings forth.

VIRGIN
Mother ....
CRONE

They carved Her name,
     Eternal Everlasting Mother,
         over the entrance to Her temple
           at the mouth of the Nile.

In Sais
  they carved in the stone:

    "I AM THE GREAT MOTHER,
        MAKER AND GIVER OF ALL LIFE—[3]
    I AM ALL THAT HAS BEEN,
       ALL THAT IS, AND
       ALL THAT EVER WILL BE.
    IN MY BODY IS LIFE EVERLASTING."

That was carved three thousand years ago in stone.
But even then it was an ancient saying,

    for She was . . .

              in the beginning!

In the beginning
NOTHING
that is was.

No.   Not yet !

In the beginning
everything that is was mere Possibility,
everything that is was merely Becoming,
for everything was gestating
in the womb of the Great Goddess,
gestating
in the close-and-holy Darkness
of Her great womb.

For in the beginning SHE WAS !
In the very beginning SHE is ALL that was.

SHE, The Source.
SHE, our VIRGIN MOTHER !

[*Singing on one long, sustained high note:*]

ALPHA !

[*Storyteller remains motionless for a moment. Deep, loud breaths—in and out, like the surf. After suitable pause, she shakes gourd-rattle in Seven Directions to signify and honor the wholeness of All-That-Is: north, east, south, west, up, down, and the thinking-heart at the center of herself.*]

THE END
· · · · · · · · ·
Blessed be.
Ananke.

Six
·····
MOTHER CONSCIOUSNESS

Hera as Mature Woman is Mother Teleia
(te-LAY-ah).

*T*eleia, the Goddess's Mother Person, is mature Everywoman writ large. She is Everywoman-in-her-fullness, Everywoman-with-a-zest-for-living, Everywoman coming forth like the earth in summer, revealing and reveling in the abundance of her many-faceted Self. Everywoman savors life, has many talents, develops many skills, and makes formative, sustaining contributions over time to her immediate and extended family. Everywoman can lay claim to a fertile mind, deep intuitive wisdom, a strong sense of justice, and the ability to bond with and nurture others. She typically exhibits a propensity to build communities and hold them together.

A woman need not be brilliant nor assertive nor unusually energetic to be or do all these things. Everywoman—as grown daughter, sister, niece, lover, the close, caring kin of all others—has a vested interest in the quality and direction of her whole community's concerns, desiring the benefits of a good life for herself, for her loved ones, for all whose lives touch hers. Like Hebe, Teleia symbolizes love and concern for Self-as-Other and Other-as-Self.

UNIVERSAL MOTHERHOOD

Not every woman will want to be, nor be able to be, a biological mother, although everyone behaves at some time to others in motherly, nurturing ways. And of prime importance: *everyone*—female and male—*has had a mother and would like still to have a good one at the center of his or her life.* (For those of us who do not have such a mother, or even such a Model, the Great Mother internalized can fill that need.)

Praising mothers and mothering is not meant to force or limit any woman's options, as too often happens with this archetype in patriarchal traditions. The commendation here is meant to reconnect us to the concept of sacred Motherhood, which had important societal ramifications for primal peoples, enriching and expanding the meaning of everyone's life, even the men and women who were not mothers. Looking at motherhood as a centering cultural device has many benefits that we can profitably explore for our own mythos today.

The Goddess tradition has endured for so long—at least for thirty thousand years, during twenty-five thousand of which She was the primary deity of our kind—because She does not focus attention on the achievements of one spe-

cial personality or individual at the expense of all others, but rather draws attention and accords prestige and value to all of Her children—human and non-human—and to the non-dominator mothering PATTERN in which Nature and all caring, wise women and men always participate to some extent. No one is left out. She personifies "that which nurtures, bonds, sustains, and endures." Men can bond with, nurture, and sustain themselves, others,

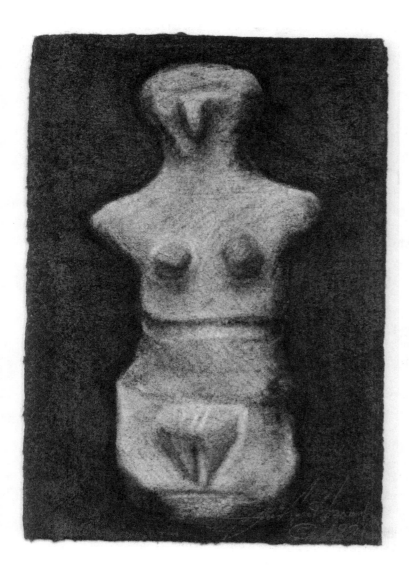

The Divine Female. Enduring stone Bird Mother, "The Source." Aegean Islands, 2500 B.C.E.

and the earth, oftentimes as well as women.[1] But since these qualities are more evident in the female body and more typical of a woman's life, female-associated images and signs long ago came to symbolize those universal human values and their continuity—in a great variety of representations of the Great Mother Goddess.

Through our mothers each of us can demonstrate a biological, emotional connectedness to the large, all-encompassing web of relationships that is humankind. Each mother evidences in herself the full range of human ties: she can in her lifetime be everything from new-born to great-grandmother, both the receiver and giver of life. Primal matristic peoples accept this as the basic principle or central mythos around which they organize their lives and values. But it is a truth in more than a symbolic way. Ova contain genetic material called mitochondrial DNA that is passed on by mothers to all offspring—to sons as well as to daughters; it is given whole and unmodified by any male contribution. Everywoman's eggs—used or not—literally and symbolically relate her in an unbroken inheritance to all humans who have come before and to all who are yet to come.[2]

The French feminist Luce Irigaray, in a phrase that is the title of one of her books, describes women as *This Sex Which Is Not One*.[3] One example of this observation is the pregnant woman who incorporates another being inside her body, an *Other* within her *body-Self*, Self and Other vitally interconnected, yet each retaining its own integrity and authenticity. Similarly, at the level of experience and perception, the oldest grandmother of a clan contains the whole group; every Other member—while having his or her own integrity—is contained within her web-Self as part of herSelf. Symbolically, metaphorically—even literally to some extent—*every* woman contains the whole group in herSelf—including all the many generations before and after her, without end. Men or childless women, as extensions of their mothers and grandmothers, also carry the whole group in their bodies—a psychological and cultural inheritance that is the birthright of us all.

Except that most of us today don't receive that inheritance. Patriarchy is designed to blot out that web, break its connections. Obsessed with individuation, we don't even value the *idea* of being so tied to others—*especially* to our mothers. Nothing in our mythos tells us that our mother-line is a blessing, that it is part of our vital inheritance as whole human beings. The Bible—like all patriarchal censuses—records only male-name inheritance lines, only lists of males who begat. We need a mythos that will value the story of our mother-line, our mother-web—so that we can claim the gifts and rights that go with it.

Carl Kerenyi, the mythologist who collaborated with Carl Jung in developing his archetypal symbols, observed the significance that motherhood had for early peoples:

> [Motherhood] gives the individual woman a place and a meaning in the life of the generations, so that all unnecessary obstacles are cleared out of the way of the life-stream that is to flow through her. At the same time the individual woman is rescued from her isolation and restored to wholeness. *All ritual preoccupation with archetypes ultimately has this aim and this result.*[4]

That is, regardless of whether we are each a mother, the Mother archetype takes each of us out of our isolation and restores us to direct kinship with the All and thereby to wholeness.[5]

What unites all people of all time, is not that we are all mothers but that we have all been born of a mother who was born of a mother who was born of a mother. . . .

Through reverent feelings for their own mothers, early matristic peoples conceived of the all-inclusive sacred lifeway (notice the word religion is not used here) of the Great Goddess, who was for them merely an extended Model and image of Everywoman and Perfect Mother.

This Goddess—or anyone, *in Her image*—embodies the joyful, releasing experience of timelessness, of being outside of linear time, of being one with the All. As a physical embodiment of the endless cycle of life, each of us *in Her* is removed in some sense from death, has become a living part of the endless cycle of life, a participant in the Eternal Present of the cosmic Life Force.[6]

For some women the culmination of their lives comes with motherhood. Nonetheless, motherhood—anyone's capacity to nurture—is enriched when other skills are developed too. In pre-classical times many young maidens went away from home to all-female schools (in the seventh century B.C.E. to Sappho's school on the island of Lesbos or to Artemis's temple) where they—the *parthenoi*—learned to belong to themselves first and foremost , not to a male caretaker such as a husband, father, uncle, or brother.

When she has acquired a strong, dependable Self, if a woman then becomes a mother, that role can be an opportunity to utilize—even maximize—each of her other talents and interests. Not everyone needs to become a mother in order to be a Teleia woman and have a strong, rich, centered Self. But if motherhood comes to a well-Selfed woman, it will not circumscribe and limit her being or her participation in the fullness of her possibilities. It is possible for the role of motherhood to center all of her other abilities and desires, expand her *raison d'être*, bring everything in her life together into one whole, and foster a further webbing or flourishing out.

THE OLD WAYS

Women were accorded much esteem in matrifocal, matrilineal societies, even though women did not dominate or rule their families or groups as men are accustomed to doing within patriarchy. Without having to do anything—just by being—early women served to center and give visible and emotional continuity to all relationships. This centrality was sustained and reinforced by the Model and symbol of the Goddess and also by the underlying philosophy of matristic tribal systems, often called the Old Ways.

The Old Ways are evidenced in the lives of the earliest human groupings as well as in many twentieth-century tribes around the globe. For example, as Gary Snyder points out in his charming, edifying book, *The Old Ways*, the early Chinese people practiced what is now referred to as the spiritual tradition of Taoism:

> Taoism is, following Dr. Joseph Needham's assessment of it in [his thirteen volumes of Chinese history] *Science and Civilization in China,* the largest single coherent chunk of matrilineal descent, mother-consciousness-oriented, neolithic culture that went through the, so to speak, "sound barrier" of civilization in the Iron Age and came out the other side halfway intact. Thus through its whole political history Taoism has been anti-feudal and anti-patriarchal, so much so that Professor Needham says that in a way Taoism has been a 2,000-year-long holding action.[7]

The Old Ways do not offer a new dogma or list of facts to learn or hold up next to our own for comparison. The Old Ways is another paradigm or consciousness that helps one expand one's own experience and derive more meaning from the facts one already has—or from just Being. Tribal women's lives are different from western women's lives, but in some core ways they are the same, for our basic humanity, biology, and potentials remain unchanged.

MOTHER-CENTERED PEOPLES

Our earliest ancestors who revered the Great Goddess as Mother Nature—as Mistress of the Animals and Mistress of the Plants—were transient gatherers and foragers who lived intimately with and in wilderness, considering themselves kin to the other animals, birds, trees, vegetation, flowers. They roamed or moved from one camp to another according to the availability of food. Since there was no one particular place where they resided for more than a few weeks or a few months at the most, *home* was *wherever the mothers of a group were situated at a particular time,* caring for children and old people. Adult males who hunted periodically came and went, not to and from one unchanging place known as *home* but to and from a changing, moving group of mothers, to and from what Grace Shinell calls the "sororal commune."[8]

In these matristic clans mothers were physi-

cally central to the group's life. Their bodies formed a geographical unit, a physical and psychical center to their clan and its lifeway. But the mothers did not rule over others or dominate them as fathers have dominated and ruled over others in patriarchy, often acquiring and maintaining their prestige and authority through physical force, intimidation, and raw power. Mothers were accorded prestige and authority by their very existence, just by their presence, by their automatic centrality to everyone's life.

In 1894 a document explaining their matrilineal society was signed by 123 clan and village leaders of the Hopi Indians and sent to "the Washington chiefs." It reads in part:

Back of oracular mirror. Shows flowing pattern of fishes and double-spiraling waters, forming two four-corner designs (fertile Xs) around the sun (a word that derives from Sunne, the name of Teutonic Sun-Mother Goddess). Bronze, Aegean Islands, 2400 B.C.E.

The family, the dwelling house and the field are inseparable, because the woman is the heart of all these, and they rest with her. Among us the family traces its kin from the mother, hence all its possessions are hers. . . . Our fields and houses always remain with our mother's family. . . . [Under this system] we provide ourselves with food in abundance.[9]

Saying that mothers were *central to society* in matristic cultures means that the values intrinsic to women's roles as life-givers, life-enhancers, and life-sustainers set the PATTERNS and standards of cooperation, nurturance, and mutual support that determined all other values and priorities in peoples' lives. Mothers were central to life: just by being—being-in-community— mothers created families, clans, societies. Maternal qualities, duties, and joys—like feeding others, storytelling, dancing, playing, making and decorating things—created activities and PATTERNS that extended human concerns beyond those of earlier primates. Mothering concerns created care-for-others as a defining PATTERN of individual male and female lives as well as of group life that replaced the more opportunistic, selfish PATTERN of earlier primates' lives (feed yourself whenever you can, mate quickly whenever you can). Maternal priorities regarding nurture and continuity spawned the development of subtle refined language and a memory that could span generations; one result of the refinement of language, caring for others, and memory (time-factoring) is that mating became more than copulation. Mother-lines fostered the development of long-range storying and sharing behaviors that eventually made our species significantly different from all other animals. That is, the ordinary qualities, duties, and joys of human mothers produced art, culture, language, and distinctively human community. And with the sharing, nurturing, storying (time-factoring) Model as the prevailing PATTERN of both male

and female lives, our kind survived and thrived in cooperation with each other and our environment—with plants, other creatures, and the earth—*until the advent of patriarchy.*[10]

As archetypal reversal occurred beginning about nine thousand years ago with the advent of pastoralism—with the first controlling of animals, the first conception of other creatures as beneath-Self—but the proliferation of hierarchical thinking and warring began with most effect only about five thousand years ago. The big cultural and philosophical change at that time consisted basically in going from viewing the world as whole, as non-hierarchical and interrelated— as if Self were always Other in some real way— to viewing the world as divided into dyads of opposition, pitting *dominators* (a few powerful men) versus the *dominated* (all Others, including weaker men).

Competition, ownership, and the struggle to control others became status behaviors, the most attractive, desirable ways for dominator men to see themselves and be seen by others. Sadly, this is a reversion back to the general societal PATTERN that strong mothering evolved humankind *out of*; it is a reversion back to the PATTERNS of less complicated primate societies in which *alpha* males eat, mate, and fight opportunistically. The compulsive, egocentric desire of some men to have dominion over Others brought about the creation of whole societies based on hierarchical, stratified class and sex distinctions. In the Neolithic Age came the first systematically power-ruled groupings our species had experienced since it had nurtured itself into becoming a communal, storying, time-factoring *kind*, at least sixty thousand years before.

With dominator behaviors came a hierarchical, dualistic value system—including the warrior sky-father gods that model, and thereby justify and sanctify, dominator behaviors. This philosophical system—with its religious icons—

supports struggle and opposition-to-others-and-Nature as the Ideal to strive for, as the prevailing PATTERN and Model for human lives. One of the most pernicious distinctions of this patriarchal ordering has been the describing of (human) culture as "the opposite of" Nature, with humans given the burden-glory of having to conquer the earth and even their own natures, if they are to win, be successful, or just be *good*!

Give credit to patriarchy for extraordinary military and technological feats, for powerful dynasties and monumental architectural achievements. But give it credit too for the damage it has done to the human spirit. Marija Gimbutas often makes the point that we can only judge civilizations by the way in which their people treat each other, not by how many enemies they have conquered and how big their slave-constructed palaces are. She suggests we ask these simple questions to determine if a people or society is civilized or "great": Do the people treat each other in a universally "civilized" way, that is, in a humane and equal way, or have they established a permanent, suffering underclass in their midst? Do the people pride themselves on and express themselves by making art and by crafting beautiful, useful, life-enhancing things, or by making weapons, wars, and forts? By these standards one must say that patriarchy has succeeded in bringing humankind, not progress, but "the end of civilization."[11]

MOTHER GODDESS AS "THE WAY"

As I have stated, matristic peoples treasure their mother-at-the-center idyll so much that they posit it as the basic societal value and PATTERN for their lives. The All-Mother Goddess functions thematically and experientially as the Perfect Knower, Doer, and Model of the *Mother's Way* of living for everyone to emulate.

Teleia as Mother is Life-Promoter, Life-Sustainer and Life-Nurturer. She models savoring life to the fullest, building and enhancing community with HerSelf as hub—with her extended, out-going, gathering *Self as center and home* rather than having a circumscribed, delimited place or edifice serve that function. She does not rule or command. She models myth-making and storying, meting justice, giving food, comfort, and love plentifully. Teleia's three interrelated aspects—Virgin-Mother-Crone—model Woman-in-Her-Fullness. This Model celebrates the interactive experiences of our bodies-in-the-world and extols our bodies-in-the-world as the only possible source of knowledge. Outside authorities, lifeless texts, or revelations from heaven might contribute to but cannot replace one's own knowing, cannot supersede Ananke the Yolk. This Model embraces all of one's Self, excluding nothing—not anger, not lust—but strives to have everything functioning *in right relationship* (which is determined by Ananke, the core [*Kore*] of one's Self, not by rules, custom, or fixing boundaries). This Model accepts life as a vibrant process full of transitions, sacred variety, movement, and potential.

The word *teleia* is a variant on the Greek word *telos,* which means "goal" or "aim" in patriarchal consciousness. *Telos* has come to mean something external to one's Self that requires singleness of purpose and an unrelenting dedication to the future that puts *living in the present* on hold and gives it less value than *the goal,* than *telos* itself. *Teleia* means something quite different. Teleia is not dedicated to some long-term achievement in the future that puts the present on hold; She is just the opposite. In Teleia's image, one can have perseverance, plans, and dreams, but these concern the maintaining and sustaining of one's precious enduring life itself—not some future goal external to one's Self that encourages or allows us to bypass days or hours of living and Being-in-the-moment for the goal's sake. The main "goal" in Hera's Model is to be nourished and informed by life in the organic moment—to be aware of the subtle processes going on in our experience right now. This Model encourages us to keep in focus what is needed and wanted *to sustain our happiness and health over time*—including the future as an extension of the enduring present—and to remain alert enough to let life's processes lead and direct us . . . with diversions encouraged. She bypasses *fulfillment* or being *fully realized* if that condition depends on achieving a goal external to the Self, or if it means one expects to "finally arrive" or "become full" once and for all.

A mature woman's body undergoes constant transformation—to a much greater extent than a man's body—from pregnancy to pregnancy, from month to month and menses to menses, when the swelling and ebbing of her womb parallels the swelling and ebbing of the moon. The changes that go on constantly in women's bodies—periods, cycles that go from birth to death to rebirth—identify women with the incessant monthly and seasonal changes going on constantly in Nature. Trying to keep one's body or life from undergoing natural changes (having plastic surgery to stave off aging or taking diuretics to stabilize one's shape during menses, for example) would be considered a vain and false value in this consciousness.[12]

So like Hebe, Teleia entertains Ananke, the voice of authenticity that comes unbidden from one's core. No one tells Hera Teleia who She is or ought to be; She recognizes and identifies Her own Self. She guards, promotes, and nurtures that Self, yet melds with and supports Others and Otherness. She is the Self that is in flux, that is More-than-One, that is fulfilled by giving of HerSelf, by continually embracing and adding Others into HerSelf, not by separating HerSelf from Others.[13]

In Teleia's image, Everywoman knows well her own body's cycles and needs and how to satisfy herself. A Teleia woman appreciates and celebrates what she has in common with all other women, but she accepts no absolutely fixed or predetermined goals or characteristics of womanhood. So although she is always female, a Teleia woman is never obliged to be feminine or ladylike, never obliged to sacrifice her Self to any cause.

MOTHER TELEIA CONSCIOUSNESS

Just as Hebe the Virgin-Maiden is springtime and personifies budding and the renewal of the Earth, Teleia is the summer aspect of the Goddess, *the Fruiting One*. Summer is the time of Nature-in-Her-Fullness; it is Mother Earth's season of abundance in which She nurtures and sustains life from the wealth and resources of Her bountiful Body. For archaic Greeks All-Mother Earth was often called Pandora—the Giver of Gifts or "the all endowed"—or Anesidora—the Bringer Up of All Good Things.[14] Teleia represents Everywoman in her season of ripeness, her body at its most abundant fullness, her mind and heart flowing with bounteous gifts of her Self, fulfilling the aspects of her Self in as many ways as possible. Teleia's attributes are boundless; whatever Everywoman or any women at any time can fantasize about or realize is a Teleia attribute.

Teleia's *mana*, or consciousness, comes from living fully and in flux around one's authentic center or hub. A woman in Teleia's image is sociable, creative, conscientious, and reliable, but also easy and playful. So a Teleia woman is capable in a great variety of ways; she asks for what she wants and needs, and she hopes to realize her dreams. She sets standards for herself, reasons well, makes decisions and choices but urges no compulsive work ethic. And no fixed or linear achievement goals apply to Her. Her plans come from Her own authentic needs and dreams; she always sustains and nourishes herSelf so that the fullness of her Being endures without interruption.

A woman experiencing Teleia's consciousness

VIRGIN
Mother ....
CRONE

*Nut, Sky-Mother Goddess, Whose blessings flow down from
Her ever-giving breasts and vulva. Egypt, 1080 B.C.E.*

knows that all knowledge and ultimate satisfaction comes first from experience in our bodies in the world, and she welcomes and appreciates each opportunity, finding the gift in all that comes to her. She is alert and aware of the ebbs, flows, and currents in all relationships. Her basic attitude is one of acceptance, trust, and inclusion, encouraging communion, treasuring her experiences, resisting unnecessary, objectifying analyses of them. *Mind*fulness, for her, is not just in the brain but rather is a whole-body awareness, a savoring, knowing in and with the whole body as it interacts with the world.

For Teleia, *responsibility* means one's *ability* to *respond* fully and well. Response-ability is allowing Ananke to manifest and grow. Response-ability comes from deep within the whole Self, is

not imposed on us by our brains, nor from outside by doctrine, custom, or manners. (For more on *response-ability* see Chapter 11.)

Mother consciousness makes women aware that their bodies and lives are the thread and web that connects all of humanity. And that web is boundless. Because she is in the image of the Cosmic Mother Goddess, a woman's sexuality and creative powers also reflect the divine life-giving, nourishing energies and powers of the universe.

Teleia is the ideal Mother we all want and need, but that some of us might not have unless we use Her as a surrogate to fill that role for us. She carries the Other within, therefore does not model the setting of fixed boundaries or oppositions between people. She freely absorbs difference and allows variety, for She is the One-and-the-Many, the Much-at-Once. She models justice, sharing, egalitarian relationships, Self-as-Other, transforming, shape-shifting, and the inter-penetration of beings.

MATRISTIC VALUES

What exactly are matristic values? How are the values of women-centered societies different from those of patriarchal societies? Might they be better for us? The work of many women scholars can help us understand and evaluate these archetypes and their inherent values for ourselves.

Native American scholar Paula Gunn Allen recognizes the Goddess religion and ancient matristic ways in the traditions of her own people. She writes:

> Many of the tribes of the western hemisphere were organized along gynocratic lines [*gyn* is the Greek root indicating "woman"] prior to contact with European patriarchies in the fifteenth century. Gynocentric communities tend to value peace, tolerance, sharing, relationship, balance, harmony, and a just distribution of goods. . . . In gynocratic tribal systems, egalitarianism, personal autonomy, and communal harmony were highly valued, rendering the good of the individual and the good of the society mutually reinforcing rather than divisive.[15]

Grace Shinell observes that for early peoples daily life was saturated with sacredness and that this intertwining between the ordinary and the sacred is typical of the "sororal communes" of early women's lives. She explains how sacred women's circles and schools for *parthenoi* promoted and sustained peaceful non-hierarchical arrangements throughout their societies: "Among ancient women, any assumed divinity does not appear to have been a status of individual power"; rather, it was a result of one's "ability *to divine*," to effect trance-like states,

perform therapeutic touch, make healing potions, and carry out the functions of sibyls, shamanesses, water-bringers, and light-bearers—all activities and roles that kept life going, at the same time keeping it rich with significance and meaning.[16]

Shinell points out that these roles "required communion, not dominion" and were taught through oral interaction . . . "by groups in groups." She adds, "Oral teaching drew on a common past. A sense of heritage induces more than self-respect; it induces collective identity and a regard for the transmission of wisdom through life processes" rather than through lifeless texts. Under these circumstances, she says, "Group concourse takes place through harmony and rhythmic flow, not through personal challenge and hustle."[17]

Culture, tradition, and love of life were transmitted in woman-centered, Goddess-revering societies daily and all at once through "inspired movement: dance."[18] Reflecting on Jane Ellen Harrison's observations and musings, Elise Boulding sums up early women's ways of knowing, communicating, and governing that came out of treasuring themselves as whole bodies-fully-involved-in-the-world: "Through dancing, concepts of order, leadership and religious projections are developed. The Cretans danced their way into culture and civilization."[19]

MATRISTIC SYMBOLS AND SIGNS

What all men and women have in common that is of societal consequence is that *each is borne by and born from a mother*. All of us bear the permanent mark of our unseverable relationship to our mother on our body: an *omphalos*, a navel. This mother-mark had great meaning for primal peoples, constantly reminding them of their blood kinship to their mother and of her ongoing, lifelong centrality in their lives. Sometimes they decorated it, for instance, by wearing jewels in it.

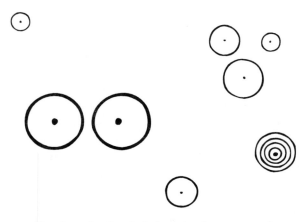

"Cup" marks. Symbols for eyes, breasts, navel,
vulva, womb, centrality, hearth, home, fertility
(sometimes a real seed is pressed into center), of
mother as Source.

Matrilineal people—men and women—trace
their family, or blood kinships, through their
mother, taking their name from her: "See my
navel, my birthmark? It says I have come from
the blood and body of Ruth. Without a doubt,
you see, I am Ruthsdotter" or "I am Ruthson."
Or Helensdotter or Helenson. Of course, there
are no such names as Johnson or Williamson or
Harrison in a matrilineal society.

The symbol for navel—the mother-mark—is
one of the most commonly carved images in all
of pre-history: a circle with a dot or small well
carved in the center, or a circle with a seed
(Kore) pressed into the middle. When a seed appears in a symbol, it is in some respect a sign of
the Virgin-Pregnant-with-Possibility, that is, the
Daughter of Mother Earth. This dotted circle, a
bull's-eye, or more accurately a *cow's-eye*, suggests the centrality and birth-giving powers of
women and the Goddess. Sometimes called a
"cup mark" or a "cupule," it is found by itself,
also in side-by-side pairs that represent the
Goddess's eyes or breasts, often in multiples for
emphasis (like a target whose concentric circles
emphasize the center).[20] This numinous mark
sometimes also depicts the Goddess's oracular

mouth (one of Her creating places) and seems to
announce: "I—the Divine Woman—am here" or
"This is the Goddess—feel Her presence here."[21]

Some of the most sacred places of antiquity
exhibit a natural feature resembling a birth
opening in their typography, and often some
Earth Mother was specifically honored there.
Hence the designation of such a site as an
omphalos, or navel place. Delphi in archaic
Greece was called an *omphalos*, the great dark
cleft in its craggy cliffs mimicking and celebrating the labia-vulva of the Creatrix, the Earth
Goddess Ge or Gaia (the word *delphi*, literally
meaning "womb" in Greek). The kivas of the
Pueblo tribes of the North American Southwest
are also described as womb places, dug into the
earth, each with its *omphalos*, a navel hole connecting the Pueblo people to the creative energies of the Earth, to the Mother of All.

These navel-womb practices and places are
central symbols in the myths and celebrations of
mother-centered peoples. When such female images, places, or stories are in abundance in a
culture's tradition, it is likely that those people
had a matristic heritage and to some significant
extent practiced matristic values.

GODDESS BREASTS

The Mother Goddess's breasts are the most
sacred, numinous symbols of Her nurturing, life-
sustaining powers and abilities. By regarding the
Great Mother's breasts as sacred symbols, Her
people held up the natural motherly activities
connected with them for all men and women to
see so that all could be reminded of and mimic
the nurturing behavior PATTERNS and ideals
that breasts represent. Men—even little boys
and girls—can use this Model, for they too can
happily and successfully parent or "mother,"
can love and comfort, sustain and nourish themselves and others. There is an old African saying:
"It takes a whole village to raise a child"—including all the men and other children.

*Singing Stone-Mother Goddess with cup marks for eyes, breasts,
mouth, navel, and vulva. England, Neolithic.*

*Stone-Mother. Menhir with three-line emphasis around breasts.
Italy, 3000 B.C.E.*

The ordinary woman's bosomed body— universalized as a Mother Goddess—expresses the nurturance of Self and Other-as-Self as a cultural priority, symbolizing and exemplifying the highest standard and PATTERN of coopera- tive and mutually supportive human behavior for all to follow. No male deity can model these things as well as She.[22]

In mother-centered foraging groups nursing mothers are an ordinary, daily sight at the heart of every community. Breasts are not concealed, and breast-feeding is done openly. All male and female children would have breast-fed for as long as possible,[23] which meant at least into a child's fourth year; a mother's final child might nurse until age five. According to a report made by one of the first anthropologists to visit the Amerinds, however, a Hopi child was seen nurs- ing at age seven. As grown men and women, children who nursed to such ages would keenly remember their intense connection to their mother's body and life.[24]

Ethnologist Marjorie Shostak recounts the great contentment and lack of crying in the ba- bies of gathering-hunting societies everywhere, for the obliging mothers carry their babies with them almost every minute of every day, the child upright, almost continually touching the mother's body with the entire length of its own body, and having ready access to a breast on demand—twenty-four hours a day. Anthropolo- gist Annette Hamilton observes that Aboriginal babies are always in physical contact with oth- ers and are fed so often they never have an empty stomach; infants are actually *never al- lowed to have the sensation of hunger*, and therefore do not have to cry to get fed. Whereas European babies do get hungry and often must whimper or cry to get fed, according to Hamil- ton's observations, on the average Aboriginal in- fants younger than two months are fed every half hour or so, and two- to six-month-old ba- bies are fed every hour and a half. She points

out that children this well fed grow up with the expectation that although eating is an irregular activity, one need not worry, for there will al- ways be plenty of food—and *that breasts are the source of contentment and bounty*.[25]

Shostak reports that among the gathering- hunting !Kung people today, men and women still typically speak fondly and longingly of nursing; they remember relishing the milk and the security and closeness of their mother's body—and everyone remembers hating to be weaned.[26] Hamilton reports that among the Arnhem people she lived with in northern Aus- tralia "feeding is a ritual of attachment [between mother and child], not just a way of filling a hungry stomach." The mother's breast retains its significance to the child for a lifetime, be- cause that society does not give its children "transitional objects" such as bottles, "blankies," dolls, or other toys. Children have only breasts to play with, only breasts to feed from.[27] In gathering societies sons would have felt no personal inclination nor any societal pressure to separate themselves emotionally from their mothers at any age, much less to the extent that men of European descent are urged—or forced—to separate as completely and as early as possible.

Under primal circumstances emotional needs are sufficiently met so that mother-son relation- ships never develop the distressing Oedipal dis- tortions common in our society and the breast fetish typical of American men (quite likely a reaction formation to infantile deprivation) can- not happen.[28] Each adult man and woman, while living among constantly nursing mother- child units, could say unself-consciously, "I too nursed and I remember that I received great comfort and happiness from it," perhaps point- ing with love and pride "at the breast of that old woman there."[29]

Not surprisingly, an abundance of prehistoric artifacts represent divine female bodies, and many have pendulous breasts, swollen and hanging down as if dropped by the weight of their milk. The image of pendulous breasts obviously eventually came to be equated with—came to be a symbol for—an endless supply of nourishment both from one's human mother as well as from the Divine Mother, the Earth-Sky.

MALE MOTHERING

Nor Hall, a mythologist and the author of *Broodmales: Men in Childbirth*, has made an extensive study of *couvade*, the widespread practice among primal peoples in which men mimetically go through the experience of pregnancy and birth—both its joys and its pains—along with their wives. In earliest times this practice was one of honoring the primacy and essentialness of the life-giving, birthing experience of women, but later, qualities of jealousy and possessiveness appeared in men's couvade practices, even "priestly piracy," the stealing of seemingly exclusive female prerogatives—like birth-giving and breast-feeding—to give to men and gods. Eventually one sees the male usurpation of the female role of creating or giving birth to new life recorded in at least two ways: first, there are those preposterous unnatural supermen who give life out of their bodies as if they were women, except that their wombs are *contrived*: like Zeus, who killed Earth Mother Metis, took the fetus from Her womb and carried it to term in his "head womb" whence he later "birthed" Athena, or like Adam, who "birthed" Eve out of his "rib-cage womb." Male theogonies present such births as supernatural, but they are merely unnatural. Other cases of couvade completely deny that female bodies, or indeed *any* human bodies, are involved in the creation of human life, as if *matter* or the *material* world—named for Dea Mater (Latin for "Mother Goddess")— were not sacred. Some male deities conceive and give material life by means of pure thoughts and words (Logos), "birthing" matter out of their reasoning minds rather than out of their viscera.

Nor Hall has examined the initiation rituals that transformed boys into men from many different times and places, including the ceremonies that took place in Paleolithic caves, which were from early times celebrated as wombs of Mother Earth. Hall concludes that even very early practices of couvade were initiations that represented the archetypal course of boys becoming mature men *by discovering their capacity to mother!*[30]

SWEAT LODGES AND MOON LODGES

There was a time not too long ago when I was attracted to vision quests, sweat lodges, and other mostly solitary pursuits that combine endurance tests with spiritual journeying. The hope was that through exertion, fasting, kneeling, purging, or dedication I would find my wholeness and purpose in life. Indeed many women have had wonderful, beneficial experiences on such quests, inviting deprivation and hardship in order to effect an altered state of consciousness in which enlightenment or improved understanding can come to them.

Sweat lodges, in the opinion of Chris Knight, Susun Weed, and many others, are environments created to give men an altered state of consciousness that women receive naturally, as an unbidden gift, when menstruating. Sweat lodges, quests, and other similarly heroic endeavors can be important, even essential, for men. But for women these experiences are oftentimes dizzying, confusing, and always unnecessary. In a sweat lodge men can *with effort* emulate the situation in moon lodges in which bleeding women receive the gifts of heightened psychic awareness and inner vision *without effort*. In addition to gaining for men the sacred gifts of insight and keen sensory experience, energetic sweating can also reduce or eliminate excess male energies that can tend otherwise to go

toward hostilities or unproductive rambunc-
tiousness. Sweat lodges occupy men in a place-
set-apart in significant, tiring efforts, while also
giving them sensory awareness similar to what
women have in their place-set-apart.

The Divine Female, the behavioral Model for
many human activities, has often been beneficial
for men. Some Tantric and Taoist philosophies
have long deemed it in the interest of society at
large that all men learn sexual practices—
kundalini, for instance—that center on with-
holding or delaying male tendencies toward too-
brief, too-opportunistic ejaculation. Robert
Lawlor writes in *Earth Honoring: The New
Male Sexuality* that by cultivating such techniques and values, men can emulate the more
prolonged PATTERN "of the female orgasm . . .
which is associated with the idea that sexuality
and ecstatic states are instrumental and necessary for people to obtain an opening to the spiritual world and for their own spiritual development."[31]

Rather than sweating energetically or quest-
ing far afield in search of Wisdom as men typically do, women could be tending to the Charge
of the Goddess that says, *"If you do not find the
Mystery and Wisdom inside, you surely will
never find it without."* Women could profit in
very special ways by spending their time in
moon lodges with other women, reclaiming the
power of sisterhood and an understanding of
the age-old Mystery of Life that makes its presence known and felt in women's synchronous
body functions. In a moon lodge we could—
with no exertion—focus our awareness and become more alert to the Wisdom inside ourselves
and each other, allowing awareness to manifest
unbidden, unhurried, in its own time. Women
do not have to force sweat, fast, actively seek,
quest heroically, or do anything at all to precipi-
tate an altered state or to provoke vision or Inner Sight. Our periodic female-hormone surges
and flows bring that propensity to us naturally,

every month, as a matter of course. All we need
to do is notice and cultivate our enhanced tendencies at those times, appreciate the miraculous
gifts that come with the bleeding, allow them,
go with them.

No pursuit or quest, no goal-directed
behavior—no matter how lofty sounding or up-
lifting in the moment—can be good for women
or for humankind in the long run *if women do
not come back from it more in tune with
Ananke, with their own yolks, and more aware
of their female bodies—more aware of their
breasts, vulvas, periods, emotions, Wisdom,
Mystery—more capable of identifying their
special magic, more in love with womanliness,
more empowered as females!, more in touch
with sisterhood, more in touch with the ways in
which they are stronger for experiencing sororal
bonds regularly, more confident in the strength-
ening, nurturing, secure kind of intimate support systems that are only possible between
women who have shared together-as-One hor-
mone surges, dreams, insights, visions of the
future. . . .*

This sacred ritual of gender solidarity, this
magical Mystery used to take place in Hera's
temple—at the Heraion—every month, at the
Dark of the Moon. The world would be transformed and strengthened today by seeing and
honoring the togetherness and personal empow-
erment that could come to women should we
once more acknowledge the flow of pheromones
between our bodies and let that cross-flow syn-
chronize our menses again *en masse.* The gift of
physical, emotional, and cosmic community—
the interrelatedness that only women can give to
each other—begins at home, at the Source, in
our bodies, in sororal communes.

In discussing the "descent into the underworld" as part of women's initiation into female
Mysteries—which would include women's
monthly synchronous bleeding rituals in the
Heraion—Sylvia Brinton Perera writes that the

131

process "involves exploring different modes of consciousness and rediscovering the experience of unity with nature and the cosmos that is inevitably lost through goal-directed development." The unifying mode of consciousness that celebrates the Mystery and Necessity in women's bodies "forces us to the affect-laden, magic dimension and archaic depths that are embodied, ecstatic, and transformative; these depths are preverbal, often pre-image, capable of taking us over and shaking us to the core."[32]

OTHER MOTHER GODDESS SYMBOLS

Some of the other symbols that carry the *mana* of the Mother Goddess and that therefore should clue us to suspect that a matristic consciousness was operative in a culture if they are found in that people's relics are:

- fertile, pink, nippled pigs
- far-seeing hawks
- protective lions, lionesses, and other large cats
- butterflies or double axes
- pomegranates
- cauldrons and vessels for carrying and preparing food or for mixing potients
- fish *(vesica piscis)*
- valleys with running streams, chalices containing red liquid, and other wombs-with-amniotic-fluid prototypes
- wombs, caves, storehouses
- vulva prototypes like cowrie shells, lozenges, hooked lozenges
- Xs, which as center-locating devices are similar to *omphalos* or cow's-eye—as in "X marks the spot"—and identify the Mother or Source as central to a people's concerns
- crosses or turning crosses; that is, swastikas (symbols of the sun's annual cycle)
- Xs and crosses together, which make the

Inanna's Gateposts. Highly stylized symbol of Her vulva. A curtain rod went through holes at the top of the posts, which were placed at sides of entrance to dark, cool caves (or other storehouses) where the grain, dates, and other bountiful gifts of Her Earth Womb were kept.

"fire symbol," or the eight-pointed star that signifies one sun cycle or the Wheel of the Year—in Gothic cathedrals this is called a Saint Catherine's Wheel or Rose Window—which is the equivalent of one annual Goddess-Body cycle
- patterns of woven threads, like nets, which also represent wombs.[33]

Single or multiple Xs, squares, lozenges, and woven net PATTERNS are all connected symbolically to each other and to Femaleness. When an X is drawn through the heart of a lozenge (a diamond-shaped rectangle or square with one corner pointing up), four other (equal) squares are created inside, and the symbol for "planted" or "fertile field" is formed. A square or lozenge can also be a vulva, and when repeated enough times these shapes become a net or woven PATTERN, signifying womb-container. An X with feet (often in partial or full circles) is a swastika, which indicates the four cusps (two equinoxes and two solstices) that divide the year into four equal seasons that are ever-turning, transforming, being reborn. The cycle of the year follows the ongoing generational PATTERN of women's lives: from spring Virgin-Maiden to summer Mother to fall-winter Crone to spring Virgin-Maiden again—unceasingly from Birth-to-Death-to-ReBirth. Nets and other woven designs represent transformations from one thing (wool, cotton, flax) to another (thread and fabric) through women's spinning and weaving, the transformation of non-containers into containers, that is, the original "things" are transformed into wombs in which more births, creations, and transformations can be expected. And so on, without end.

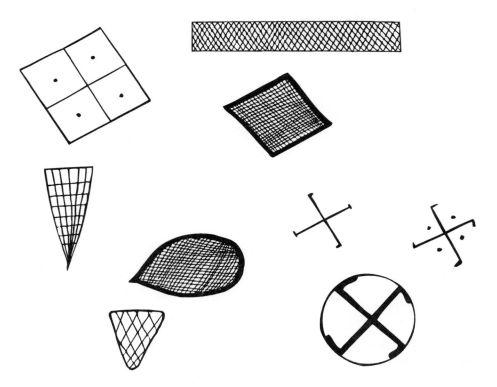

Xs, squares, lozenges, and woven net PATTERNS   [DW]

Seven

· · · · · · ·

ATTRIBUTES OF FULLNESS

*B*efore we tell the myth of Hera, the Triple Goddess, there are a few specific things of interest about Her mature aspect that need to be recounted, because the significance and values of these attributes sometimes go against our expectations in the west. As was detailed in Chapter 6, "Mother Consciousness," there is more to this Person then biological motherhood. Teleia is also described as Woman-in-Her-Fullness. Some of the attributes that go into Hera's Female Fullness are as follows.

TELEIA'S SEXUALITY

From archaic times one of Hera's three temples typically housed a Sacred Coupling Couch, for *ecstatic sexuality is essential to Teleia's rites and nature.* In this respect Hera's sacred practices closely resemble those of Inanna, a beloved Sumerian Goddess whose marriage bed was also a central part of Her hymns and myths. "The Courtship of Inanna and Damuzi" is the oldest extant written narrative that has thus far been found (written in cuneiform about 1900 B.C.E.).[1] The poem is also wonderfully erotic. In it, both Inanna and Damuzi, Her consort, take initiative in the lovemaking; both honestly acknowledge lust and joy in sexual congress. Reading this verse narrative startles, mainly because neither of the partners in full-body-sharing objectifies the other.[2]

Greek Aphrodite and Roman Venus are fragmented descendants of the Great Mother. These classical deities—so-called love goddesses—are to a great extent deified patriarchal sex objects who model eroticism isolated from the rest of life. A worshiper goes to a sex goddess for one thing, and when one leaves her, one leaves her hegemony—her authority in that one thing—behind. Isolating any human attribute from the whole person fractures the Self and makes ecstatic union with the All impossible.

Teleia, a cognate of the Great Mother, is not a deified sex object. Teleia's sexuality is synonymous with deep, profound knowledge of Self and Other, of healing and bonding. Teleia's holy Couch fosters sacred play, delight, and the Oneness of all human experience. When sex is perceived as a powerful, whole-making sacred act, the dualistic struggle between spirit and body disappears, for acts of sacred sex demonstrate that human bodies are inseparable from human spirit and the Holy, that physical and psychological health are one, that human bodies are part and parcel of the most sacred profound Mystery of life and creation.

One need not have sinned to take advantage of sacred sex as a means of being ReBorn. But men who had committed crimes like murder could go to the priestess of the Goddess to be cleansed and renewed, as Deena Metzger's novel *The Woman Who Slept with Men to Take the War out of Them* suggests. In acts of sacred sexuality the universal cycle of Birth-Death-ReBirth was recapitulated, so that temple sex could be a kind of Self-giving that brought on the death of the despoiled-Self out of which a renewed Self was born. Healing took place through ecstatic Self-expression and union with a sacred Other and, through the Goddess's representative, union with the All.

There is no reason to believe that any form of the Great Goddess, including Hera, modeled only heterosexuality for Everywoman. In antiquity the Couretes of Crete, swarms of women, retinues of the Great Mother, danced together over fields and through forests, eventually per-

forming wild sexual rites among themselves. Drunk with themselves, intoxicated with the Goddess and Nature, other groups were seen in different millennia participating in the Goddess's cyclical Earth rites, sometimes clad in animal skins, often waving billowing scarves and flowered branches over meadows, most always drumming, releasing life from the womb of the Earth in spring and summer by their festivities and raptures.[3]

The drum was one of the Great Goddess's special gifts to humankind. Myths specifically say Kybele, Rhea, and later Dionysos invented it and gave it to women to transport them into ecstasy and invigorate their surroundings. The drum was for early peoples a most sacred instrument, used in their shamanic rituals. Only in patriarchal societies has the drum been demonized, banned from sacred rites, and turned over to warriors to invigorate their warring.[4]

Dionysos is an androgynous god of sensuous pleasures who inherited the orgiastic rites of the Great Mother when matristic peoples were conquered and their sacred Goddess rites banned. His female followers celebrated their rapturous rituals away from men with entranced singing, passionate drum beating, and sensual play with one another.[5]

In the religion of Artemis, young and adolescent girls were sent to live in same-sex circumstances, to become *yellow bears* in the Goddess's temple, for years of training in running, crafts, shooting bows, and other womanly arts, and to abstain from sex with males lest they become pregnant and have to call short their Self-development. Grace Shinell writes that "sisterhood must be firmly understood to include a sexual relationship, providing the emotional-spiritual ties and life-supporting strength of the same-sex bond. From the root for tribe (Greek *tribe*: 'the act of rubbing'; cf. *tri-ba/o*: 'tri-based') comes a cognate term, tribadism, exclusively defined as lesbianism."[6]

On the island of Lesbos there were several famous schools for young women (*parthenoi*) led by renowned teachers, including the poetess Sappho, Gorgo, Andromeda, and others. Undoubtedly there were such schools elsewhere too. "Relationships within these circles were artistic, affectional, sexual, and religious."[7]

The Sumerian Goddess Inanna is famous for her ritual marriage to the god Damuzi and for their heterosexual lovemaking. But Betty Meador writes that Inanna travels "throughout the landscape of her sexuality, enjoying each scene to the fullest. She sanctions sexuality in its many forms as the surging of the life force itself. To suppress a viable expression of sexuality, such as homosexuality, would be anti-life to Inanna and would go against the creative force of her nature."[8]

TELEIA AS MOON

Hera Teleia—Woman-in-Her-Fullness, threefold Changing Woman—is often imaged as the Moon. This is an obvious and convenient metaphor, for both moon and women constantly change and cycle together in a 29.5-day period. Women, Hera, and the moon all also have three aspects or phases: Becoming or Waxing (the Virgin), Fullness (the Mother), and Waning or Dying (the Crone).

Religious historian Mircea Eliade writes that the complex and rich image of the moon has been used by humans for practical reasons (as calendars for predicting herd comings, for instance) as well as for religious reasons for at least thirty thousand years. See thirteen *moon marks* on the crescent in the hand of the Earth

The World Tree. Axis Mundi, Hub of the Universe, home of the All-encompassing World Serpent. Also called Yggdrasil (in Norse myth), meaning "generative source," a word akin in sense and etymology to "egg" and "yoni." Scandinavia, 18th century painting.

Mother of Laussel see pages 18 and 81). Eliade urges us to note "the considerable role of the moon in archaic mythologies, and especially the fact that lunar symbolism was integrated into a single system comprising such different realities as woman, the waters, vegetation, the serpent, fertility, death, 'rebirth," and so forth.[9]

TELEIA AS TREE

One of the oldest symbols of fullness, wholism, and unity is the World Tree. Mythically this sacred Tree holds everything in the cosmos together. It reaches both up into the sky and down into the underworld, pulling both of those areas into the middle—into the world and our lives—and holding the three realms together, bonding them, making them all more accessible to us, relating them, keeping them from flying apart, from seeming to be separate, unrelated places. Thus Hera as Tree links all three realms—heaven, earth, and the underworld—into Oneness, into the unified fullness of All-That-Is.

The tree further dissolves differences in that it can be seen to require both light and darkness for its life. The leaves and branches reach up into the heavens toward the sun for the life-giving properties of light, and the roots reach down into the earth for water, stability, and the life-giving properties of darkness. Remember: *if one exposes the roots of the tree to light and air, the tree dies.* No dualisms here—no opposition between up and down, no struggle between light and darkness, between a sky-father god and an Earth Mother. *The tree* lives by the gifts of all: the light and the darkness, sky and earth, up and down, all together at the same time. The world perceived through the tree's existence and function is *unified and whole.*

Teleia consciousness means being constantly aware of the wholeness of Being. Teleia consciousness resembles being a fully leafed summer tree, taking what she needs while giving of Self

Goddess as Tree-full-of-Birds. Crete, c. 1400 B.C.E.

abundantly, reaching both into the sky and into the earth, unifying the cosmos and one's life, experiencing everything as a conduit into Oneness. The Goddess as Tree mimics the mother who holds her family and clan together, the bonding in which diversity celebrates commonality. The Tree Goddess was frequently sculpted as a wooden or stone pillar. The marble columns of ancient temples honor this Goddess in Her

"Woman displayed" or Birth-Giver as Tree of Life [BW]

guises both as individual tree and as protective, nurturing grove, as Manyness-and-Oneness, as the One and the Much-at-Once.[10]

Another form of the Mother Goddess as tree or branching stalk that has been found across many cultures in unbroken continuity "for nearly three thousand years in many locations from West Africa to the Far East, even to the North and South American continent" is, according to artist and historian Mary B. Kelly, the "birthing" or "displayed woman."[11] This female tree-fertility PATTERN—with arms upraised and "legs outstretched to display her vulva"—is often found in traditional Eastern European embroidery today as well as painted or carved on the clay and stone artifacts of prehistory. It was prominently featured in Çatal Hüyük, the Anatolian city that flourished around 6500 B.C.E.[12] This "heraldic symbol" has a central up-and-down line or trunk with a top lozenge for the head and a bottom lozenge for

the vulva; bent lines that splay to the sides are both branches and arms and legs.[13]

The fruit tree, especially the apple, has been associated with the Mother Goddess's Abundance and with Her Tree persona from early Neolithic times, playing a lead role in many of Her myths, as well as having prominence and significance for other reasons in the cultures of matristic peoples. Apples, date palms, and other fruit-laden trees symbolize Her food gifts and the bounty that comes from Her to us from the earth, Nature, and the summer season.

Linguist Thomas L. Markey cites research showing that all the words for apple in Indo-European languages—most tongues from westernmost Europe across to India—come from pre-patriarchal, Goddess-revering peoples. Wherever patriarchal Indo-Europeans migrated, they "simply borrowed words for 'apple'" from the Megalithic matrifocal farmers whom they found living there, tending orchards, telling stories about an abundant, benevolent Great Mother.

The Indo-Europeans borrowed words for apple, but they stole the *mana*, the divine Goddess powers that apples symbolized. Remember how the apple tree was first associated with the Tree of Knowledge in patriarchy's Garden of Eden and then was diabolicized? "The dramatic focus of all of the earliest apple legends is an attempt by members of one (patristic Indo-European) pantheon to steal apples [and their *mana*] from the members of another (matristic non–Indo-European) pantheon."[14]

TELEIA, THE HOLY COW

Matristic peoples obviously valued motherly, mothering things, like a mother's miraculous ability to feed others with milk from her own body. Since the cow did this miraculous thing all the time, the cow was experienced as one powerful, explicit manifestation of the nurturing, food- and milk-giving Mother Goddess. Indeed, the most common animal epiphany for the Mother Goddess in Her role as Nurturer was as the Great Milky-White Celestial Cow—white like the Moon, with two horns that look like crescent Moons.[15] Hera Teleia was one such

Cow Goddess Europa, in human form, being carried off by Zeus as bull. Roman antiquity.
[JWW]

Celestial Cow, the Milky Way regarded as Her Breastmilk.

The most familiar Cow Goddess to us, though, is probably Europa. One myth says that Europa mated with Zeus-as-bull and birthed another bull: King Minos of Crete. Inanna of Sumer, Isis and Hathor in Egypt, and Io in Ionia were also Cow Mother Goddesses. And many other Goddesses—Kybele and Ishtar, for instance—are pictured with bovine horns and are said in their myths to give birth to bulls (or to Golden Calves).

Christians call the symbolic eating and drinking of their deity's flesh and blood the Holy Sacrament of Communion. Hera's people considered ritually eating a sacred cow's flesh and blood also to be "Holy Communion" with Her.[16]

So Hera's people raised sacred cows and bulls for sacrifice and for eating. The pre-patriarchal Olympians sacrificed one hundred bulls and one of Hera's sacred cows all at the same time once every four years. This gigantic sacred feast occurred after every running of the Olympic Games, which consisted originally of three foot-races run only by women in three different classifications, unsurprisingly: the virgins' race, the matrons' race, and the crones' race. The winner of the virgins' footrace was designated to consume ritually the flesh and blood of the sacred cow that symbolized Hera's living presence at the Games.[17] This ritual communion honored cows and bulls for their sacred Life Force, and celebrated the *mana* and energy that the cattle exchanged with humans in the sacrament of eating.

HERA, THE QUEEN

In telling the Myth of Hera I have used Her archaic title "Queen of Heaven, Earth, and the Underworld," even though the notion of queen as autocratic ruler is not appropriate for the immanent Goddess of pre-history. Thorkild Jacobsen, a historian of religion, notes that kings and queens do not appear in human affairs until the third millennium B.C.E. in Sumer, and neither do divine kings and queens of heaven appear in myth or sacred images before that time. All Sumerian deities before the fourth millennium B.C.E., he writes, were immanent in Nature, but when earthly rulers first came to power in the next millennium, the immanent deities changed and acquired the same royal roles and titles that powerful men and women had recently acquired. Most likely, the deities' autocratic heavenly titles were designed to give celestial authorization to the tyrants who invented them.[18]

Most likely the first rulers adopted the crown and throne for themselves because such things already had powerful symbolic significance. As early as the seventh millenium B.C.E. Mother Goddesses wore crowns as signs of their (the Earth's) wisdom and wealth. Wearing a crown enabled one to know all, to see hidden treasures, and to understand the language of animals and birds.[19] After the advent of patriarchy, the title of Queen or Lady, or its equivalent, was used for some time for goddesses who were not married to Indo-European gods, but who continued to be powerful in their own right.[20] It is easy to see, however, that none of this symbolism has anything to do with a caste or class system. The crown does not bestow on its wearer authority to rule over other people, nor does it affirm that the wearer has more worth or deserves more favored treatment than anyone else.

The Neolithic Mother Goddess is often found on a mound or chair exuding such numinous Self-possession that the viewer gets the clear impression some kind of throne or at least a symbol of Self-power is intended. In the seventh millennium B.C.E. the Goddess is depicted seated prepotently between two leopards on what is presumed to be a throne (see illustration on page 96). The throne of Egypt was specifically said to be the Goddess Isis's body, and when the pharaoh sat on this divine, regal chair, he was said to be sitting in Isis's lap. Chairs still are spoken of as if they were bodies—they have arms, legs, backs, and so forth. So the title of "Queen" feels appropriate for Hera, although many of the assumptions that westerners tend to bring to this title may be inappropriate for Her.

THE PRIESTESS

Evangelis, the official title of the priestess at the Heraion on the island of Samos, means "she who is the messenger of good tidings." Our word "angel" comes from *Evangelis*. On Samos one of Hera's names was *Antheia*, meaning the Earth, or the Flowering, Abundant One.

I have invented a priestess to tell the story of the triple Goddess Hera, the flowering Earth Mother. In the tradition of the Heraion on Samos I call my priestess Evangelis.

Evangelis is a passionate, even rabble-rousing advocate of matristic society and the sacred traditions of the All-Mother. She speaks in this myth, or more accurately, in this mythic evocation, about earlier times and the outlawed mother-centered tradition to a group of women assembled in secret. This audience mimics a Women's Secret Mystery Religion convocation. (The women and men in my audiences take the part of the ancient women when I tell this myth.) Evangelis has no patience with the new-fangled sky god Zeus, of course; she regards him as one who unjustly subverted her Goddess to his tyrannical, selfish purposes, so she never even mentions him.

Here is the devoted priestess Evangelis to tell us of her Hera—not Hera the Wife, but Hera the Triune Goddess, the Much-at-Once, the Great Mother of pre-history in all Her miraculous Fullness.

She the Three-in-One. Three red lilies in one plant, from ritual "Room of the Lilies" on island of Thera, in which all depictions are of red three-in-one lilies. Thera, Aegean Islands, sixteenth century B.C.E.

Eight

· · · · · ·

THE MYTH OF
THE TRIPLE GODDESS

An Evocation of Hera,
Virgin-Mother-Crone

[*Hera's priestess, Evangelis, whose name means "she who is the messenger of good tidings," speaks to a group of women who have gathered to learn about the Goddess's Secret Mysteries from her. In performance the women and men in the audience will take the part of Evangelis's listeners, who sit in a large semicircle in front of an altar covered with a gold cloth. Three special instruments are on the altar: Hebe's shell-chimes, Teleia's sistrum or tambourine, and Hekate's deep drum. As the sound of exhilarating sonorous drumming begins, Evangelis starts dancing in a large circle, chanting exultantly "Hera!" over and over. She stops upstage with arms and three scarves raised:*]

Hera!
Hera!
   Miraculous Mother!
   Three-in-One!

VIRGIN
Mother . . . .
CRONE

[Evangelis dances in three large circles, dividing the open space in front of the altar into three round temple areas. While making each circle, she displays the appropriate scarf and the appropriate sacred instrument. In the left circle-temple she leaves Hebe's white scarf and Hebe's chimes, indicating that is Hebe's temple. In the middle circle-temple she leaves the red scarf of Mother Hera Teleia along with Her cistrum-tambourine. In the right circle, the temple of the Wise Old Crone, Evangelis leaves the dark crone scarf and the deep-sounding drum of Hekate. At each temple she intones the appropriate one of the following appellations:]

Hebe—Mother of Creation!
Teleia—Queen of Heaven!
Hekate—Wisdom of the Ages!
HERA! BLESSED TRINITY!

Trinity!
Three-in-One!
VIRGIN   MOTHER   CRONE!
Yip! Yip! Y I I I I PPPP ! ! ! !

[Drums stop.]

Triple Goddess as three Tree-Pillars with nesting doves (sensuality symbols).
Clay, Knossos, Crete, Early Palace Period.

VIRGIN
Mother . . . .
CRONE

[*Priestess speaks to women:*]

    Oh, women!

        I have come to tell you of
            Threefold Hera.
        Hera, Virgin Mother Crone.

        Of course, Hera is not
            three different Goddesses.
        VIRGIN MOTHER CRONE are the three phases
            of women's lives,
            the ordinary cycle and phases
            of ordinary women's lives.

        So our Goddess is not an impossible Ideal
            "out there" somewhere.
        Hera is each of you, all of us.
        She is Everywoman writ large—
            the Mirror of Ourselves,
            the Model of our Wholeness.

So . . .

Let me take you into Hera's three temples:

one temple is for Hebe the Virgin,
one for Teleia, Mother or Woman-in-Her-Fullness,
one temple is for Hekate, the Wise Old Crone.

Three temples, women,
But you will find in them no rules;
no goals,
no lessons,
no quests.

In Hera's temples we celebrate
the rhythms and cycles of our lives,
the natural passages and
transitions of our lives.

In Hera's temples we find Possibility,
Insight,
Wisdom,
Gifts that come unbidden—
In Hera's temples we find the Community of women.

Come with me, women.

VIRGIN
Mother  . . . .
CRONE

[*Priestess goes into Hebe's temple and once more holds up Her white scarf for audience to see.*]

Come with me into the temple of Hebe.

And listen well!
For as I tell you of Hera Parthenia,
    I shall be telling you
        about yourselves . . .
        and your VIRGIN Power!

[*Priestess goes into Teleia's temple and holds up Her red scarf for audience to see.*]

Come with me into the temple of Teleia.

And listen well!
For as I tell you of Hera in Her fullness,
    I shall be telling you
        about yourselves . . .
        and your WOMAN Power!

[*Priestess goes into Hekate's temple and holds up Her dark scarf for audience to see.*]

Come with me into the Temple of Hekate.

And listen well!
For as I tell you of the Wise Old Woman,
    I shall be telling you
        about yourselves . . .
        and your CRONE Power!

[*Evangelis places all three scarves on the center altar.*]

Miraculous Mother!
Three-in-One!
Hera, Trinity!
    the Mirror of OurSelves!

[*Priestess goes singing into Virgin's circle-temple stage left:*]

HEBE, the VIRGIN!
HERA PARTHENIA!

*Kore, the Seed, Virgin Daughter of Mother Demeter, the Earth.
Acropolis, Athens, 530 B.C.E.* [JWW]

HEBE, the Budding One,
>Bud of Youth,
>Budding Earth,
>Budding Female Child of the Earth—

Spring's daughter,
>Full of Herself and Her blooming,
>>Her Becoming.
>Her skin, flowering fresh petals,
>>dew-pink, golden, or brown.
>Her blushing parts vibrant,
>>burgeoning with Possibility.

>Oh, the Possibilities in Herself!
>the blossoming of Herself!
>the belonging to Herself!

HEBE, VIRGIN!
>Not belonging to mother,
>>not to father,
>>not to lover!
The Virgin belongs to Herself alone!

PARTHENIA!
Youth exultant!
>Exulting in Her first bleeding!
>Exulting in Her connection to the earth!
>Exulting that She cycles with the moon!
>Exulting in Her magically transforming body!

VIRGIN
Mother . . . .
CRONE

She — waxing, incipient . . .
She — the sliver of New Moon . . .
          barely becoming . . .
Hebe — the Virgin Moon!

THIS
THE TEMPLE
OF HEBE
VIRGIN.
IN
THIS TEMPLE
WE CELEBRATE SPRING AND ALL
NEW BEGINNINGS, STARTING OVER, RENEWING OURSELVES.
IN THIS TEMPLE WE CELEBRATE GIFTS
THAT COME UNBIDDEN, BEING
FULL OF POSSIBILITY,
PREGNANT WITH
POTENTIAL.
THIS
THE TEMPLE
OF BECOMING! HERE
WE CELEBRATE BELONGING TO
OURSELVES. THIS TEMPLE NESTLED
AMONG LYGOS BUSHES, LYGOS BUSHES THAT
BLOSSOM RED, LIKE THE FIRST FRESH DROPS OF A
MAIDEN'S MENARCHE. THIS THE TEMPLE OF BUDDING BY
THE SIDE OF FLOWING WATERS, BY THE BROOK PARTHENION:
VIRGINS' BROOK, FREE-FLOWING VIRGIN WATERS, THE VIRGIN
WATERS THAT WASH AWAY THE OLD, AND GIVE BIRTH TO THE NEW.
FREE-FLOWING VIRGIN WATERS, BY THE SIDE OF THE VIRGIN'S
TEMPLE. SHE — HEBE PARTHENIA — THE VIRGIN MOON

WAXING,   BECOMING,

transforming . . .

into . . .

*Flowing. Water, snake, egg, vortex, Xs, meander.
Clay, Minoan Crete, 2000* B.C.E.

VIRGIN
Mother . . . .
CRONE

[*In mid-sentence priestess cycles slowly from Hebe's circle-temple at stage left into Teleia's circle-temple in center area:*]

TELEIA!
GODDESS as the full golden moon!

TELEIA!
WOMAN in the full golden time of life.
Mature, fertile, nurturing, nourishing,
Self-empowered woman!
She who births the family,
builds community,
centers the tribe, and is
at the heart of the nation.

Dazzling TELEIA!

    She: the quivering, radiant Falcon!
    She: the all-seeing Hawk-eyed one!
    Fierce protectress!   ARRRRgghhh!
    Lioness!   ARRRRgghhh!
    Serene Guardian of the Mother Clans!
                      Prrrrrrrr . . .

Primordial Mother of Civilizations,
    She who taught Her people
          to sow and reap the crops.
    Meter of justice,
    Composer of songs and revelries!

    She of the ripe, honeying BODY,
    She of the magically transforming BODY.
    Hera's BODY:
        swelling, ebbing . . .
        swelling, ebbing . . .
    Hera's WOMB the earth:
        gibbous, growing, giving . . .

Female symbols on face of cow. Goddess's quatrefoil (X) and three chevrons beneath crescent horns. Crete, c. 1600 B.C.E.

HERA!

> Splendid cow-eyed Goddess!
> Soft-downed heifer of succulent breasts!

HERA TELEIA!

> Dynamic, fulfilled Woman!
> She, the Mirror of Ourselves!
> Queen of Earth, Air, and Heaven!

THIS
IS THE
TEMPLE OF
TELEIA.
HER
TEMPLE HIGH UP!
BUILT HIGH! ON A HIGH ROCKY LEDGE OF MOUNT EUBOIA TO
HONOR THE HIGH QUEEN OF HEAVEN! HIGH
UP NEAR THE STARS, NEAR THAT
SPILL ACROSS THE SKY
OF HERA'S BREAST-
MILK. HERA
TELEIA!
THIS TEMPLE A HIGH,
HOLY PLACE FOR VIEWING
THE PLAINS WHERE HER BEAUTIFUL,
SACRED CATTLE GRAZE, A HIGH HOLY PLACE
FOR VIEWING HER FERTILE VALLEYS AND TOWNS. A
HIGH HOLY PLACE FOR VIEWING HERSELF—THE MOON—
AS SHE TRAVERSES THE HEAVENS, THE ALL-SEEING MOTHER
OF ALL, WHO LOVES ALL THAT SHE SEES. THIS TEMPLE ON A
HIGH FLAT TERRACE FOR DANCING . . . IN CELEBRATION OF WOMEN'S
MATURE BODIES! IN THIS TEMPLE IS THE SACRED, COUPLING COUCH
ON WHICH HERA MAKES LOVE TO HERACLES—IN A SACRAMENT OF UNION
UNDER A FULL MOON.   IN THIS TEMPLE WE OFFER BACK INTO THE EARTH
SOME OF THE BLOOD OF OUR WOMBS, AS A LIBATION TO OUR MOTHER FOR
ALL SHE HAS GIVEN US. IN THIS TEMPLE WE LEAVE OFFERINGS ON HER

STONE   ALTAR.

WE SEEK OUT OUR MOTHER IN THIS HIGH TEMPLE,
FOR ALL OF THOSE WHO TASTE OF HERA'S BREASTMILK
SHALL HAVE LIFE EVERLASTING!

In this temple is the ivory throne,
    draped with a white cowskin,
On which the Heavenly Queen sits to be seen,
    Her back against golden carved doves,
    Her feet on the sacred tripod footstool,
in each hand a symbol of eternal life:

In one hand a golden wand
    topped by a BUTTERFLY.
        BUTTERFLY,
Symbol of life everlasting from Her body,
    for as a chrysalis the
        BUTTERFLY eternally dies
    in its cocoon,
    the womb
    out of which it is eternally reborn as
        BUTTERFLY.
    Hera, the MONARCH of heaven and earth!
    She,   the DOUBLE AX!

Hers the power of gentleness!
Hers the power of everlasting love!

Hera, Queen of Heaven and Earth, dispensing everlasting Life.
Marble, Greece, 480 B.C.E. [JWW]

VIRGIN
Mother . . . .
CRONE

In Her other palm a POMEGRANATE—
POMEGRANATE—
full of its own red juices and
the seeds of its own rebirth.
POMEGRANATE:
Like Hera's womb,
full of its own red juices and
the seeds of Her own rebirth.

POMEGRANATE!
BUTTERFLY!
FULL MOON!

Symbols of eternal rebirth,
Symbols of life everlasting
from the body and blood of
MOTHER HERA! TELEIA!
But the Full Moon wanes . . .
into a dying crescent.
And the pomegranate dries and dies . . .
goes to seed . . .
PHhooooff . . . PHhooooff . . .

For
The POMEGRANATE-GONE-TO-SEED
and
the WANING-MOON-CRESCENT
are the sacred symbols of
the Wise Old Crone.

[*In mid-sentence priestess cycles slowly from Teleia's circle-temple in center into
Hekate's circle-temple at stage right.*]

Gold butterfly, representing fullness, maturity, the cycle of Birth-Death-ReBirth. Mycenae, sixteenth century B.C.E.

Earth Mother as Oracle, Goddess as Wisdom and Prophecy. Malta, c. 3100 B.C.E.
Bulk can often be read as an indication of "great substance," signifying the earth.

[Priestess picks up deep-sounding drum and sounds it softly and slowly, pronouncing Crone's name in loud rasping whisper.]

Kah! . . . Kah! . . .   HEH-KAH-TEH!
Old woman!
Beyond the peak of Her body's ripeness and glory!
But entering Her period . . .
          Her period of great Wisdom.

Hekate!
          Wise old woman!
          Owl-eyed healing woman!
                    HOO-hoo!   HOO-hoo!
          She who sees clearly in the darkness
                    the web that connects all of life.
                    HOO-hoo!   HOO-hoo!
          She who stirs Her cauldron
                    unceasingly.

Hekate!
End of bearing, end of harvest.
Goddess of the Waning Moon Crescent!
Goddess of Decay, winter, and Death!

VIRGIN
Mother . . . .
CRONE

Hera Hekate, the Old One, who withdraws
to be alone,
to contemplate and heal—
Herself and others.

HEKATE,
old Earth Mother,
receives us back into Her Body
for renewal,
for rebirth—
Hekate calls us back into close-and-holy Darkness
for healing
and transformation.

[*Priestess spirals slowly around and into the center of Crone's circle-temple. Then after "not afraid!" she quickens pace and spirals out again to upstage-center for ecstatic Crone-praise.*]

THIS
THE TEMPLE
OF HEKAT,
OLD
WOMAN LIVING
ALONE IN REFLECTION.
THIS TEMPLE DUG INTO THE EARTH,
INTO THE EARTH AT THE SWAMPY EDGE OF LAKE STYMPHALUS.
IN THIS TEMPLE IS THE INNER SANCTUM, THE
CLOSE-AND-HOLY DARKNESS INSIDE THE
EARTH. HERE ONE DESCENDS INTO
THE SPIRAL LABYRINTH OF
TRANSFORMATION!
OLD HEKATE!
GODDESS OF TRANSFORMATION!
SHE LEADS US . . . INSIDE . . . AND DOWN
INTO THE CLOSE-AND-HOLY DARKNESS OF THE
EARTH! HEKATE! GODDESS OF INNER JOURNEYS!
SHE LEADS US INTO THE CLOSE-AND-HOLY DARKNESS
OF OUR INMOST SELVES. GODDESS OF REFLECTION! SHE LEADS
US INTO THE CLOSE-AND-HOLY DARKNESS OF OUR MINDS AND HEARTS
AND WOMBS . . . DEEP INSIDE WHERE WE ARE TRULY ALONE . . . BUT NOT
AFRAID! FOR HEKATE, THE LOVING MOTHER WHO LEADS US INTO DARKNESS
LEADS US OUT! HER WOMB IS THE SOURCE OF ETERNAL LIFE! GODDESS OF
CREATION! GODDESS OF RE-CREATION! GODDESS OF CREATIVE CHANGING! OF
BEGINNING AGAIN! GODDESS OF RENEWAL! MOTHER OF DARKNESS, DECAY,
AND DYING! GODDESS OF DEAD SEEDS! OF REBIRTH! GRANDMOTHER

HEKATE!   CRONE!

Women, . . .

The withered, dried body of the old woman
   is as sacred
      and precious
         and necessary to life
As the withered dried seeds-in-a-pod are to Nature.

And that womb blood that creates life,
   the blood that contains the
      WISDOM of the ages in it?
        Mother-Daughter
        Mother-Daughter
        Mother-Daughter . . .

That WISE BLOOD
     no longer flows out of the Crone.
No . . .
Grandmother Hekate
    keeps Her WISE BLOOD inside.

So look with love on the old woman, women.
   SHE WHO KEEPS HER WISE BLOOD INSIDE,
   She is the source of WISDOM and
       healing visions.

Look with love on the withered old crone, women.
   SHE WHO KEEPS HER WISE BLOOD INSIDE, . . .
   She is the FUTURE!

*Polished, red Mother-Daughter Goddesses. Three repeated
for emphasis in neck bands, breast chevrons, hands.
Cyprus, Early Bronze Age.*

HERA HEKATE.
HERA PARTHENIA.
HERA TELEIA.
Three names, three Persons,
But always One.

*Bird Goddess as Queen Mother Goose, She the Water-finder, She of the
Three-fold Bounty and the three-toed foot Who lays the Golden Egg of
Creation. With quatrefoils, cup marks, spirals, water signs, threes repeated for
emphasis. Serbia, Balkans, second millenium* B.C.E.   [JWW]

[Evangelis cycles in a large circle from one temple to the next:]

Remember, women, . . .

THE
TEMPLE
OF
HEBE IS
FOR CELEBRATING
THE POSSIBILITIES,
THE
POTENTIAL
IN OUR LIVES!
FOR CELEBRATING
NEW BEGINNINGS AND
BELONGING-TO-OURSELVES
NO MATTER WHAT OUR AGE.

THE
TEMPLE
OF
TELEIA IS
FOR CELEBRATING
OUR
FERTILE,
GIVING MINDS,
METING JUSTICE,
FOR COMPOSING SONGS,
AND LOVING OUR MATURE,
HONEYING BODIES.

THE
TEMPLE
OF
HEKATE IS
WHERE WE LEARN
NOT TO FEAR DEATH AND
DYING
BUT LEARN TO
CELEBRATE THE SACRED
DARKNESS OF OUR MINDS,
HEARTS, WOMBS, AND EARTH.

VIRGIN
Mother . . . .
CRONE

Three sacred Persons in Hera.

Three sacred phases to our lives.

Three temples to help us celebrate ourselves,
unify our lives,
ease our transitions

from Death . . .
. . . to ReBirth.

[*Priestess makes a large circle, cycling through one temple after the other, naming in each temple the particular association each of Hera's Persons has with Death and ReBirth.*]

In the temple of HEBE we celebrate:

DEATH of winter . . .
. . . BIRTH of spring.

DEATH of childhood . . .
. . . BIRTH of womanhood.

Spring lilies, spring birds. Fresco from "Room of the Lilies."
Thera, sixteenth century B.C.E.

VIRGIN
Mother . . . .
CRONE

In the temple of TELEIA we celebrate:

DEATH of carefree youth . . .
. . . BIRTH of others from our bodies.

DEATH of belonging to ourselves alone . . .
. . . BIRTH of mature responsibleness . . .
of nurturing others . . .
of fullness . . .
wholeness . . .

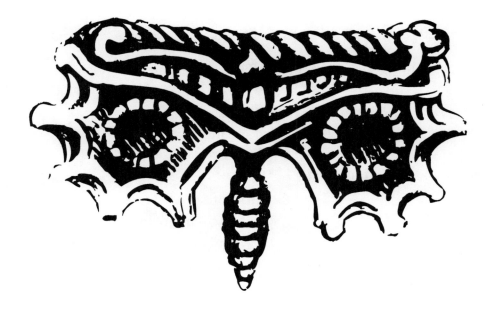

Goddess as Butterfly with All-seeing Eyes. Symbol of maturity, fullness,
realization. Gold pendant. Mycenae, sixteenth century B.C.E.

VIRGIN
Mother . . . .
CRONE

In the temple of HEKATE we celebrate:

the DYING of our bodies . . .
the BIRTH of Wisdom and healing vision.

HEKATE:
Goddess of DEAD seeds . . .
. . . She who gives BIRTH
and new life to the DEAD seeds.

*"The Seed-Vulva." Flowery X, #, or four-line grid as sign of
"fires-of-transformation," womb-vulva lozenge in center.
Çatal Hüyük, Turkey, seventh millenium* B.C.E.

VIRGIN
Mother . . . .
CRONE

[*Priestess continues cycling around and through all temples.*]

There are THREE TEMPLES OF DEATH-AND-REBIRTH,
For ALL DIES and is Born Again.

[*Priestess continues cycling as chanting intensifies, speeds up, as spiral tightens,
grows smaller.*]

All Nature . . . . dies and is born again . . .
Seeds . . . . die and are born again . . .
Plants . . . . die and are born again . . .
The years . . . . die and are born again . . .
The moon, the sun . . . . die and are born again . . .
We . . . . die and are born again . . .

Mother-Daughter
Mother-Daughter
Mother-Daughter

THREE TEMPLES celebrate
the unbroken cycle of our lives!

HEBE !
TELEIA !
HEKATE !

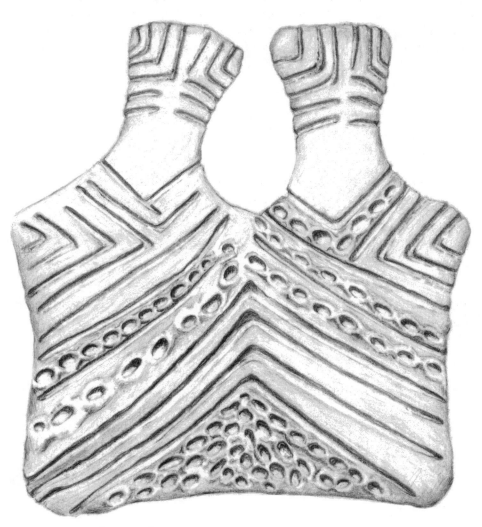

Mother-Daughter Goddesses with chevrons and egg-shaped depressions.
Clay, Anatolia, Turkey, 1600 B.C.E.

VIRGIN
Mother 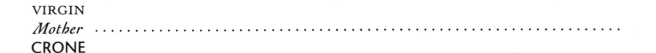 . . . .
CRONE

[Priestess reaches center of spiral. She stops. With hands in shape of crescents she mimes the moon cycling in unending circles: first, her left hand forms the Virgin-Moon crescent down at her left side and she slowly raises it over her head where the right hand in shape of a crescent joins the left; together the crescents form a circle or Full Moon over her head; then the left hand crescent falls away as right hand in shape of crescent arcs down. Then the circle repeats: left-hand crescent rises, both hands form full moon, right-hand crescent descends. Again and again in silence. . . . Then:]

Our lives cycling . . .
The moon cycling . . .
Our lives cycling with the moon . . . unendingly . . .
The moon . . . the measure of our lives . . .
The crescent moons:

[Priestess puts left-hand crescent and right-hand crescent on either side of her head—like cow's horns:]

The horns of our Great Cow Goddess, HERA.

MMAAA—MMMAAAA HERA !
MOO—OON HEIFER !
MOO—OON GODDESS !

Women, . . .

Did you know?
The first races at Olympia,
The first Olympic Games were
            MOON RACES—
            MOON RACES
                    run in honor of our MOON MOTHER, HERA?

178

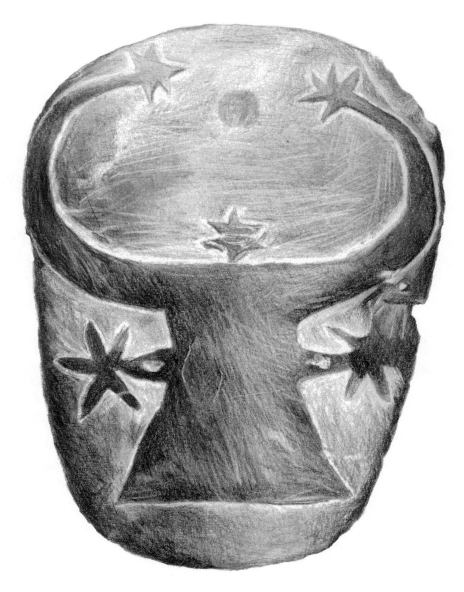

Star-headed female. Arms upraised like crescent horns and moons suggests
Celestial Cow Goddess. Egypt, pre-3100 B.C.E.

VIRGIN
Mother . . . .
CRONE

Oh, yes, women . . .

    The first Olympic Games were
           foot races run only by women!
               at the Full Moon,
               near Hera's temple
                   at Olympia.

    There were three MOON RACES!
      so that all the women could run:

          One race for the old women—
             those old Hekate Crones
             who run like Hebe colts!

          One race for the matrons,
          One race for virgins.

How the girls anticipated
      their first show of blood!
How they celebrated it when it came!
      for that meant the girl had become a woman,
A virgin, who could run in the MOON race!

MOON RACES!
All the women running with hair unbound,
All the women running free
      and full of laughter.

Young Goddess emerging from sea or ritual bath. Marble, Rhodes, third century B.C.E. [JWW]

But running in earnest too!
For the winner of the virgins' race
          had the honor and responsibility
          of choosing the next king!

The virgin winner would choose
          HERACLES, the king who would rule
                    for the next four years.

With garland-bedecked kin and kine,
With noisy rams-horn blastings,
A great procession swept the winner up,
Her cheeks still flushed with victory.

Having run and won the glorious prize,
     she was led to the Virgin's Brook
     where she disrobed
          in preparation for

          HER NUPTIAL BATH.

[*Priestess bathes at the edge of the Virgin's temple, using tinkling Virgin's chimes for splashing Virgin waters which she "scoops up" and lets fall over her arms, head, back, singing:*]

          HEBE VIRGIN!
          HERA PARTHENIA!

VIRGIN
Mother  . . . .
CRONE

[*Rising from the stream-side, Evangelis announces loudly:*]

And there was a great feast!

And the SACRED COW WAS SACRIFICED !
     the sacred cow
     that was the body and blood of the Goddess Hera—
And the VIRGIN ATE AND DRANK OF IT !

For by partaking of the body and blood of Hera,
     the virgin *became* Hera.
For it is as Hera that she will perform
     the sacred ritual
         on the Goddess's Sacred Coupling Couch
           under the Full Moon.

Yes, it is as Hera that
     she will mate with Heracles!

The women put star-flowers in her hair—
     a-stars,
       five-pointed asters—
And she is led up Mount Euboia . . .

[*Priestess cycles upstage center to Teleia's temple.*]

To the temple of TELEIA, . . .

To Hera's holy House-Body
    where Heracles
        waits . . . for her!

    where the new-crowned king of her choice
        waits . . .

            . . . for her . . .

    where the sacred bed has been prepared . . .

            . . . for her . . .

[*Priestess stops where scarves lie in pile on golden altarcloth representing Teleia's Sacred Coupling Couch upstage center.*]

        . . . for Hebe the Virgin . . .
          . . . Who transforms . . .
            . . . becoming . . .

          TELEIA!

*Goddess of sensuality and love-making. Marble, Hellenistic
Greece.* [jww]

[*Singing:*]

> Oh, see me . . .   I am become TELEIA !
> See my beautiful Goddess body!

[*Evangelis sinks sensually onto the pile of scarves, still singing:*]

> When they bring him to me . . .
> When they bring my sweet honey man,
> He will adorn me with agates,
> He will share his rich cream with me.
> Then when he and I have burgeoned with love,
> All gardens will flourish luxuriantly!
> All gardens will flourish luxuriantly![1]

[*Rising to knees; speaking:*]

> Women, . . .

> Such is the power of Hera's body,
>   of Hera's sexuality,
> That the coupling of Hera and Heracles
>   energizes all the forces of Nature!

> Such is the power of Hera's body—
>   and Her temple is Her body,
>   Her house Her body,
>   Her house Her womb,
>   Her house-Womb the
>   Sacred Vessel of all Creation—

VIRGIN
Mother . . . .
CRONE

Such is the power of Hera's Body, that
    when She bedded Heracles,
    their coupling
        moved the earth,
        burst the seeds,
        pushed the air,
        swept the winds, and
        turned the heavens!

HERA'S UNDYING LOVE CYCLES ALL OF NATURE!
HERA TELEIA!

[*Priestess again mimes the cycling moon in the heavens, stopping as the waning moon falls toward Hekate's temple.*]

But as the heavens turn,
The fullness of the moon wanes . . .

        . . . and the moon dies, . . .

        . . . even as vital young men die! ! !

[*Priestess crawls toward Hekate's circle, keening, mourning:*]

Rose Window, or "the Year Wheel turning," representing annual sun cycle [2]

VIRGIN
Mother ....
CRONE

Oo—lay-loo!
Make lamentations for the lives that are lost!

Ah—lay-loo!
Make lamentations for the BLOOD that is lost—
                                        in vain!

Ah-lay-loo!
Weep and make lamentations for the BLOOD
          that is lost and spilled
                  in war,
                  in violence, and
                  in other unnatural,
                        unnecessary sacrifices!

                        AH-LEH-LOO!

Oh, women, remember!

Our blood flows
                  in peaceful, natural cycles!
Our blood is not shed
                  in violence, revenge, or anger!
No sacrifice, wound, or injury
                  causes our womb blood to flow!

WE BLEED!   BUT WE DO NOT DIE!
For our blood is the Blood of Life!
We, the vessels of Creation!

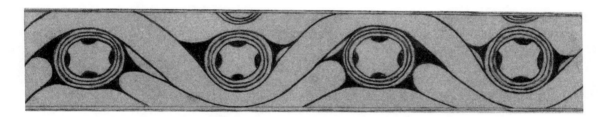

Flowing waters design on pitcher, Crete snake, egg, vortex, Xs, meander . . .
Pattern on vase, Ukraine, 3900 B.C.E.

Women, . . .

    Did you know that our foremothers
        spilled their womb blood together,
            all at the same time?

    Oh, yes . . .
        following the Dark of the Moon!

The afternoon before the Dark of the Moon
    all women
        extinguished their hearth fires, and
        left their homes,
            husbands,
            older children,
    and came together
    to claim their Sisterhood.

All of them came —
      bleeders and non-bleeders,
      mothers who were nursing,
           and crones too old to bleed.

All of them came —
      pouches full of uncooked foods
      hanging from their shoulders,
           enough for four or five days:
      honey, fruits, cheese, artichokes, olives.

All of them came
      to affirm together
           that an unbroken stream of kinship
                from time out of memory
                flowed through their bodies
                    as though through one.

Women doing ritual dance. From Hera's temple near Paestum,
sixth century B.C.E.   [JWW]

[Priestess picks up drum from Hekate's temple and beats it in units of seven quick beats at a time as she wends her way between and around the temples:]

Like the wetness that was coming,
the women poured into the streets;
flowing together into Oneness,
drumming,
shaking their sistrums and tambourines,
sounding their cymbals and gongs.

Before leaving home they had painted their faces and
decorated their bodies
with bangles, necklaces, and rings,
belled bracelets,
carved shells and stones,
ornaments of copper and gold.

Now they displayed in the streets—
preening,
enjoying themselves
for themselves.

[Priestess takes her bullroarer from her waist and swirls it around over her head, making a loud, eerie Earth sound.]

Snaking through the streets—
wildness growing—
they swirled their bullroarers
over their heads!

Yip-yip-yip-YIP ! !

And they shape-shifted—
   dancing their Power Animals—
      Lioness, Hawk, Falcon,
      Winged Cosmic Serpent!

They called themselves witches
    and chanted:

  "Old Mother Dragon swims through the waves,
  Swallows red apples, sleeps in deep caves.
  Twin wingéd Pythons, writhing in the rain,
  Die shedding their skins, then are born again!"

Ecstatic,
  they mingled-joined
    in riotous waves of love and energy,
      and carried themselves
        in one turbulent stream,
          from one time to another,
            one world to another.

Thus
  they wended their way—
    in a din of togetherness—
      to the thickets in the swamps
        where they calmed themselves . . .
        gathering branches
          from Lygos bushes.

Carved and enhanced natural vulva images in cave, c. 13,000 B.C.E.

Transported, they filled baskets with
  shiny green leaves of Lygos—
  sacred, pungent
  herb of Transformation—
    for use in the temple,
      in the Heraion.

VIRGIN
Mother . . . .
CRONE

And then,
        as the moon withdrew from sight
        the women too withdrew from sight.

At the Dark of the Moon
        the women descended into Hera's temple.
And that close-and-holy dark womb-place
        tenderly swallowed them, . . .

     FOR THEIR TIME OF WISDOM AND POWER WAS AT HAND.

              THEIR DRAGON TIME . . .

                       . . . WAS AT HAND![3]

Inside the Heraion,
      having left their Sister Din behind,
The women folded in on themselves,
       accumulated their acumen,
       became One and buoyant.

With ritual excitement
    those who would be bleeding
       began to crush the Lygos leaves,
         making piles of them,
         arranging the piles
         in friendly clusters and circles.
Crushing the leaves
     filled the air
     with an acrid, medicinal smell.

MMMmmm! stringent, but clean, invigorating!

They shared the pungency,
        letting it move and transport them.

All together—all at the same time—
        they grew more aware
                of all sensations,
                of all smells, feelings,
                of touches to the skin.

Moisture was released on their hands
        when they crushed the leaves
        and they rubbed it
                into their bellies and thighs.
Softly chanting and humming,
        they massaged and blessed each other's bodies
                with the pungent Lygos oil,
for
        "Juice of the Lygos brings on the flow.
        Sap of the Lygos brings on the flow."

Sister time was sacred time,
        time of heightened awareness of Being,
        time not to be wasted in the regular world
                doing ordinary tasks,
                distracted by small talk
                        or men.

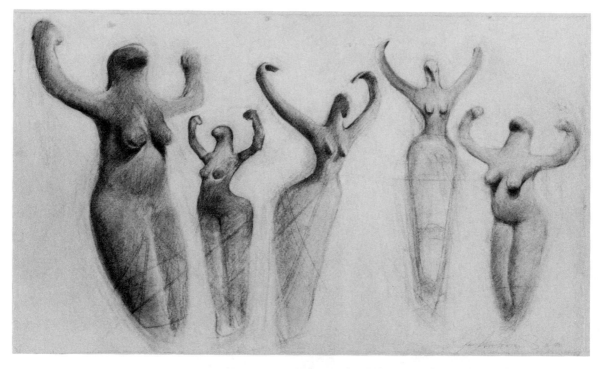

Nathor, Snake-Bird, Nile River Goddess. Terra cotta, Egypt, 4500 B.C.E.

Inside Hera's temple
    all energies went
           into togetherness,
           into meditation,
           into openness,
           into readiness and allowing.
All energies went
       to experience the Goddess
             in themselves,
      to dreaming,
      to receiving visions and
         knowledge of the meaning of life.

Flutist playing in Goddess ritual. Marble, Greek Italy, 460 B.C.E. [JWW]

Through moonless nights and restful days
    they prepared themselves
        with graceful, stretching movement,
            meditation,
            massage,
            the music
        of flutes and drums.
Then as the New Moon rose outside
    near dawn, losing its light to the day,
        inside,
        the women began losing their blood
            to the earth.

Those who were flowing
        sat bare-bottomed
                on their soft heaps of Lygos,
      their womb's blood slowly
             seeping into the spongy nests,
      into the absorbent membranes
                  of the crushed leaves.

And as the blood flowed,
      the women shared their insights,
        their visions,
             prophetic dreams of and for the future.

Sometimes they sang
        about the sacredness
        of their kinship blood,
            and its power to create, heal, reveal:

[*Singing:*]

"This is the Blood that promises Life.
 This is the Blood that promises Sustenance.
 This is the Blood that promises Rebirth,
                Renewal,
                Regeneration."[4]

Mother Niniganni as
Python, the Baga (African)
Goddess of Prophecy,
Death, and Giver-of-Life.
She has twenty-eight womb
lozenges (fourteen on each
side) for the twenty-eight-
day period of women's
menstrual cycle (only one
Dark-of-the-Moon "day" is
counted). Wooden carving,
Guinea.

Later—

    they would plow their blood-soaked nests
        into the fields
          to fructify the soil.

      Women's New-Moon blood
          enriching the earth,
             feeding the seeds and plants.

      Women connected vitally to the earth.
      Women cycling together with the moon.
      EARTH, SEEDS, MOON, WOMEN
          cycling unendingly together!

[*Priestess makes crescent moon again with her left hand and slowly raises it.*]

And then, . . .

    when the New, Virgin moon was rising late enough
          in the daytime sky
          for its light
          to last into the night,

  the women rose
      from their resting, renewing place
          in the Heraion.

It was dusk when they came out and
    went together by New Moon light
      to bathe themselves
        in the Virgin's Brook,
          in the Brook of the Freeing Waters.

The women immersed themselves in the Virgin Brook,
  celebrating the sacrament of flow and change,
  celebrating the transition
    from one period to another.
  letting the free-flowing, birthing waters,
    wash away the old cycle,
  letting the Waters ease them into a new.

And like Hera—Who is "the Spring Bough
    drenched in dew and water
    that it may burgeon and blossom anew,"
The women emerged from the waters renewed,
      reborn.

They emerged from the Waters as blessed virgins again,
  for all women are like Hera:
      Ever-Virgin!

As with Hera, so too with all women:
  the eternal, joyous cycling from
  BIRTH . . . DEATH . . . to . . . REBIRTH . . .

And so, women, . . .

  That is my story of Hera
    and Her sacred persons.

I CHARGE YOU TO REMEMBER ![5]

I charge you to remember Hera and
  to visit Her temples,
  to celebrate the cycles and
    rhythm of your lives.

IF WE REMEMBER HERA and use Her temples, women,
we will survive, thrive, and renew!

But when we women no longer teach one another
the sacraments of our bodies, . . .

When we women no longer serve our own Necessity,
we will live the necessity of others,
we will be in the service of others,
we will be profane things,
objects,
the possessions of others.

And that profanity
will end the cycle.

When we live as objects,
our days and lives will pass,
go by,
die—
without renewing us.

Our dulled bodies will go straight for the end,
without having known the joy
of rebirth,
the ecstasy of the Round.

But you *do* remember the joy!
        You *do* know what wholeness is like!
                what being ever-New is like!
I *know* you remember!

I CHARGE YOU TO REMEMBER!

Our foremothers were no one's property,
        no one's servant, wife, or concubine.
        Our foremothers belonged to themselves.

Our foremothers gave birth to their *own* children
        out of their *own* wombs, and
        gave their children their *own* names,
                their mothers' names,
                their grand-dams' names,
                their great-grand-dams' names.

Our foremothers walked confidently,
                alone in the streets,
                so respected and revered were they!

Our foremothers ran!
                free and full of laughter!

Goddess emerging from sea or ritual bath. Marble, Greek Italy, 460 B.C.E. [JWW]

Our foremothers bathed bare-bellied,
        unashamed under the sky,
            in renewing waters,
            in the womb waters
            of our loving Mother Hera,
                    the Earth.

VIRGIN
Mother . . . .
CRONE

So REMEMBER THESE THINGS, WOMEN!
Or failing that, . . .
          Dream them!
Let Hebe's voice rise in your ears afresh!
Listen afresh for a new message,
                a new message for these new times.

The Goddess of Invention lives in you.
The Creatrix never stops creating.
Call Her forth in yourSelf!

Go to the temples and proclaim loudly:

    "I am Hebe!   The Creating One!
                  I bring forth my own Necessity!
    I am Teleia!   I savor life fully!
                  I nurture myself and others!
    I am Hekate! I have the Wisdom of the Ages in me!"

      "I am my own Miraculous Mother!
      I am Many-in-One!
      I am Virgin-Mother-Crone!"

        All praises be unto Hera, women!
        Hera, Blessed Trinity!!

        HERA! GODDESS OF WOMEN!!!

          THE END
          . . . .
         Blessed be.
         Ananke.

Nine
......

CRONE CONSCIOUSNESS

Hera the Crone, the Wise Old Woman, is called Hekate
(HEH-kah-tee) or Chera (KEH-rah).

*T*he crone is a woman past her bearing years. In mother-centered societies women too old to give birth or to menstruate—those who *keep their Wise Blood inside*—have often been the most respected, most feared, most beloved, wisest members of the community. She might be called respectfully, even reverently, "the oldest of the old," even "chief," but she was chief only of counsel, meaning, "primary advice giver." Girls and women could look forward to growing old, to becoming a crone, without fear that their wrinkles or stoop would diminish their worth, influence, or the meaning of their lives.[1]

Crones were the ones most capable of offering guidance and direction to others, the most likely persons to have the wisdom, the time, and experience to heal the sick and minister to the dying. But *time-factoring was their special domain and responsability*. Menstruating women's bodies kept track of— *were*—lunar-month calendars, while the old remembering women kept track of—*embodied*—long-range events. It was their ability to respond to large cycles that kept all events in perspective. They kept records in their heads and bodies of the old days, of what happened that needed to be remembered, of what could be expected to happen—genealogies, eclipses, mishaps, summers of special abundance, recipes for healing potions, annals of deaths and births, knowledge of how to handle things, how to survive and thrive. And they recounted their litanies over and over, by heart, telling the story of their people to each new generation. Because of their accumulated experience, insight, and practiced vision, crones, more than any others, could look into people's eyes and see their character and future. They could read animal behavior and celestial movements; they knew best what was going to happen next in Nature's complex, overlapping cycles. Perhaps that is why we tend to picture the wise one bending over a crystal ball as an old woman; the one who can most reliably predict the future is quite likely a crone.

VIRGIN

Mother . . . .

CRONE

Knowledge of plants, herbs, and roots gives power to heal. And if that knowledge and power is unknown to any but the women of one family, the working of cures by their most accomplished healer—their crone—may seem to be magic. But that kind of magic has nothing to do with sorcery or using one's knowledge to impose one's will onto events or onto others. A healing hag has over decades carefully scouted and experimented with Nature's resources, has added her own observations to the wisdom of ages past that she inherited from her mothers and grandmothers, has conversed with the plants, herbs, and roots themselves, has received in trance much wisdom from them. She makes effective rites and potions through knowledge of and *participation in* the PATTERNS of Nature. She would never attempt to *control* nature for selfish or for devious reasons. What would be the purpose of defying Natural Law when one's whole life had been spent in learning the power and ecstatic peace that comes from harmonizing with Nature?

TRANSITION TIMES

Hekate—like Hebe and Teleia—is Changing Woman. But the Crone persona most especially models *healing* and *transformation*. Her most sublime gifts come from the Cycle. Those who revere Her find that serenity, health, and wholeness come from honoring the Eternal Return, the entire cycle of Birth-Death-ReBirth. One participates in Her essence—one gets Her power—when one responds to and enters into the ongoing transformation within all the moments, days, and seasons, as well as the entirety, of one's life.

The wise old woman's participation in ever-cycling, ever-changing Nature includes knowing how to make changes for the better happen. This crone magic comes from making a lifelong study of plants and herbs to learn their nourishing and medicinal properties as well as when

and where to apply her knowledge. She knows that *rituals that aspire to effect change or transition* are most effective, most powerful, most magical, when they take place during *natural times of transition*, times of cusps, times that are *in-between*—scary times that foreshadow a change.

Everyone can feel the power and aura of such times: Twice every day there are in-between times—*dusk* and *dawn*. And twice a year the *equinoxes* (that mark the beginning of autumn and spring) are harbingers of drastic changes to come in temperature and the length of night. Also twice a year there are *solstices*—those special cusps or in-between moments when the sun's orbit pauses briefly (*sol stice* means "sun stands still") before it makes a complete change in direction in the sky, reversing portentously from a southerly descent to a northerly rise, or vice versa, and bringing a significant seasonal shift—taking the earth into summer or into winter. The moon's celestial path traverses several auspicious transitions: into *Full Moon*, into *Dark of the Moon*, into *New Moon* (the word "month" means one complete cycle of the *moon*), and twice a month the moon is exactly a half-sphere, accentuating its waxing or waning, preparing to move through a cusp, leading us toward . . . some culmination. These cusps are wicca times, bending times, magic times, auspicious times pregnant with Mystery and Possibility. It is therefore exceedingly important for crones and hags—the magic-makers and transition-easers, the healers and distributors of age-old sacraments—to observe these times with awe and reverence, receptive to their opportunities and gifts.

From time immemorial crones have been associated with in-between times and their Mysteries. Such events, momentous in themselves, are also portents of other events to come. Cusps are times that hover between death and life—between the end of an old day or season and the beginning of a new one. Cusps remind one of crones most obviously because of the momentousness of crones' own coming event; because of crones' own visibly approaching death, they themselves are "in-between." The association is helped out by the Old German word *hagazussa*, which means "one who rides on the *Hag*"—a hedge or fence, a device that comes "in between."[2] One of the hag's most auspicious times has been All Hallows' Eve—Halloween—the seasonal cusp that marked the death of Earth's productive or harvest time and the start of Earth's fallow time of hibernation.

NOSE-THUMBERS

Ever-changing crones—the in-between ones—are famous for their laughter, for knowing something others don't know. Hags—experienced, confident, full of secret knowledge, with nothing to lose—get away with being raucous, brazen, bold. In my personal experience crones do not always feel bound by manners or tradition. With no time to waste, they sometimes dress and behave eccentrically, unceremoniously disregarding restrictions or conventions that they find unnecessary or bothersome. Some crones I know, full of accumulated wisdom and newfound freedoms, have become innovators of personal style. They assertively "walk their talk" and are willing to throw caution to the wind, even court danger, as they thumb their noses at what people might say in order to go on to spin their new ways—and to cackle.

> *When I am an old woman I shall wear*
>   *purple*
> *With a red hat that doesn't go . . .*
> *I shall gobble up samples in shops and*
>   *press alarm bells*
> *And run my stick along the public railings*
> *And make up for the sobriety of my youth,*
> *. . . And learn to spit.*[3]

TEACHERS BY EXAMPLE

Tenacious old women, primed by a broad philosophical overview of things, are likely to take the wisest path, not the quickest. Even in infirmity, an old grandmother often assumes the role of guardian of youth, the group, and the future. Such elders teach steadfastness, not by laying down the law or rules but by the example of their lives and minds.

The crone teaches by modeling a keen ability to respond—*response-ability*—to what goes on in-between two live beings. With momentous things on her mind, precarious work in her fragile hands, a crone's transmissions may from time to time be cranky, rambling, tenacious, unnecessarily vague or fierce. So add the following to her skills and her potency: teaching indirectly through body language, teaching the need to watch and listen, teaching through her own abilities to perceive intentions and the subtleties of inner communications and the knowings that can happen indirectly in-between persons, in-between beings, where the Mystery takes place.

A reverence for the Wise Old Woman archetype and her in-betweens can give women a teacher for being a keen observer and respecter of life, a Model for experiencing the power of waning, an example of living advanced years with energy, pride, and eagerness. There is joy in continuing to make important contributions to one's community—or just continuing to contribute to one's own life's meaning-adventure. In our tradition old women—as soon as they are past their prime as breeders—are usually treated by others and themselves not as teachers but as throwaways. Feeling worthless as one gains in maturity and wisdom is a ridiculous waste of human resources and lives.

THE GODDESS AS CRONE

Hekate the Crone is the Decay, Death, and Regeneration aspect of the Goddess, the personi-

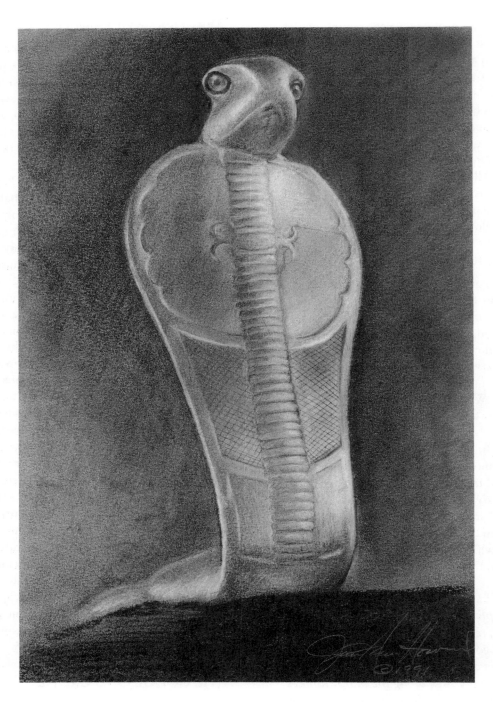

*Goddess Neith, Creatrix of All, as gold Cobra Whose neck-swell was called the
Third Eye of Wisdom. Egypt, 1325* B.C.E.

fication of the eternal cosmic cycle of Birth-Death-ReBirth. Through this Goddess of Transformation every life form proceeds from and eventually returns to The One, so She contains and manifests Wholeness within HerSelf. The Wise Old Crone is the vague, scary autumn-winter aspect of the Goddess; most vegetation has died, but underearth, dead matter reconstitutes, composts, makes heat; roots and seeds retain life and hold the future, the unknown, renewal. All this the Crone embodies and manifests.

The Crone has often been the most beloved, most passionately adored, and most tenderly revered person in the Trinity. Contrary to western expectations, the Crone Goddess is the embodiment of the deepest, most profound Mystery of the Universe, personifying Eternity, Wisdom, and the Most Sublime. Some idea of how intense Her followers' affection for Her would have been in earlier millennia can be glimpsed in the fervent devotion many Hindus still bestow today on the Goddess Kali.[4]

As fierce guardian of the tribe, She can assume aggressive, deliberately offensive, frightening stances and persona, like the Crone-Goddess Gorgon and Medusa did in ancient patriarchal times while protecting their group. It was said Medusa actually turned men to stone; that is, She is the Death-bringer Who precipitated *rigor mortis* in them.

Hers is the ostentatious, all encompassing Third Eye of most profound Wisdom and insight; sometimes this eye is in Her forehead, but it appears on the front of Her neck when She manifests as spiraling, skin-shedding, healing Cobra. She embodies the Mystery of the coming and going of life, and the unification of all forms of being through the mixing and remixing that goes on throughout the universe in Her cosmic cauldron, without ceasing, in the eternal cycle of Birth-Death-ReBirth.

According to one version of Hera's classical myth, when She had finally had enough of hus-

band Zeus's tricks and shenanigans, She took the title *Chera*, which literally means "widow" (although the sense is "divorcée"), and withdrew to Her Crone temple, a dark Inner Sanctum dug into the earth by Lake Stymphalos in central Greece, to live alone in reflection. One usually finds Hera's three Persons listed as Hebe Parthenia, Teleia, and Chera, but since the name Chera only came to be associated with Hera in historical times, after She became Zeus's reluctant wife, I do not use it in the myths here. It is an unsatisfactory label for the Self-sufficient Great Mother Goddess. I call Hera's Crone person *Hekate*, the name of another once-revered Wise-Old-Woman archetype, a Self-reliant Goddess of Dark Inner Power and Knowing, a Goddess much older than Chera, with whom Hera was intimately associated in archaic myth before such female powers were demonized and debased.

CRONE CONSCIOUSNESS

Reverence for the Crone is the aspect of matristic cultures most foreign to our own. We admire and aspire to permanence and individuation, while the heart of Crone consciousness is the ability to be comfortable with and find the sacrament in *change*—to enjoy the power and gifts of endings, of death, of mixing, adding, transforming, of renewal through shape-shifting. The nature of all life in the universe is change—in some ways regular, in some ways random, complex, and chaotic. If we stop fighting change (Changing Woman) and become aware of and sensitive to it (metaphorically, to Her), if we embrace Changing Woman as our nature, as ourSelf, we can move with Her creatively, productively, with grace. Awareness of the rhythms and cycles of change in ourselves and in Nature fosters connectedness, freedom, and a sense of openness, surprise, and unplanned, undreamed-of Possibility. It seems ironic to westerners, who long for fixity and equate happiness mathemati-

VIRGIN
Mother ·
CRONE

cally with deliberate effort and planned goals, that all of these uncertain unbidden gifts from the Crone can help one realize one's deepest yearnings for Self-satisfaction and wholeness. Like the Virgin, the Crone manifests courage, letting be, and hope for ecstatic union with the All.

Obviously, although this Person of the sacred Trinity is imaged as old, She must be prepared for, encouraged, and recognized in the very young: "Out of the mouths of babes come words of Wisdom." Her Wisdom and Potential must be anticipated, looked for in every child and youth, experienced and foretold in the raising of every girl, lauded in the Models and PATTERNS held up to all children, female and male, for without the respect, positive expectations, and trust of all the people in a community, the Crone cannot manifest Her powers or dispense Her Wisdom.

The Hekate myth that follows develops the Crone Goddess's special attributes and offers some insights into how women and men today might use the possibilities in Her PATTERNS for enriching their lives. However, the special, unique consciousness that reverence for this Wise Old Goddess archetype can instill in us is so multifaceted that I would like to discuss several of its aspects beforehand.

NO IMMORTALITY

As I brood over the metaphysics of the neolithic, I detect a language . . . ridden by fear: fear of not enough food, fear of animal elusiveness and hostility, fear of our own death. I see none of these elements of fear disclosed in the voluminous literature, both historical and ethnographic, on hunter-gatherers. And that, I think is revealing.[5]

—Calvin Luther Martin

For those who honor the eternal cycle of Birth-Death-ReBirth, *death is real and a certainty*. It is accepted without protest—even appreciated—that individual or particular forms of life always change, always decay and die. Nevertheless, life in new forms continues ceaselessly. In Goddess consciousness only Nature's cycle of Birth-Death-ReBirth can be eternal.

Blood of the Ancients
Flows in our veins.
Forms change
But the cycle of life remains.

This women-honoring chant by Ellen Klaver commemorates the inevitable change, decay, and death of all forms of life, and at the same time it celebrates the Cycle that does *not* change or die. In this philosophy no particular instance of life—no one tree, no one star or person, no galaxy or species—will have immortality or eternal, unending life.

Patriarchal religions, however, do promise immortality—"No death!"—by proposing that the essence of a human being resides not in the material body that is subject to death but rather in a disembodied spirit or soul that is temporarily housed in our temporal bodies but which itself never dies. When those heroic authors who invented immortality gave bodily life a permanent ending and the soul a fixed state, they deliberately stopped the unending cosmic cycle of Birth-Death-ReBirth—a philosophy that robs the Divine Female of Her sacred essence and power. Father-god religions further offer the possibility of transcendence as an enticement: the hope of eventually leaving or transcending this lowly earth. On the other hand, the Mother Goddess models the divinity immanent in the Earth and the promise that one needn't go anywhere or have to transcend anything in order to be holy and be at home on sacred ground. One's

ters fear of death. It is born of the impossible desire to separate one's Self from Nature's material stuff and from Her cycles. It comes from a vain quest to find one's identity in being unattached, in striving to be so individuated that one needn't participate in the All.

What the ever-changing Goddess and Her cycles stand for, however, is the very stuff and functions of all life. For the gathering peoples who first devised Her image as the Divine Shape-shifter, no forms were perceived as fixed—other than the Cycle. They had no sense that decay was their enemy—and no fear of death.

CRONE AS RAPTOR

It is possible for us to communicate with snowy owls provided . . . we dissolve the boundaries [we have so carefully constructed] to our own animal nature, separating us from the snowy owls.[6]

—Hans Peter Duerr

Raptors are birds of prey. It is their nature to kill and to eat the dead, so they are easily associated with death. Hekate and other Crone Goddesses are therefore often imaged as a raptor or carron bird: especially as Vulture, Hawk, and Owl.

The raptor symbolized most especially *the wisdom and knowledge that comes with knowing when to bring an end or death to something*—a relationship, an apprenticeship, a job, a journey. . . . *This power to kill, to end something or bring about a transformation—along with the wisdom to know when and what needs ending or changing—is the special* mana *of the raptor,* part of the Crone's special consciousness, one of the unique gifts and responsibilities that She models for us.

physical, ever-changing body is sacred, as are one's living, ephemeral relationships to other physical beings. Theorizing about the highest achievable state as "immortality without bodies" does away with the perception of immanent divinity within matter. Promising to fix or cement life eternally into unchanging form—as a constellation, a soul in heaven or in hell, and so forth—takes the meaning out of Matter and the enduring truth out of the ever-changing Cycle.

Looking at the concept of immortality in this context makes "No death!" appear to be a masculine ego concept working in two ways: *First*, it is a heroic attempt to separate or individuate one's Self from the Mother: that is, the core of the Self is removed from matter (derived from the Latin word *mater*, meaning "mother") and from the body-in-the-world regarded as holy. *Second*, it is an attempt to straighten the ever-turning unpredictable cycle into a more controllable, fixed linear concept. The notion of immortality creates false hopes, therefore a sense of frustration, failure, and anxiety and also fos-

Raptors are predators, and they can also be carrion eaters that will consume the flesh from the bones of bodies left exposed after death. This is the origin of stories of the Goddess's "eating" Her children, an act that sounds sordid if taken literally. But if one can appreciate the metaphor of the Creating Mother, the Goddess of Death and Regeneration—Mother Earth, Mother Vulture, or Mother Owl—receiving or actively bringing Her children back into Her Body-Cauldron-Womb—*from our Mother's Body we were born and back into Her Body we will return*—a sense of great personal power will result: a feeling of closeness, comfort, and kinship with raptors and loss of any disgust of decay or fear of death.

Paintings and carvings of the Goddess as Vulture were dramatic and plentiful in Çatal Hüyük. There, as in many other places, people exposed their human dead to the raptor birds, whose claws, beaks, and appetites hastened the sacred process of *transformation* from life to death-and-decay. Reducing the human body down to its hard white essence—down to white bones—was perceived to be a sacred process, "the White Goddess at work."[7]

No sense of outrage clings to this image or elemental process of raptor-assisted decay. The Great Mother of Transformation, the Vulture who takes Her children back into Her Body at death, was painted in red at Çatal Hüyük with an egg inside, indicating that after consuming one of Her creations, She would later give birth to its life energy in another form. Thus the Raptor and Her Great Cosmic Egg symbolize the eternal cycle of *transformation* that promises rebirth to all life forms in other forms, but always and ever as vital parts of All-That-Is.[8]

DARKNESS

Eventually the Raptor—as the Wise Old Owl, for instance—came to symbolize not just death, but also the kinds of wisdom associated with Darkness: intuition, Self-knowledge, omens, prophecy, foretelling the future, and, by extension, wombs, new life . . . the wisdom of the entire cycle of Birth-Death-ReBirth. Learning to find wisdom, comfort, renewal, and personal power in Darkness—in roots and wombs, for example—in an essential aspect of Crone consciousness. Her Wisdom—like the owl's—manifests in the close-and-holy Darkness: the Darkness inside ourselves, under the earth, and in-between one another. Grandmother Twyla of the Native American Wolf Clan (the teaching lodge of the Seneca Nation) draws attention to the powerful Crone medicine that comes from the badger's dark burrow with all the healing roots that grow and hang down into it.

Darkness is essential, necessary to life. Germination often requires darkness. Seeds and fetuses and pippins need darkness to grow. When

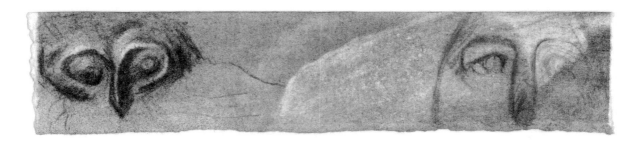

Eyes of Athena as Owl. Gold, Athens, sixteenth century B.C.E. *Drawing on stone, Egypt, 105* B.C.E.

Inanna's Vulva, "Door to the Underworld." Mesopotamia, c. 2000 B.C.E.

we are thinking, sometimes we close our eyes, cover them, for thoughts germinate in darkness too. As does love. Small animals seek close dark places for refuge and healing. When ill, I want to be in dimness or darkness; I heal better there.

Darkness is for reflection, for looking inward, for intuitive perceiving, for healing, for renewing. Winter is the dark season, a propitious Crone-knowing time, a period for lying fallow and taking stock.

Sounds travel better in the dark; our body is more primed to listen at night; stars only give their wisdom at night; the Three Wise Men were black astrologers.

Monica Sjöö fears that people who are afraid of the wild forests, and of night or underearth creatures, will soon destroy the earth and all life on it in their attempts to bring light to everything. She laments that many are still trying to clear-cut the Goddess's sacred groves where the despised darkness hangs on even in daytime. Many pollute the air and waters in their search for more energy to light the darkness; neon is everywhere twenty-four hours a day, she notes. Sjöö feels that these fearers are trying to keep themselves from facing the blackness of the shadow of death. But death will come; their fears only prevent them from having access to a source of profound insight, knowing, healing, comfort.[9]

Remember Tiresias, the wise old "breasted one" in the Greek myths who came to help Oedipus discover who was polluting Thebes? The aged seer—in earliest times female, only later male or androgynous—"sees" what and when others cannot, although, of course, Tiresias has no eyes. Blindness (and its darkness) was part of the ancient metaphor about how to obtain self-knowledge. It is no mere accident of history that mythical Homer is described as blind, for he too was considered a great "seer." Oedipus—blind by choice—discovered that in darkness one can see inner things that one can readily miss in the light.

The year and its days are on the average half light and half dark. There is no reason for using the model of competition or struggle for this phenomenon. We need not talk about one's banishing the other; we can legitimately say: light and dark take turns, for both are necessary to life.

Darkness has long been a euphemism for women's wombs and for human emotions and intuition. So why does anyone seek to "banish darkness"? Darkness belongs inside our heads and hearts and wombs, just as a tree's roots belong in darkness—for they *cannot live in the light.* Banishing darkness means banishing or repressing femaleness and female-associated ways of being and knowing. But the darkness—like femaleness and the Crone's consciousness—is something to treasure; it is where all life begins. Baby, seed, or tree—all are rooted for dear life

in the darkness, the Source of their nourishment and strength. Light, yes! In its time and place. And the Crone's close-and-holy Darkness too! Yes!

NO DESTRUCTION

Notice that I call Hekate the Goddess of Decay and Death, but I do not call Her the Destroyer. The habit of opposing Creation to Destruction comes to us out of a dualistic vision of Reality. "Destruction" is the linear end of something—final! finished! *fait accompli*! To say that something is destroyed implies it is done away with completely; the cycle has stopped. This means that re-creation would have to start at an absolute beginning, would have to come from nothingness. *Decay*, on the other hand, brings about death while participating in the ever-repeating cycle—without ending the cycling at any point, without destroying any matter, only trans*form*ing its form.

In the Goddess's cycle nothing is actually destroyed. Although things die constantly, everything that dies is merely reorganized, redistributed, re-formed, then reborn, recycled back into the process, back into the whole.

If we posit that the Goddess is ever full of potential, *nothingness cannot be a part of Her nature.*[10] She would not create *ex nihilo*[11] as the transcendent male deity is said to, for She who is always pregnant with Possibility has no emptiness about Her. She has no ego and no Plan. But She always has the raw materials for new forms in Her belly, womb, or cauldron. She is always stirring them, constantly changing, renewing, re-forming, re-creating them. As a model of non-linear, non-dualistic reality, the Goddess is always *in medias res,* already *is* from every moment. She always has been—and has always been full of Potential. A periodic Big Bang is Her way of getting things reshuffled and reenergized from time to time.

It used to be said that there was "empty

space" out there. But now we know that space is full; there is "pervasive physical activity in space . . . gravity . . . trajectories and vectors, lines of tension and strain . . . dynamic process . . . energy propagating itself in the void . . . fields of force . . . transient aggregates of energies impatient to be on their way,"[12] radio waves, light waves . . . She is the Dark Cosmic Mother of Transformation . . . and She is full to overflowing . . . as are we *in Her image.*

The use of "emptiness" as a sacred state is too dangerous to be worthwhile. There have to be better metaphorical ways to describe and experience our wombs and hearts. Sylvia Brinton Perera warns women that perceiving their "inner space" as *empty space* "can make a woman feel empty, lifeless, hollow, as if without food or substance—an oral cavity—due to lack of mother or lover. She then craves to be filled and is susceptible to abject dependency on an outer or animus impregnation. She can lose her soul in the bliss of melting into her lover."[13]

The Crone as Raptor transforms, digests, dissolves, brings about decay and constant change, but She is never empty nor is She the Void. See the Egg in Her belly? See the new life growing inside Her? No matter how old we become, new life and potential grow inside of us, and even when we die, new life will come from our decaying bodies. The Death Goddess rearranges matter, kills and reconstitutes life—but She never destroys it. She is never nothing; She is always and ever full of potential, like the endless spiral or like the hungry Raptor's Cosmic Egg.

GRIEF AND KEENING

Hekate is important as the Goddess of Mourning. Keening and loud wailing are natural expressions of sorrow and are appropriate responses to great loss, although our culture tries to repress deep sorrow and disapproves of loud grieving. But repressing any natural feel-

ings diminishes our experience of life and delays or prevents healing and renewal. In earth-honoring traditions death is accepted and honest grief is allowed, even encouraged. Great sorrow at the loss of a loved one is expected, expressed, shared, and dignified by an outpouring of tears and lament. Mourners' recovery is hastened and eased by a proper *getting rid of* or letting out of their anguish. So mourning was ritualized by early matristic cultures as a sacrament, as something essential to do to confirm an ending, so that one could begin to feel again the cycle of life returning, so that one could begin to renew.

It is said that Egyptian Mother Goddess Isis invented the wail—the "Ah-le-loo" or "Oo-le-loo"—and taught it to women as a magical device to bring about rebirth out of death. Ancient women ritually mourned with these ululations at the death of the grain god as he was "buried" in the earth at planting time. The Semitic Goddess Ishtar also wailed "OO-loo-loo"—like a woman having birth pangs—in Her annual effort to bring about the successful return of creative energy to the body of Her dead son Tammuz, the grain god who had been buried (planted) into the earth, and there awaited rebirth.[14] "Oo-le-lu!" is the cry that brings up the deepest grief as it lets out the most profound joy for life begun again.

There are many Goddesses associated with women's loud wailing—with their "alleloos," the cries that simultaneously recognized and honored deaths and births. The sacred weeping of women in archaic ritual dramas had enormous power of transformation in it; their ritual keening helped bring about healing and renewing wholeness. Such wails—at once real *and* symbolic—mixed death with birth-giving—"Alleloo!"—for the women of those times refused to separate human experiences or emotions into opposed categories as the classical genres of tragedy and comedy did. Women's universal cry—"Alleloo!"—is an enactment and re-enactment of the entire spectrum of human emotion and life in one sound, a full-bodied sound-Model for eliciting and maintaining the perspective and ideal of wholeness in ourselves.[15]

Our tradition demeans any public expression of deep feelings. I, however, long for an honest public expression of such feelings. I welcome Hekate's loud lamentations. I have cried "Alleloo!" in deep grief and joy—but have wished I were not so embarrassed by doing it.

FAMILIAR CRONES

The names Gorgon and Medusa come from pre-patriarchal times when these were awe-filling, Mystery-full forms of the Great Crone Mother. But the classical myths in which they appear demonize them, devalue the worth of all Crone Goddesses, reduce them from their earlier status and ridicule their powers. The *mana* of Kybele (or Cybele), the Magna Mater of classical Rome, was experienced in a black meteorite; one form of the name Kybele was Kubaba, Mother Goddess of the Hittites, a name directly related to the black meteorite in Mecca called the Kaaba. Seed Goddesses, dead but containing future life in them, often have both Virgin and Crone *mana*—Persephone and Kore, for example. The White Goddess, subject of Robert Graves's book of that name, brings transformation and death, reducing us to our essence—down to our white bones.

Another famous Crone—Goddess of Transformation and the eternal Cycle—is *Hel*. Hel is an Anglo-Saxon Goddess—Her face half golden, half black as is every cycle—who takes the dead back into Her Womb of Creation, the Underworld, where burn Her Fires of Transformation. *Frau Holle* is another version of Hel, and Holle's land is Holland, still known as the Netherlands. Saint *Hilde* and Brune*Hilde* are other memories of this Teutonic Crone Goddess.

When we become aware of how we today categorize Hel, this sublime Goddess who was once beloved by Her people, it is easy to see the extent of the archetypal reversal that began in early historical times as an attempt to diabolicize the Great Goddess and devalue all things associated with women's powers.

CRONE GODDESS SYMBOLS

Some of the crone's symbols are:

- webs and spiders
- the spiral
- brooms or combs (both instruments of change and transformation)
- pairs of all-seeing eyes, or one eye (called the Third Eye of Wisdom)
- hardened nuts and dead seeds
- wise old owls
- egg-laying, flesh-eating vultures
- cauldrons for stirring ingredients of Creation together
- the inner earth or nether lands as Her Womb or Vessel of Creation
- fires that hasten the process of decay, transformation, and creation (like Hel's fires or Saint Catherine's fires)

Vulvas and dark wombs of rebirth belong to the Crone as well as to the Virgin, for the entrance to a cave is the entrance to the underworld, the vulva of Mother Earth's womb-tomb; it marks both the place of one's birth-into-life and the place of one's grave. The Goddess's vulva and a cave entrance are therefore each said to be "a door that goes two ways."

CRONE-VIRGIN COMBINATIONS

The mixture of the Crone with the Virgin—of Death with Birth—permeates ancient myth. The Greek Goddess Artemis of the Forest and

Her Roman cognate Diana are both Virgin Goddesses, both Mistress of Animals, both midwives of all new life, and both huntresses. Both are symbols of Creation. And yet both have a sacred Death aspect, evidenced in the bows and arrows they carry and are ready and able to use to kill at any moment, demonstrating in their archetypal natures the inseparability of death and new life. The combined names, Artemis-Hekate and Diana-Hecate, are common in ancient lore. Furthermore, as Hans Peter Duerr points out in *Dreamtime*, Frau Holle was identified with Diana.[16]

By classical times Persephone had become the Daughter archetype, a maiden, the narcissus spring flower, but many scholars feel that Persephone was originally the Crone, as evidenced by Her title: Queen of the Underworld, She who presides over the halls of death.[17] Obviously, Persephone contains both Virgin and Crone in Her nature.

Writing about the Crone mythos, invoking that Goddess consciousness into my own life, both quickened my pulse for life and slowed my anxiety about death. I am most eager to share my evocation of Her with you.

Ten

. . . . .

THE MYSTERIES OF DEATH
AND TRANSFORMATION

An Evocation of Hekate, the Crone

[*A priestess of Hekate—a passionate old woman—joins an assemblage of women and girls where three roads meet in a Y. She comes to speak about the Goddess she serves. Strong emotions permeate the telling of this myth—awe and respect for the powers of Decay and Transformation in the cosmos, an obvious craving to live fully and long, a sense of the drama of life, anger at its brevity, yet playful, teasing intimacy with Death. There is no fear, because for the priestess—as for all who experience Nature's rhythms and cycles as sacred—death goes with life; it is an ordinary, natural aspect of living, to be savored and entered into in its time with contentment, tenderness, a sense of completion.*

The priestess sometimes addresses the women, sometimes Hekate.

The women form a ritual circle and enthusiastically drum, dance around a fire, chanting Hekate's many names, raising a cone of power with their voices and bodies. After awhile they settle into quiet expectation, and the priestess raises her hand.]

> Hush-sh-sh . . .
>> Hear them?

[*She pauses, then softly returns a dog's howl:*]

>>> Ah—OO—OO—OO—OO!
> The dogs go seeking Her at dusk.
> Dusk is Her time—
>> but all transition times are Her times,
>>> Mother Hekate's times.

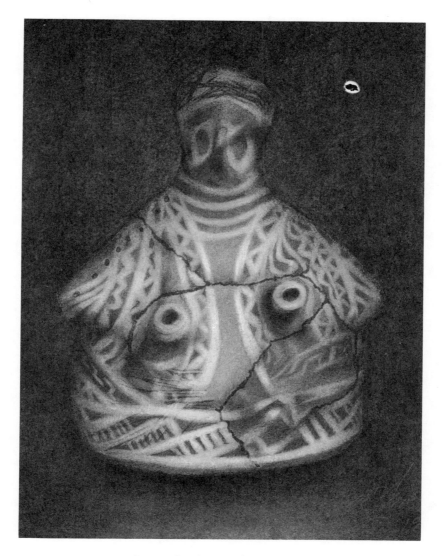

Breasted owl jug with water-snake-womb markings.
Terra cotta, Crete, Early Minoan.

Hear them? Hear their OO-hoo?
The owls greet her too.

[*Returning the call:*]

OO-hoo!

VIRGIN
Mother . . . .
CRONE

It is time, women.
Let us also greet and welcome Her.
Repeat the litany after me:

"Come, Hekate.
 Beloved Grandmother.
 Blessed old Walnut Face!
 Goddess of Transformation.
 Goddess of sacred Comings and Goings."

"Dried, withered, cackling Sweetness.
 You dependable old fire-breathing Guardian.
 Tail-whipping Dragon Lady!"

"Mother of One Million Kah!
 Mother of one million magical, healing words!
 Kah Mother! Heh-kah-teh!"

"Beloved Great-grand-dam.
 Bringer of life—too short but ever-lasting.
 Ageless Vulva—eager to birth, eager to reclaim."

"All-consuming Hecuba.
 Hovering Succuba.
 Goddess of Decay and Death."

*Sheela-Na-Gig: Frog Mother, Whose Vulva is Door of Birth and Death.
Stone carving over door of Christian church, England, ninth century* C.E.

Ah, yes, women, . . .

    She is all of that:
    our own sweet Hekat!
    The All-Embracing One!

Who can remain unmoved by such devotion?
Who can resist such constant Mother-Love?
Who would not go tenderly into the night
       to find Her,
       to thank Her for life
          and for Her promise
            of eternal Oneness with the All.

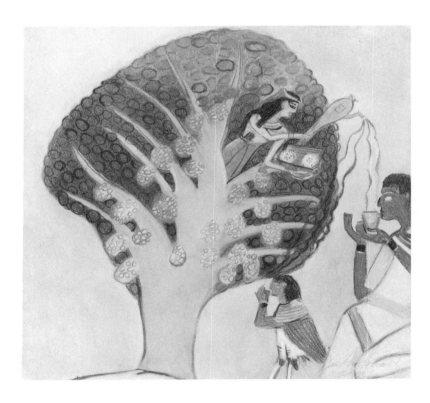

Egyptian Tree Goddess dispensing food from Her sacred sycamore,
sixteenth century B.C.E.

So . . .
> Come, women.

> Come, laughing, howling, sick, or well,
> > but come.
> Come to the Three-Way Place.
> Come where the road forks.

> > At the Three-Way Place,
> > at the Trevi—
> > > Trevia,
> > > > *tres vias*—the Three-Way Place,
> > > > the Y Place,
> > Make circles and magic.
> > Light fires in honor of Hekat-Trevia.
> > Drum up Her powers and your own.

> He-kah-te! He-kah-te! He-kah-te! Heqt!

> Drum up Her powers and your own, women, for
> She is your guardian,
> > that old snaky Mother, Hekat-Medusa.
> An old blustering Gorgon too!
> These two scare off enemies—and boredom . . .

[*Sudden, scaring:*]

GAHHHHH!

[*Cackles:*]

Ah-ha-ha-ha-ha-ha!

VIRGIN
Mother ....
CRONE

Gather.
And pour into a crafted cauldron
        wine of black-red grapes and
        milk from a black ewe or nanny-goat.
Mix in herbs of such appointed powers
        they grow by moonlight only.
Blend in soma, fleshy fruit of the moon tree,
        soma that opens to us
            the wisdom in ourselves,
            the wisdom in darkness,
            the wisdom in Hekat's brews—
                Her wonder-working, healing secrets.

And brew.
And drink.

And pause.
And listen intently for your own deepest voice.
        Listen . . . and allow it to rise.
        Listen to,
            Reclaim! your sacred sister,
                your Animal Power;
        Dance! Her into your Self.

Drink.
And rekindle kinship with the All.

[*Exultant*:]

        Ah-OO-oo-oo-oo!

Life Force as wild Goat and Butterflies. Bas-relief vessel, Crete, 1500 B.C.E.

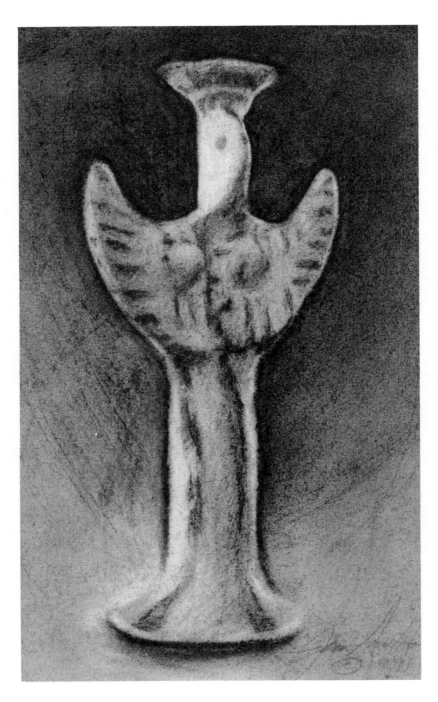

Bird Goddess, "drawing down the moon," with snake-water
markings associated with cosmic Creating Mother. Terra cotta,
Mycenaen Crete, fourteenth century B.C.E.

Trevia-Hekt!
Shape-Shifting Goddess!
Goddess of ten-thousand names and guises!
Heqt! the Much-at-Once!

Seek Her, women, at the Three-Way Place, for
The three-way sign
        —the uncertain, shifting Y—
             is Her Body.
Arms out and upstretched,
    She draws down the moon,
       pulling "the All" together into "the One."

In Her image and manner
    let us do likewise,
    let us too reach up and draw down the moon,
       beckoning its embrace,
       pulling the ever-changing cycle,
          the unchanging silver cycle
          into ourSelves:
       the ever-changing, unchanging cycle of
       Birth-Death-ReBirth
       Birth-Death-ReBirth.

VIRGIN
Mother ....
CRONE

But be prepared
       when you reach and shine, for
The moon impregnates with divine lunacy.
She will take you over!
You will find yourself behaving just like Her,
                         the old hound.
You will find yourself leaping and howling:

             Yip-Yip-YIPP ! ! !

Go ahead.
Neigh and prance as She does,
       cavort as Old Night Mare Heqt does.
Lose yourself in Her!
It'll happen one day anyway . . .

     . . . that you will lose yourself in Her.

So
Come where three roads meet.
And at that arms-up place
Drum up power
      and leave offerings of ambrosia
            and sticky golden honey, for
         She is the ecstatic coming together
              of all things,
         She, the blessed holder-together
              of all things,
         Who laps up libations, and
              adoration, as well as
              Her children.

Yes.
Honor Trivia.
But then depart.
Pass on.

VIRGIN
Mother . . . .
CRONE

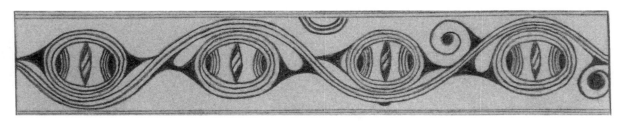

Flowing, becoming. . . . Water-snake-egg motif.
Pattern on vase, Ukraine, 3900 B.C.E.

You cannot stay long in a Three-Way Place,
              it is a Transition Place,
              a flowing, watery place,
              a place where one Way ends.
You can veer to the right or veer to the left,
       but veer you must—
              transform you must.
For here, one
              way
              dies.

Prepare to lose yourself.
And to end something:
    to end something:
            a stage . . .
            a phase . . .
            a relationship . . .
            an apprenticeship . . .
            a period of mourning . . .
            a dream that has died . . .
            a day . . .
Prepare for death, for
Trevia is a Killing Place.
Death-dealing is part of Trevia-Heqt's gift.
So use your birthright:
    the Eye that Mother Gorgon-Heqt has willed you.

Use your dark wisdom, your insight Eye, and
Look right into the Truth.
Stare to death
        anything that needs to die.
Stare to death
        whatever strangles or impedes
                your Becoming.

Let it go!

Do not hesitate.
Killing
Eating is the obligation
      of all who would live.

Just remember:
What dies is Sister and Self.
Hold that in your heart!
Kill—but with great love for the dead.
      Say grace and benediction;
      go through proper mourning.
      Consume, extinguish—go ahead. But
      lay to rest with honor and love.

Maintain right relationship, women.
Be on good terms with what you kill.
      Love it and its gifts,
            for the past ever lives on in you.

Owl-Eye Goddess carved in stone. Malta, fourth millennium B.C.E.

The name Kybele on clay shard. Southern Italy, sixth century B.C.E.

She comes blazing, our Mother of Dark Wisdom.

    Magna Mater!
    Kybele!
    Kubaba!
    Alli-Kubaba!
    Sili-Kubabat![1]

        Black Stone!
        Flaming shooting-star Stone.
        Black star-to-earth Stone.
        Fiery sky-earth Mother,

Brilliant Astarte-Kybele-Heqt!
Mater, Meter, meteorite Mother!
Flaming, heaven-lighting Goddess of Transformation!
Come-and-gone Goddess of Decay.

VIRGIN
Mother . . . .
CRONE

She comes flying, our Mother of Death.

      Car! Carmen!
      Black Mother!
      Blood Mother!

         Bird Mother!
         Wingéd cycling One!

Owl, Hawk, Vulture!

        carrion-eating Car,
        carcass-eating Car,
        death-dealing Car,
        who carries
        the ever-regenerating Cosmic Egg

                  within . . .

*Vulture: Death-bringing, Egg-laying Goddess of Life, Decay, and Transformation.
Painted in red, Çatal Hüyük, 6150 B.C.E.*

She comes gnawing at our entrails, our Blood Mother.

      Car! Charm! Chartres!
      Carmenta! Car's Wisdom!
      Sophia!
      Hagia Sophia!

She, our Wisdom:
      the knowing in one's guts,
      the knowing
          about communion,
              eating,
                drinking,
      about living together on this planet.

Car . . .
Car . . .
Carm . . . mmm . . . menta . . .
Mmm . . . Mmm . . . Mmm . . .

Vulva-incised clay Seed stamp.
Ivory, c. 1900 B.C.E.

Mmmmmmm . . .

She, the Mmmother of Mmmystery.
She, Sublimmmme Oneness,
  but not *a* One,
   not a "One of Something."
She, the Mystery of the Communion and Oneness
     that permeates the All.

All honor be to you,
  old wizened, wisened Crone!
Praises be to you,
  you two-faced Mother
   of Death and ReBirth!
Praises be to you,
  you shriveled, seed-inside Honey-date!
  You egg-inside Vulture!
   hovering around, day in and day out,
   jealous of the life you give,
   loving with such All-consuming passion,
    you prey on your own flesh and blood,
    unashamed
      to take back the Gift!

Succuba!

Ecstatic Goddess with poppy-head trim on crown with omphalos *(womb symbol) on top. Terra cotta, Crete, 1350* B.C.E.

The gift!
How I love the gift . . . this life . . . this brew!
Hail, Brewer!
Hail, Mother of this Bubbling Cauldron!
Mother of fermenting hops!
Brew delights!
Brew life-enhancing delights!
Brew change.
Brew new life.
Brew revelry and springtime.
Brew an end to the old.
Brew death!

Yes.
Brew death . . .

The brew kills,
        is meant to—that's the gift!
        Endings bringing hope and new life.

Hekate,
        red poppy
                gone to Seed.
Ecstatic Mother,
        making me dizzy
                with so much going and coming,
                with so much seeing and becoming!

VIRGIN
Mother ....
CRONE

I am grateful for your gifts,
        Artemis-Heqt—
                        you old Night Dog,
                        Red Star,
                        Hound of Heaven—
But I have to watch you,
        offering your head to my lap!
You are liable to set yourself and your pointy teeth
                on me,
                to have me back before I am ready.

Stay awhile, sweet Bitch!
I have an eternity to try out the All-at-Once.

Even though
I share your need for Oneness,
I nurse with an unremitting hold
        on the teat you have loaned me here and now!
So, yelping Mother,
Stay your love awhile!
Stay the Oneness . . .
        awhile . . .

Artemis-Hekate as whelping-nursing bitch. Roman antiquity.

VIRGIN
Mother ....
CRONE

For now
I am Hekate
The Extravagant!
Hecate
Crow!
Caw! Caw! Caw! Me-She! She-me! Caw! Caw!

Oh, Hekate, you glossy ravaging Raven,
            you black shining scavenger
                        picking at bones and life!
Sweet Mother!
Let me, in your image, see treasures everywhere!
Let me too notice every bauble,
            every shiny beetle's eye,
            every rainbowed fly's wing,
            every wriggling bit of life
                        and nourishment in the grass,
            every sparkling crumb of fool's gold,
            every shining bit of paper, and
                        broken glass.

Let me treasure it,
        love it, and
        throw it back!
        to be found again
        and treasured anew
                    by me . . .
                        someone else . . .
                        you . . .

Oh Trivia!
'Tis trivia!
Why keep it!?
Let it go!
Let it die!
There's more!
More!
Trivia!
I am past storing up treasures—
I am Hekate's daughter,
I am flowing with life and possibility!   Caw!   Caw!
Hekate and I can find more of everything!   Caw!

Oh, Mother of Most Intimate Knowings,
    Mother of Sexual Stirrings.
You are a sensuous shape-shifting leprechaun!
              Yes, you are!
Snaking in and out of your skin,
        dying,
           only to go off new-born!
Again!
And again!
And yet again!

We grow old—and yet,
            watching you,
We feel the flow,
    the shifting,
    the coming . . .
        Watching you,
Our fragile blue-veined hands and thighs
        flirt with spring and
        entertain numinous possibilities.
Our sweet-soaked almond vulvas pulse still.
        Still!   Are we not Car's trees
                —Caryatids—
        solid with blossoms
        before the green comes.

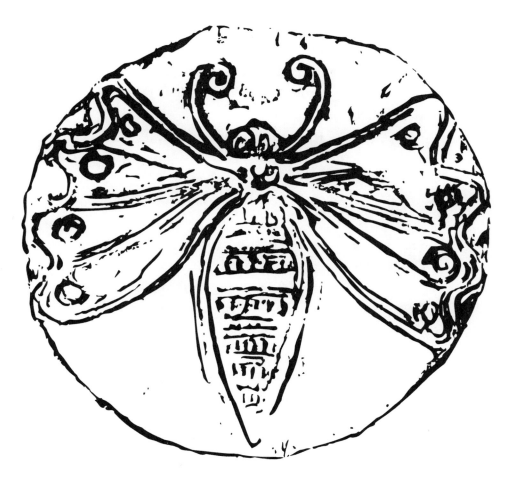

Shape-shifting Goddess of Transformation as gold butterfly.
Mycenae, sixteenth century B.C.E.

VIRGIN
Mother . . . .
CRONE

We—
Hekate's aging daughters
     (aging no matter what our age)—
        grow slowly old as does the earth.
As the earth has seasons
     (the spring always comes)
So, even to the end
     some part of us feels springy,
        feels a rising potential,
          a newness.
Even at the end some part buds!
Though wrinkled and stooped
     Still! we are Car's spring-bursting nut trees!
     So what! if the shell eases around the core
        and hardens
        and dries.
Is not the nut full of new life and potential?
Is not the dried old nut *full* of Becoming?

And remember, . . .

     the All-at-Once . . .

          will be something new . . .

*Caryatid, from Acropolis, Athens. Remembrance of Goddess Car
as almond Tree-Pillar-Column, almond also being a symbol for
Vulva and the ever-renewing cycle of the Seed.* [JWW]

At the Y Place,
At the arms-up place,
      where the sticky honey and
           all else come together,
      where we lose ourselves,
      we reach into the All-at-Once,
           soaking up bliss and oblivion together.

So, my sisters,
Laugh!
Don't be on guard.
Stick out your tongue at play-safe advice!
The tongue is part of the dance of life.

     "Oh, I could just eat you up!"

The old Mother wants you to learn where the joy is
      while there's time.
She wants you—in Her image—
      to keep your Eye on your bliss,
      to reach out your tongue and lap it up.
Fiercely eat of it!

Oh, . . .
      But what if we grow warts
               on our faces or hands?
     What if they call us: Hag!
              despise us, and
              say we're hexed with
                  signs of the frog?

Yell back:
      "Praises be to the Frog!
      Praises be to Old Heqt,
             to our Hagia Sophia,
                  Holy Mother of Wisdom!
      Praises be to our warts,
             our froggy nipples.
      They are marks of wisdom!
    Praises be to Old Hex, the Hag!"

Breast-shaped, nippled libation cover with frogs, c. 3500 B.C.E.[2]

Our croaky Mother comes forth from primeval waters
       green with life and potential,
    alert,
    Her throat pulsing
          (swelling, ebbing
           swelling, ebbing)
       as She contemplates the All
       from lotus pads and muddy banks.

Proud of Her shining lumps
She feeds with Her long tongue . . .
         thoop! thoop!
processing pond neighbors into HerSelf.
        thoop!

         Life . . . thoop!
         Death . . . thoop!
         One and the same.
         Thoop! thoop!
         One and the same . . .

It's all the same.

So
prepare no defense, women,
Rather do circle dances,
        drum up power and prance and howl
        in Three-Way Places.
Hold forth in wild exaltation,
        and for now,
        obstreperous Hekate
        will cackle and make merry with you.

                Ah-ha-ha-ha-ha-ha! ! !

It is no offense that one day
    —in the midst of riotous merrymaking and chaos—
Our healing Mother-Nurse
        will mend the rift and
            hug you back into
                Her close embracing Self.

Yes.
At some time or other
        Hekate will ease you out of yourself,
And with the leavings
        make more life
            without your knowing or caring.

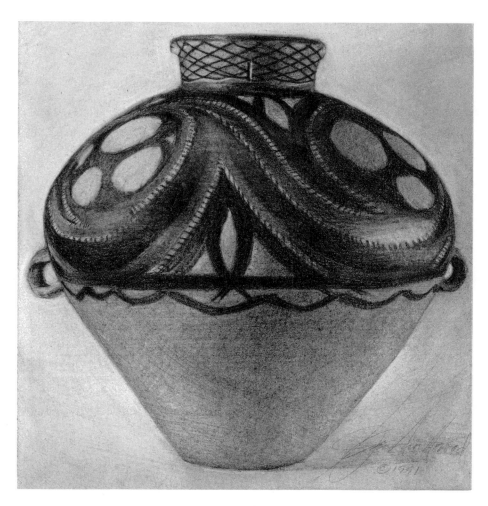

*Funerary urn, She the Vessel of Creation and ReBirth, with
egg-spiral-water-net motifs. Clay, China, second millenium* B.C.E.

VIRGIN
Mother . . . .
CRONE

In death
    old women and old men
        come together
           in Her Body, the Earth.
Great Coitus.
Great Climax.
Blessed be!
Heaven and bliss are ours
           in the Earth,
           in our Cosmic Mother's Lap.

My life?
To Heqt with it!
To Heqt, the Oldest of the Old.
To Hekat,
    the One.

      My Mother!
      Oh, Mother . . .

THE END
. . . .
Ananke.

Eleven

. . . .

MALE & FEMALE DEITIES
WHO CREATE THE UNIVERSE

The Differences

One of the fundamental premises of mythology, theology, philosophy,
and psychology is that procreation is the antithesis of creation.
Procreation is relegated to a "merely" physical status, while
creation—seen as spiritual, metaphysical, and symbolic—is the
paradigm for rituals, narratives, and belief systems. . . . Traditional
myths of cosmogony fail to integrate beliefs, myths, and rituals
surrounding pregnancy and birth, thereby compromising the full range
and complexity of creation and procreation.

[But] in the myths of many cultures, giving birth to a child can be
recognized as the fundamental act of creation. . . . The privileging
of metaphysical and spiritual over physical
creation is by no means universal.[1]

—Marta Weigle

*C*reating deities serve as Models of Perfect Knower and Perfect Doer for
the cultures who create them, for the people who tell of their creating exploits
with pride. That is true of primal peoples as well as of us. Joseph Campbell is
one of many who has seen of late that our modern western predicament can be
traced to a cultural reliance on nomadic patriarchal values and models of perfection that come out of the Genesis version of Creation but that are no longer
edifying.[2] Thomas Berry laments that we in the west in the main ignore the
plight of the earth while focusing on our own personal salvation, relying on
the traditional interpretation of Creation in Genesis for our goals as if that
were a universal description of the world and human aspirations.[3]

263

VIRGIN
Mother . . . .
CRONE

The Biblical tradition began in Neolithic times among patriarchal pastoralists. Therefore, the story of Creation in Genesis posits a tribal, masculinist, desert herders' Model of ideal human behavior. This Model seemed natural and good to those wandering people who sought a permanent home through wresting what they called *their* "promised land" from its owners, their enemies. Unfortunately for us, the reasonings that guided the Hebrews in their wanderings, the tactics that helped them get their homeland and adjust to desert living were so successful they were adopted by successive generations—even after their wandering, landless days were over. Remarkably, those reasonings, tactics, and values remain our modern western guidelines for living; they still largely determine what kinds of adjustments and orientations are considered good for us.

Whether or not we are believing members of the Jewish or Christian community, all of us in the west are caught up in Biblical ethics and politics. Our lives are influenced and determined by the gendered values and social constructs of the ancient Hebrews: their patriarchal perspective on life, the hazards of desert living, their fables about their legendary oasis, the Garden of Eden. "Certain ideas—in particular, ideas concerning sexuality, moral freedom, and human value—took their definitive western form during the first four centuries [C.E.] as interpretations of the Genesis creation stories, and . . . have continued to affect our culture and everyone in it, Christian or not, ever since," concludes Elaine Pagels.[4]

Genesis records the observations, fears, and consequences that seemed inevitable to the homeland-hungry Hebrew patriarchs. But can we afford to apply those ancient images and ancient reasonings to our modern lives? Can we still afford to use as our Model an authoritarian Creating Deity who establishes rigid dogma and grants to a chosen few—dominant males—exclusive ownership of prime land, merciless power over their enemies, and absolute authority over women's lives?

FIXITY, PERMANENCE

One of the particular attributes traditionally associated with the Biblical God as creator is his divine immutability: that he is the Unmoved Mover. Although this principle has modeled and fostered dogmatic tyranny for millennia, it is still held to be part of what is ideal here in the west. It has become an intense theological preoccupation: as Catherine Keller sums it up: "Western thought has been riveted to the ideal of unchanging perfection."[5] This Ideal of *unvarying consistency* comes primarily from ancient Greece, from Aristotelian metaphysics and Platonic reasoning, even though it is generally thought to have originated in the Hebrew Canon, usually attributed to Genesis. No western Model or value is so unchallenged as this supposed *virtue*. "No tenet of Christian theology has stood so firmly—and with so little scriptural justification—as the divine unchangingness. Since Plato, change has been taken to imply imperfection: a perfect being is eternally—already—all that it can be.[6]

Divine fixity has significantly informed all western values, determining inviolable standards for how one should think, form opinions, do things; "right the first time" is widely considered the ideal. By this standard, lack of change implies integrity, so that making up one's mind early and never changing it shows more admirable character than if one has grown and learned something since first making a decision and has over time changed one's mind. If Yahweh, the Unchanging One, is our divine Model, then we will all aim for that same dogmatic, unchanging perfection in ourselves and others.

The supposed divinely ordained unchanging "story of reality" in Genesis is also the basis for what is called creation science, an assumption that Yahweh created All-That-Is not only instantaneously *as it is now*, but created everything exactly *as it should be*, and therefore no evolution in the original forms is possible now, or has ever been possible. Since the never-erring Creator *got it right the first time*, fish have been and will always remain fish and will never evolve into land-walkers; monkeys have been and will always remain monkeys and will never become hominids, and so forth.

Nor is any change in the hierarchy possible in creation science. The Great Chain of Being—the order of the importance of species—is inviolable: God over angels over men over women over children over animals over plants over the earth. . . . In this PATTERN of reasoning *good people* are those who accept this hierarchy as natural, right, and good; they are those who are obedient to handed-down authority, to God's immutable laws, to his written commandments; *good people* read and do God's will, not their own.

Taken from a written (specifically *non-oral*) tradition that claims not to have changed over thousands of years, this mind-set depends on hierarchical, dualistic assumptions about unchanging perfection—and therefore about what goodness and evil (or abomination) are, about who "God's people" are and who "Mine enemies" are—now and forever. This mind-set projects distrust of human variability and fear of a constantly changing, non-linear world. It proclaims eternal life for one's undying, immaterial soul while it instills disgust for decay, death, and all natural cyclical functions of bodies and matter. It associates light with what is most holy and darkness with evil. These assumptions necessitate strong controls over human emotions, women, human nature, and Nature, as in the Biblical injunction to Jehovah's patriarchs to "multiply" and have "dominion over . . . every living thing that moves upon the earth" (Genesis 1:28), commandments that are bringing us close to worldwide ecological disaster.[7]

Continuing to multiply, however, and continuing to carry intense fears of flesh, world, and darkness—and maintaining the inflexible controls over women and Nature that result—obstructs our ability to mete out justice, to appreciate, love, and nurture the earth or ourselves as we are today, here and now. It impedes our ability to think our way out of today's social and ecological difficulties, often preventing viable solutions to our non-Neolithic, non-desert-herder problems from being tried.

Biblical truths are based on the assumption of a fixed, unwaveringly dualistic universe, on claims that creation consists of fixed, hierarchical, competing pairs of entities, of dyads locked in unresolvable opposition—"and ne'er the twain shall meet"—like God/human, spirit/world, mind/body, reason/emotion, good/evil, man/woman, light/dark, Self/Other.[8] As I have shown in the Introduction and earlier chapters, these dyads are not in unresolvable opposition; each of these entities is actually infused with its Other. Simone Weil insisted that evil is always the perversion of some good. Positing dualisms as an innate part of everything from human relationships to cosmic order encumbers us in every way—socially, politically, personally. It restricts what science can envision and accomplish by prescribing ahead of time the perimeters of how the world manifests. That certainly limits what we can know about the world and about ourselves. Falsely assuming that dualisms exist in the laws of the universe encourages prejudgments about who is a *good person* and discourages tolerance of "deviants" (bad persons), which then impedes personal choice and social justice for all.

OUR FATHER-MOTHER, HE-SHE . . .

Some suggest that revising Biblical language to include female as well as male words for the

Spiraling spider web

deity would soften the God of Abraham, making him less tyrannical, therefore more acceptable as a Model. But calling God "Our Father-Mother" and sometimes saying "She" in addition to "He" will not alter Jehovah's basic character or archetype. As the quotation that opens this chapter illustrates—with its comparison of creation and procreation—the origin story in Genesis is deliberately devoid of any divine or authorizing female rituals or bodies; there are no womanly concepts or values, no sacred cyclical processes honored there. Absent are any female modes of organization, of conception, or of creation. Certainly the male act of creation is lacking in metaphors or prototypes of the sacred Spiders, the divine Websters and Spinsters who weave and spin their worlds out of their own body-substance, which is a decidedly female way of creating and is the concept behind calling a Creating Mother *Spider Woman.*[9] Re-gendering Biblical pronouns will in no way give us a Divine Female Model who

creates new life by giving birth to it out of Her sacred limitless Body-Self. Calling Jehovah "Mother" is a hollow device that only puts a skirt—a meaningless female decoration—on a totally masculine *transcendent* deity.[10] One would not look up and say of the Goddess: "Our Mother Who art *in* heaven"; Hera our Mother *is* the air-sky-heaven itself! The images and story line that would celebrate Her *immanence,* Her cyclical, bleeding, gestating, nursing Body as Source are not in the Bible, while the language that belittles such recurring, embodied, bloody, messy doings as contemptible, dirty, and base is ubiquitous throughout.[11]

Please notice that there is no claim in this book to any moral superiority for women as a sex or as individuals. The myths here illustrate only that the Female is a richer, more effective Model and norm for men and women, better for what I deem to be our basic, sustaining human PATTERNS, than the Male Model and norm can be.

ASKING PROFITABLE QUESTIONS

Some questions each of us might ask as we search for the Perfect Model for ourselves are: What attributes do I prize most highly in human beings? What values promote simultaneously the welfare of individuals and of the whole community or nation? What is the most desirable form—or combination of PATTERNS—for human community to take so that our societal groups will encourage and be effective guardians and promoters of peaceful, creative lives for us and our children, now and for generations to come? What aspects of our environment are essential to life as we need and want it to be? What is necessary in order that human, animal, and plant life continue? *Which values—if storied far and wide—would provide for maximum self-realization right now, and at the same time sustain the future of humankind and our essential environment?*

She Who is penetrated while retaining Her integrity and wholeness.
The Crick Stone, Cornwall, England, 1600 B.C.E.

When we have some idea of our personal values through our own answers to these questions, then we can each begin to fashion for ourselves images and metaphors that can inspire and model those values for us. Of course, your answers and your Model do not have to agree with mine, or anyone else's.

TWO DIVINE MODELS OR PARADIGMS

To help make clear what I have deliberately left out of my Model and what I am trying deliberately to put into my Model, I offer the brief summary on pages 268 and 269 of the main points I have considered in composing the myths and Mysteries in this book. Common attributes of the western male creator appear in the left column; my Goddess's attributes are to the right.

CELIBACY

Theologian Mary Condren documents in her book *The Serpent and the Goddess: Women, Religion, and Power in Celtic Ireland* that celibacy was not a theological issue at the beginning of Christianity in Ireland. Rather celibacy came about as a political device, a reactive position

VIRGIN
Mother . . . .
CRONE

GOD'S DIVINITY

God's divine self expressed as *spirit,* a way of being that claims to transcend baseness of material world.

As spirit he is *celibate,* expressing himself mainly via his calculating *intellect* (Logos), his *will, mind,* and *thought.*

A *good person* will try to escape embodied human nature, will try to avoid "the sin of our iniquity . . . the sins that flesh is heir to," and will strive to behave "like an angel" or even yearn to become pure spirit.

He is the model of a *great (extraordinary) supernatural individual,* quantifiable as "one" being, a category unto himself, *exclusive* of Others. He penetrates Others while remaining unpenetrated.

He is *spirit,* and his *mind* intervenes against and dominates nature (that is, mind over matter, mind over bodies).

His followers honor—in his image—the will to power (of Self over Others and the world).

Necessity is: *burden, limitation,* what one *submits* to. He is TRANSCENDENT, *rules over* and is *above* all else in value; his nature is *different from, better than* ours. He models *hierarchy* as Good.

He is a *dualist;* his law emphasizes *traits that distinguish* at the expense of traits that are shared. He allows evil, has an arch-adversary.

He is *Unmoved Mover, the unchanging Absolute,* eternally the same. He created *Fixed Ideal Forms* that endure throughout time without changing.

His laws are inviolable; the universe is planned and is in order.

GODDESS'S DIVINITY

Goddess's divine Self is expressed as the *Knowing Body* of the *World-Universe* itself.

As *Body* She is *sexual* and expresses Herself via *Material Forms* and *Relationships.* Her thinking-intuition-feelings work together, inseparably.

Every person is a reflection of divine Nature; all matter is Her Body and *good* by its very nature. Human bodies and emotions—including lust, anger, fear—are precious gifts from Nature that bring us useful information about ourselves and the world.

She is the general *PATTERN of All-That-Is,* completely *inclusive,* never a "One" except as the All or as the Unifying One-ness-of-Manyness, the *Much-at-Once.* She is malleable, interconnected and interpenetrating.

She is self-renewing *Nature, Matter, all Bodies;* no one form (all manifestations of Her Self) rules over any other.

Her followers honor—in Her image—the will to live and enjoy sensuous pleasure.

Necessity is: what *inspires and fulfills* the Self. She is *non-hierarchical* PATTERN and is IMMANENT in whole Universe, all of which is interconnected, interrelated and reveals Her Nature to us.

She Models *Wholeness* and traits that *join, share,* and *cooperate.* Things can go wrong, but not because an adversary is causing them to.

She Models *Constant Change and Variety;* She is every Form so no form is ideal or better than another; She is the PATTERN of Eternal Chaos; that is, the Unchanging Cycle of Birth-Death-ReBirth.

She is Changing Woman, constantly renewing, re-creating Herself and the cosmos, sometimes even randomly or by Chance.

GOD'S DIVINITY

His priests learn dogma and hand down fixed orthodoxy.[12]

He promises there will be *NO DEATH* for our individual immortal, immaterial *souls* and *spirits;* each one of us has "one" soul or spirit.

Important: mind-spirit, mentalisms, facts, being right.

He teaches lessons via pain; he maintains power to punish; he imposes Necessity. Even some natural occurrences require penance, cleansing.

He is revealed through linear (progressive) history—also through his Law and Plan for his people.

The world is an occasion for *sin, submission, or lessons to be learned*, and one hopes to achieve a better realm eventually. Material forms are illusory or undesirable.

He is unchanging, *stern, ethereal, ascetic*, often *severe*; limits sexual activity to procreation; prizes celibacy.

GODDESS'S DIVINITY

Her shamans lead all to discover what is sacred for themselves—without dogma.

Death accepted as a *real, natural part of life's cycle.* We all share and create human spirit (which is never one quantifiable thing); we share in the life of the cosmos, which endures eternally through cycle of Birth-Death-ReBirth.

Important: experience, mind-body synthesis, empathy.

She expects Inner Necessity to motivate and inspire. All points of the cycle are holy, none sinful or punishable.

She is outside his-story—Her cycles have no progress, no absolute ends or beginnings. She renews but has no plans, likes to surprise Herself.

The World is an occasion for *blessings, mutual appreciation,* and allowing among all Creatures, the place for obtaining *Divine Wisdom;* all material forms are desirable and real; all realms are real, part of what's Natural.

Her changeableness is often playful and generous; She promises sexual ecstasy; She is *Shakti, Karuna,* and *She who rejoices—"la mère qui jouit . . . qui a jouissance."*

· ·

taken by a male priesthood seeking to preempt ordinary women's influence and religious power at that time. Early official Church letters reveal that the proposal to value celibacy over sexuality was made in an effort to disempower women, whose potentially fertile wombs and capacity for erotic ecstasy gave them much prestige in pre-Christian society and so much authority that the priests experienced women as rivals and threats to their power.[13]

Celibacy only became the official "highest way to live" for all Christians long after Jesus's death. The Gnostic Gospels, for instance, paired Jesus sexually with Magdalene (see the Gospel According to Thomas).

"ECSTASY NOW!"

In our tradition the ideal mother is imagined neither as erotic nor as full of laughter. Traditionally she can be that way before marriage perhaps, but not afterward, for many men want their wives—who are, after all, the mothers of their children!—to be as *pure* and virtuous and serene as they remember—that is, as they imagine —their own mothers as being. Hence, the long spiritual love affair many Christians have had with the ever-celibate Virgin Mary, who many Christian writers and theologians have claimed was impregnated through her ear or who gave birth through the top of her head or conceived (did "it") by means of other supernatural tricks that preserved her vulva as unsullied, untouched by the action. The list of elaborate denials of her having been penetrated or having engaged in any genital activity, in or out, is long.[14]

Absent from ascetic religions of the east and the west is a Divine Female Model that equates sexuality and motherhood, a Model that gives approval and encouragement to women to be sensual, to be full of joyful laughter and sexuality, to fulfill the Goddess's promise of "Ecstasy now!"—*in the present-enduring tense.* The Buddhist and Christian traditions have glorified celibacy and urged men to abstain from sensuality whenever possible, supposedly because a woman's body focuses a man's attention and energies on the flesh, here and now, while he should more properly be focusing on his spirit and the Void or on God and the hereafter. This dualistic way of perceiving life—that the heavenly reward that comes later is better than the earthly one available now, and that a "pure" spirit is better than a sensuous body—pits the virgins (in our modern sense of the word, meaning those who have never engaged in a sexual act, who never have had their bodies' boundaries penetrated and therefore have not been sullied by Otherness) against the whores (who have all-of-the-above). Virgins are assumed to be too "pure" to care about sex or sensual touching; whores are said to like sex but are called sinful for it. This philosophy encourages a judg-

mental mind-set that constantly pits women against each other—supposed Good Women against supposed Bad Women—and each woman against the normal facets and attributes of her Self.[15]

In Asia, however, there is the Tantric tradition, a woman-centered sect of Hinduism and Buddhism that glorifies sexuality and worships the Goddess Shakti along with Her consort Shiva (two deities who personify the yoni and lingam) through special, *sustained* sexual practices. Shakti represents both divine sexuality and "the innermost, animating soul of man or god," a concept that dissolves the dualism proposed by the ascetics who *religiously* and vigorously keep *god-spirit-discipline* separate from *body-pleasure-sex.* The word Shakti can be translated both as divine *Cosmic Energy* and as *female genitalia*—as yoni or vulva. "Shakti is the active power of any deity." (Notice the association of *action* with the Female Principle.) "Every god needed his Shakti, or he was helpless to act." The Tantras say that "the female principle antedates and includes the male principle, and . . . this female principle is the supreme Divinity."[16]

The Tantric tradition also gives us *karuna*, a

term for the basic quality of mother-love, directly experienced in infancy and ramified in adulthood to embrace all forms of love: touching, tenderness, compassion, sensual enjoyment, and eroticism. . . . It was understood that *karuna* must be learned through physical and sexual contact comfort, by adults and children alike. . . .

The ancients well knew that the experience of being in love recapitulates the mother-child relationship in its intimate physical attachment, trust, and dependence. . . . It has been shown even in the animal realm that adequate sexual functioning in adulthood depends on satisfactory relations with the mother in infancy.[17]

The French feminist theorist Julia Kristeva describes a model that recapitulates *karuna* and

Shakti for westerners. She calls this model—which is both maternal *and* erotic—*la mère qui jouit*—a good mother who enjoys good sex.[18] I love this model! To me the Goddess in my myths is *la mère qui jouit . . . la mère qui a jouissance*.

Jean Graybeal, a philosopher of religion, elucidates Kristeva's phrase by writing that *jouir* means "to enjoy, to revel," or to be "in an ecstatic moment," while the nominal form *jouissance* means "enjoyment, . . . pleasure, delight." She explains that the Latin root *gaudere* means "to rejoice" (as in gaudy, joy, enjoy, rejoice). "*Jouir* is connected to the history of words with 'joy,' 'enjoyment,' and a sense of 'religious fear and awe.'" And she adds, "Contemporary French idiom uses *jouissance* as a common term for orgasm." Obviously, this word has several meanings at once that we tend to think of as belonging to separate experiences; it has sexual, spiritual, physical, and conceptual significance all at the same time.[19] *Jouissance* implies that sensual play and pleasure, revelry and cavorting are of this world and sacred at the same time.

And furthermore, *jouissance* describes a Self not as if it were an atom or a solitary "one thing-in-itself" but as a long continuum! Jane Gallop refers to the observations of Kristeva and Luce Irigaray (*This Sex Which Is Not One*), when she writes, "You can have one or multiple orgasms. They are quantifiable, delimitable. You cannot have one *jouissance* and there is no plural. . . . [Female] sexuality is a '*jouissance* enveloped in its own contiguity.'"[20]

La mère qui jouit is Everywoman (and Everyman); we all share her potential, which like the Great Mystery is not quantifiable. Like the Great Mystery Herself, all women potentially carry "the Other" within themselves and therefore cannot theorize or abstract themselves as a solitary "one" as easily as can western men who are trained to separate themselves as soon

as possible from their mothers—in dread of an Oedipal attraction—and from their emotions, from anything even vaguely female or "sissy."

ANDROGYNY AND SACRED SEXUALITY

Many who agree that the Model of Perfect Person should not be exclusively Male conclude that God should be neither Male nor Female. I have heard countless times: "What about an androgynous deity? Why does a deity have to be of either sex? God should be above such things!"

"Androgyny?"[21] "Above?" Then are "such things" as one's sex (maleness or femaleness) to be dismissed from our ideal Model? And is one's sexual activity to be regarded as lowly? Those questions seem to me to be *part of the problem* that needs to be corrected by a different creating deity. When the Highest Principle is sexless, our Perfect Model is sexless, and our own sexuality remains, as it is in our present system, unsanctified.

I feel that we need our sexuality and sexed personhood to be sacred, so that we will treat this aspect of our Selves as a manifestation of Life Force, respected and honored. I would like

for our sexuality, our fullest, most natural Self-expression, to become truly a sacrament and for all sexual activity to occur between people who honor and respect what they are doing as well as themselves, their partners, all bodies, all Others. That is the cure to the abuse of women, men, and children; it is the solution to the abuse of any Self or Others. Perhaps if Tantric practices were widespread—or some other practices that would esteem the present tense, our sexuality, and our intimate relationship to all Others as sacred preoccupations—the war would be taken out of all of us, delight would rush into the vacuum, and *jouissance* would fill our lives.

A CATEGORY OF ONE

I heard Dr. Paula Gunn Allen speaking at Colorado College in April 1990 about her Native American heritage. She emphasized over and over in response to comments from the audience that westerners tend to value most highly *individual* instances of things, "the thing itself," and they like to quantify things, striving to isolate and locate each "thing itself" into a single precise category. But she stated repeatedly, *"My people do not understand how there can be only 'one of something.'"* Things always exist in a context, things only have meaning in a web of relationships, so how can there be a "thing itself." The "category of one" includes *one definitive moment at which something begins and one definitive moment at which something ends.* The philosophy that images All-That-Is as a Great Web of Being and as a cyclical continuum does not value—cannot even *imagine*—such singularities. Primal philosophy perceives all categories as easing into one another with no single definitive moments of separation.

Allen's people do not sacrifice their authenticity or uniqueness by incorporating Others into their own Being; they do not feel that the way to become an authentic human Self is to isolate or separate themselves from Others—from other humans or from the four-legged ones, the flying ones, crawling ones, swimming ones, and so forth. For primal peoples who revere an immanent deity, species are not valued hierarchically, for they all are a form of divinity manifest. Such people are enriched by sharing the PATTERNS of different Other beings. Primal peoples achieve authenticity by their own unique arrangement, webbing, conglomeration of the common categories they share with equal Others.

To some extent all people live unique, singular lives, but that linear, historical dimension of life is considered banal and profane by those who regard life and the world mythically and who think of their lives as having meaning in terms of their core relationships, in great Webs of Being. To such people, one's singularity is less valuable than what one shares with eternal forms and enduring PATTERNS. Many consider the western preoccupation with isolated singularity a non-adaptive "cult of indiv*dualism*"—that is, an extension of our other dualisms.

Primal relational philosophy brings to mind a contemporary observation about the different ways in which men and women experience their bodies and being. Feminists today are noting that only women can have the experience of having an Other inside and they pride themselves on that ability, while men often pride themselves on not allowing themselves to be penetrated by an Other (a value that encourages building fences, setting fixed, inviolable boundaries, creating "no-fly zones" over embattled areas, wearing armor, carrying arms, and so forth). But a woman can be penetrated during love-making and is penetrated by a whole Other Being during pregnancy with great benefit and pleasure and without any violation to her Self. This inclusive, unarmed, unboundaried female way of Being is perhaps a better ideal Model for *human Being* than the male warrior experience that is so keen to set boundaries that discourage or even deliberately prevent intimate exchanges.

RESPONSIBILITY

But what about an individual's responsibilities to his or her Self, what about one's responsibility to protect and care for one's Self? Is Self not a legitimate, proper "category of one"? No, not really. *Responsibility* literally means *ability to respond*; it refers to how fully and sensitively one can take in and react to what has happened in a situation, not as an isolated entity but in the moment of an experience-in-the-world. To have responsibility means being able to have an appropriate give-and-take with the world; it means developing an ability to size up a situation and persons, becoming sensitive and able to perceive what and who one wants to be near and what and who one should be distanced from at a given time. The most effective *ability to respond* would be an unset, fluid way of being and perceiving Self and Other. One's responses should be flexible enough to allow for changing needs and changing circumstances. Learning to enhance our abilities to respond-in-a-changing-world is a more versatile and profitable skill than learning to set fixed boundaries and establish strong defenses around one's Self. Becoming more responsive and pliable will be much more effective, safe, and response-able in the long run than learning to use armor, shields, and weapons in Self-defense—all toys of the dominator model. Such defenses set and congeal limits, allowing an individual to remain isolated, encouraging people to be *un*responsive to Others. Any process that makes us less hemmed in, less singularly isolated, that makes us more responsive, more adaptive, more able to tap into more varieties of coping and relating skills is worth considering for its rich possibilities.

CYCLES—OR BEGINNING IN THE MIDDLE

The aborigines are not interested, as we are, in the episodes of the past. The important things to them are the cycles of life: the development of the individual from infancy to old age; the path of the initiates from ignorance to knowledge; the yearly round of the seasons; the movements of the celestial bodies; and the breeding time of the creatures. These cycles are full of meaning to the native people, but to them the remote past, the present, and the future are and will be changeless.[22]

—C. P. Mountford

Our familiar creation story is linear; it starts with an Absolute Beginning—from Nothingness, from the Void—and *progresses* from there. But the creation myths of primal peoples are non-linear; concerned as they are with the Always-So, they have no Absolute Beginnings and do not progress. Rather, they spiral and cycle, often beginning in what we would consider the middle. Perhaps others have been as confused as I was when I first began reading creation stories that began: *"Changing Woman, the Creator of the Navaho People is the Mother of All; She was born at the foot of the Mountain on a bed of flowers."*[23]

How strange, I thought! This is supposed to be a creation story! Where do they think the mountain or bed of flowers came from? Didn't these things have to be created by Changing Woman, if She is the Mother of All? I have learned since not to be so quick to expose my ignorance. Primal peoples' stories do not have any *one definitive moment at which everything literally began.* Beginning *in medias res*, in the middle of things—rather than making up a hypothetical "absolute" place from which to begin—is both a dramatic storying device and reveals a wise philosophy of life.

I have come to understand that the seemingly simple-minded myth-tellers from long ago (who couldn't see what was so obvious to me about the need for Absolute Beginnings!) have long known some important things that I did not know and could not have appreciated until recently: that creation is not a machine-like activity, not a predictable sequence of progress, neither a linear nor a mental construct, and that our preference for pinpointing an Absolute Beginning—in our science as well as in our mythos—comes from our preference for logic, linearity, abstractions, and for control-over-things, not from a passion for the Life Force manifesting where and when it may. Positing an Original Void does not foster an appreciation for our whole, multidimensional truly ever-changing cosmos nor does the notion of Emptiness help us picture or value the non-linearity of Creation. N. M. Williams explains how the Aboriginal Yolngu people, for instance, "perceive time as circular, so that from any particular time, what is past may be future, and what is future may be past."[24]

Or as the Native American Pulitzer-prize-winning author N. Scott Momaday puts it: "We feel that time is collapsed so that we are all a part of all important events in the universe."[25]

The *Great Round of Becoming*—an eternal cycle of comings and goings, births and rebirths—is like a wedding ring in that *it has no beginning and no end*, no goalpost, no clear past or future. We use the metaphor of an endless circle to seal our vows when we marry, a time when we are caught up *in hoc tempo*—in Mythic Time, in the Eternal Present, in the Always-So—because "it feels as if I have always loved you and always will." At such a time we tend to speak as if we are a part of something timeless, as if there were some ways in which our feelings just "are" without any beginning or

end and *without any progress taking place*. The wedding ring symbolizes those non-linear feelings.

Just so with the creation myths of primal peoples. They could tell the story as if it had an Absolute Beginning if they thought the idea of an Original Void could make a significant contribution to understanding ongoing creation. But they have something else to say about creation and the process of creating that is more important. They are more interested in the enduring, constant, continual nature of the act of creating (which is not the same as evolution). They celebrate the act of creating over and over again during the year as if the universe and their lives were constantly and literally beginning over, as if *they were actually participating in that renewal as co-creators*. They begin their myths *in medias res* because there is no other place to begin on a continuous circle.

Still, I imagine others will also think—as I used to—that it is odd to begin a creation story in the middle instead of at the beginning. This tack can be an initial problem for my listeners and readers. So I do not begin my telling of the creation story in the middle of things—although that *is* the authentic way of primal peoples.

Many readers will have noticed that I start with the linear phrase, "In the beginning. . . ." I do this out of my concerns as a performer-playwright, not as a theorist. Usually an audience or a reader can be moved to experience something new more successfully if the story starts with what is familiar, if it begins with something the reader is already comfortable with. In my creation myth I deliberately begin with quickly recognized words because I want to set up immediately the expectations listeners and readers should have for hearing a sacred story. Only when I have established the proper mood do I move into the unexpected, cyclical, unfamiliar ideas that the Goddess embodies and stands for—like the Great Web of Being and an absence of any completely singular categories, an absence of any instances of absolute individuality.

VAK, THE GODDESS AS VOICE

We in the west have a tradition about creation that says, "In the beginning was the Word." For us "the Word" is Logos, related to *logic*, reasoning, an activity of the so-called disembodied Mind. The Hindu religion has a similar—but importantly different—tradition, maintaining that Being, Matter, *and* Thought first manifested in the primordial Silence as Song *embodied in* the Goddess Vak, primordial Creatrix. Note that Vak is a patriarchal Goddess and that this is a linear story. But there still is something in Her image we can use, something primal and wonderful about Vak as metaphor, something powerful to have in a Model for humans as the beings who story themselves, the beings who sing praises about life and the cosmos and thereby co-create themselves, for Vak is the Creating Mother Who sings the flowing Universe into Being as Poetry-Matter. Gary Snyder describes how Vak, the Goddess of Song and Poetry,

> becomes the universe itself as energy. Of that [singing] energy all sub-energies are born. Now, Vak, in Indo-European philology, is the same as the Latin "vox" or the English

"voice." This goddess takes on another name too: she's also called Sarasvati, which means "the flowing one," and she's recognized today in India as the goddess of poetry, music and learning. She's represented as wearing a white sari, riding a peacock, carrying the vina [a stringed instrument] and a scroll."[26]

Vak, the Flowing One, the One who endures and continues like the Waters, unceasingly. She, the Creating One, is all possible rhythms, the Music of the Spheres! She is the universe as Energy, the cosmos—and ourselves—as Song being sung. Omm. She is all Learning and Knowing manifesting as Music and Sound. Vak is the universal myth sung and recreated again and again in and by us. She is the Innermost Voice in each of us, our Being and Becoming.

Vak's depictions resemble those of the original Hera in many ways. Even the exquisite peacock that was sacred to Vak was also sacred to Hera. And Hera too was the Creatrix, a Virgin Mother who gave Her human children justice, dance, poetry, and song.

So we end where we began: with the Oral Tradition. With singing and telling. With celebrating womanhood and human nature. With creating ourselves.

Blessed be.
Ananke.

EPILOGUE

. . . .

The Oral Tradition

"I would ask you to remember only this one thing," said Badger. "The stories people tell have a way of taking care of them. If stories come to you, care for them. And learn to give them away where they are needed. Sometimes a person needs a story more than food to stay alive. That is why we put stories in each other's memory. This is how people care for themselves."[1]

—Barry Lopez

Socrates, "the wisest man of antiquity," is thought to have had serious misgivings about literacy, about relying on writing for keeping records of personal or national histories. One of his students, the Greek philosopher Plato, wrote a dialogue entitled *Phaedrus* in which he gave his famous teacher a speech expressing apprehension that people will become less self-reliant and less self-confident if they learn to read and write. Socrates says:

> If [people] learn this, it will implant forgetfulness in their souls; they will cease to exercise memory because they can rely on that which is written, calling things to remembrance no longer within themselves.

And Socrates practiced what he preached. Although he was one of antiquity's most respected and most quoted men, Socrates, like Jesus, never wrote anything. What we know about the famous Greek gadfly—as well as what we know about Jesus—was written by others. They both were expert practitioners of the Oral Tradition.

Many American poets have advocated returning to this primal way of teaching and learning, urging that we return to communicating all information primarily through song and dance. Walt Whitman and Ezra Pound wrote verse that was intended to be read out loud, part of a deliberate and specific attempt on their part to retrieve the oral, physicalized schooling methods of Sappho's academy on Lesbos, a wholistic pedagogical system that tolerated no separation between daily life, the performing arts, what is important to learn or remember, and what is sacred.

Human beings have written down their stories for only about four thousand years. Before that, everything that needed to be taught or learned was spoken or shown. Family and tribal history, common values, blood ties, vital information about the location of water and fruit trees—everything was communicated person to person, usually face to face, and in a poetic form (to make it easier to remember).

Many primal peoples, although aware of writing, have chosen not to use it. Writing—even of a sacred text—seems to disrupt the sensual bonds between people that talking to one another creates. Exchanges of information through writing can prevent relationships from growing; telling stories and singing songs together can keep relationships strong.

Primal religions had no priests or dogmas. Everyone learned their group's traditions firsthand from the mouth and gestures of someone who loved him or her. Everyone in turn was expected to contribute to every ritual and therefore to the continuing life of the group and its habitat that the rituals helped to sustain. This kind of universal participation—oral and full-bodied—in the sacred work of sustaining human life and Nature gave incalculable meaning to each person's life. "Everyone feeds the living reservoir of knowledge, while receiving in return an answering flow of information" from Nature and one's group.[2]

There are still some primal peoples who retain this enviable Way because of the benefits and personal satisfaction it offers. Being a teller of tales, the storier of Nature, makes one an ongoing, living, long-lasting part of one's community, even a vital part of the world around. A storyteller could look forward to growing old in such a community, one that treasures and holds

in high esteem those who have many remembrances and songs to share.

Most of us have lived all our lives within the western, dualistic worldview. This hierarchical, competitive model has formed and trained our thoughts, our eyes, our muscles, our bodies, until it's so automatic to think dualistically that it seems *the only way* to perceive the world. Surely it must be "just the way things are." Many may need to read or hear wholistic, woman-honoring stories over and over before they can begin to live from a non-dualistic way of perceiving the world and their lives, before they can experience a different kind of embodiment, a different PATTERN of thinking. Some of the rhythms and ideas of the myths in this book may need to be experienced more than once before people raised in the west can make the principle of cyclical time that the Goddess stands for their own time, or before they can experience in a visceral way how a woman's life and body do not fit naturally into our culture's linear notions and constructs.

PERFORMANCE: THE BODY AS A WAY OF KNOWING

The presence of a living, breathing teller is always presumed in my stories; always the presence of a *sensuous, thinking, fully feeling and behaving body*—that of the storyteller—is a vital ingredient of what is being communicated. Our performing bodies—that is, our living, breathing *whole* bodies—are essential components of becoming all that we can be. We cannot have good inner Truth Detectors unless our muscles and sinews are a part of the way we know ourSelves, part of our response to Others, and therefore a part of how we know what is good or true.

Oral enactment implies wholeness, for it honors and celebrates the entire knowing body, including feelings and movements in addition to the cerebrum. Try singing gustily and feel how the full use of the voice puts you in touch with more of your body-Self than does just sitting and thinking. Oral enactment manifests wholeness, for our whole inner world—the mind, breath, body, emotions—as well as the whole world out there are brought into simultaneous play together when we perform.

By *embodying* my ideas I show that the paradigm of wholism is a real-life possibility. When stories are effectively told by a live teller-performer, they become real and vital enough to be absorbed into viewers' bodies—empathically, mimetically. Dance and song, moving images, infectious sounds, and rhythmic lines can get into spectators' viscera and give them a lived experience of a new PATTERN or Way of Being. *And it goes home with them.* When audience members leave a performance, they still have in their own bodies a living reference to the PATTERNS they experienced earlier vicariously with the performer. Enactments can become living flash cards or models of ideas for audiences to take home as memories, recallable immediately in their own muscles, sinews, and emotions.

Having new PATTERNS that we like and admire readily available in our viscera makes desirable changes in our lives possible and more probable, because those new model sensations offer us immediate options and truly viable alternatives. Muscle memories—including the chemical and emotional responses inherent in them—can be good Truth Detectors. Muscles respond—they are actually the home of *our deepest responsibilities*, that is, of our *abilities to respond*. The process of remembering in one's muscles gives us a method for evaluating options, for comparing propositions and memories right in our bodies.

I began to develop my own physical Truth Detector in acting school. (An acting technique is often described as "the ability to behave truthfully in public on cue.") The development of this acting-truthfully technique, the discovery of where in my body the Detectors reside, how every part of one's perceiving-feeling apparatus comes into play to make the Detector work, has helped me immeasurably in all aspects of my life. There have been times—for example, when something that was said has made me uneasy—when I knew in my bones (or stomach and muscles) that I was being put down. Nothing had been said that would hold up in a court of law as having been demeaning to me, but because of the way I felt in my body, I knew for sure what was happening. Since my body—my sinews—often know before my head does, I always respect those sensations. I consider them information, knowledge, clues.

Acting different roles has given me an effective way of enhancing and changing my life for the better. I was raised to be a good little girl as a boarding student in a Catholic convent school, so as a young adult I found it impossible to speak up for myself or to express anger. I was well trained to feel that such feelings were inappropriate, not ladylike, not nice, even sinful. But after repeatedly rehearsing and *playing* the role of the foul-mouthed, aggressive character of Martha in *Who's Afraid of Virginia Woolf?* I acquired certain previously forbidden PATTERNS of behavior as my own. They got into my own body rhythms and routines, into my vocabulary, for the first time. And I found them exhilarating and releasing.

Since then I have been able to speak up for myself in the loudest, most unambiguous way. Playing that role was not just *play*; it was practice in learning to live more fully; it was training for an expanded real-life repertoire. From that role I acquired new, previously unexperienced, helpful ways of behaving. From that "pretend" enactment I learned physical skills and emotional outlets with which to enrich and carry out the serious business of my life. Acting is a serious, enriching, fun thing to do. There is nothing like the Oral Tradition, nothing as rewarding as making a habit of embodying one's own and others' ideas and feelings, storing them in one's body, and trading them between your whole full body and others'.

EMBODYING THE CRONE

*An old woman past her bearing years who is in her power—an old woman who is respected and sought after for her Wisdom and Being—*is something our culture has not allowed us to imagine as valuable, so we have few crone heroines who can serve as Models for us. But enacted images of a living, breathing, powerful Crone Goddess can model this new PATTERN for us. When the Crone is seen and heard in an actress's live body, or when She is remembered later in an audience member's own alive body (in a male or female's remembering body), She becomes a living, new part of our personal and collective mythos. We can model it for others while we model it for ourselves. And this new information and Wisdom, these new standards and expectations, will give us a new way of looking at and being with an aging person (ourself or some other), something different to put into our bank of usable experiences.

Live performance has the potential to give everyone an opportunity to grow in some way. Watching an actress be a crone-in-her-power can help people envision and experience a wildly different way of being themselves in their own bodies. Such an enactment can create the real possibility that *old women are not just has-beens, that they can be admired, looked up to, and consulted for their wisdom and experience.* You can give that to others when you read or perform the "Evocation of Hekate" for them.

Writing, developing, and enacting the Hekate-Crone archetype over the years has helped me reverse my expectations that a downhill feeling would accompany my own aging. Hekate has given me access—as I enter my sev-

enth decade—to feelings of expansion, excitement, and deep satisfaction about being old.

In trying to retrain one's perceptions and thinking PATTERNS, it is especially helpful to use the Old Ways, the Oral Tradition. That is, to read the myths *out loud* in the company of others. You can get together with one or many others and take turns reading solo, one at a time or all together in chorale. Be sure to use the knowledge from your full bodies in the communication that develops and in the questions and insights you generate. Enjoy one another's impressions and feelings about what you are reading; treasure disagreements as well as agreements.

OUT LOUD? HELP!

For any who are not used to reading poems out loud, here are a few hints. First of all, have fun! There's no right or wrong way to read a line, except for the injunction Enjoy! Your voice is a vehicle of your Self, and Self-expression can be a great pleasure.

Storytelling is often best when it is simple. For the most part let the reading be as easy and natural as your ordinary breathing and talking. Don't be afraid of anything. It's no big deal if you stumble a bit when reading to others. Feel free to start over, to go back to repeat things— words or whole sections. Actually, audiences can be quite impressed and moved by watching a performer think and grow "on her feet." Your listeners—mimetically involved with you—will enjoy finding themselves thinking and growing spontaneously along with you. So don't apologize for stumbles. Turn mistakes into insights. Allow them to become part of what is happening in-between people, part of the live storytelling, part of a joint leap into spontaneous living.

Storytellers love to repeat words and sounds. If the word "whole" is said six times in one

VIRGIN

Mother . . . .

CRONE

paragraph, you might vary it each time if that makes the repetition more interesting to you: loud, soft, fast, slow, staccato, largo. Or you might hypnotically repeat "whole" the exact same way each time, stressing and opening the vowel unvaryingly, repeating the sound as if it were Your . . . Own . . . Heart . . . Beat . . .

Experiment. Try things. Play.

Varying sounds, pitch, volume, or tempo contributes to a personalized interpretation. One inspiration can come from the size of the line. Let the length pace you. Short lines are heavy: feel and hear the few words just sitting there taking up all the space in the whole line. Let them have all the time and duration they need to take up all that space. On the other hand let long lines ramble on and on for as long as they go. . . . Or you might want to speed up to get all the words into that one line-space-time.

To me words and sounds are *major* toys. I love them—I take none of them for granted. I like to hover over vowels, consonants— I find them all intrinsically powerful. They constantly delight and move me. I like all kinds of other sounds too and make lots of them in storytelling—with my voice, lips, and tongue, or by clapping my hands, stamping my feet, slapping my thighs. When we are storytelling, our whole body is our instrument. Each part has tremendous *mana* or internal magic, and all of our body parts can be played on to reveal their particular sound. Part of the fun of reading out loud is seeing how many different parts of yourself you can let have a voice.

Let music and movements come to you. Add the beat and rhythms of your pulse—sometimes steady, sometimes quickening—along with drums, bells, flutes, tambourines, cymbals. Add anything your imagination takes a fancy to. Allow the most vivid colors and tones. Allow yelps and cries and sighs. The line may read "Ohm," but for that word you can exchange any and all sounds that express the ecstasy and pain that the myth evokes in you at that point.

It is wonderful to please your audience and yourself. But try provoking them too. And try inciting them to cry, to anger, to lust, to cheer. To leap!

This book begins with the Charge of the Goddess. And my stories and singing have taken me no distance from it. I need not quest to the desert or mountaintops, seeking truth far from home, because it was ever the case that *if you do not find the Wisdom and Mystery of Life within yourself, you surely will never find it without.*

May the songs I have sung here and the stories I have told be pleasing to my grandmothers, the ancient ones, and of benefit to all beings.

Blessed be.
Ananke.

NOTES

· · · · · · · · · ·

Introduction

1. Alexander Marshack has some provocative things to say about the role of storytelling in the evolution of human nature. According to him, for at least the last five hundred thousand years two things have been a part of our basic make-up: the ability to factor time and the need to create stories (a mythos). He points out that we cannot be human without both of these, and they are so interrelated that we always use them together. Without a doubt, we human beings require story-mythos and a sense of the cycling seasons (the ability to factor time) in order to make sense and meaning out of our lives and then to communicate that sense and meaning to others. See the chapter on "Time-Factored Thought," in Marshack's *The Roots of Civilization: The Cognitive Beginnings of Man's First Art, Symbol, and Notation* (New York: McGraw-Hill, 1972), 109–123.

   In our scientific western tradition there is so much preoccupation with defining and pinpointing instances of time—so much belittling of the cyclical—that our time-factoring gifts have fallen out of favor. It is no longer fashionable to regard this way of perceiving as a vital, treasurable part of our essential human nature. The Model and Way of the Triple Goddess restores storying and time-factoring to the focal point of our lives.

2. Jean Graybeal, a philosopher of religion, reminds me that although only human beings story to the extent that we do, the more we learn about dolphins, whales, and other creatures, the likelier it becomes that other species also tell stories to each other and thereby—through storying—also modify their own group behaviors, creating their own lives and futures to some extent. Do they have the capacity to remember over generations as we do? Are they aware that they are bridging such a gap as we are? Do they use metaphors and symbols to express value and meaning as we do?

   Perhaps not, but Earl W. Count has collected much evidence to show that symbol-making and ritual behavior is in evidence in apes, elephants, bees, and termites so that myth-making is most likely "an aspect of our morphology"—in the final analysis not merely a human cultural activity but a product of "neurologic energies that are more ancient even than

mammals, let alone the primates and the line of man." From Earl W. Count, "Myth as World-View: A Biosocial Synthesis" in Stanley Diamond, ed., *Culture in History: Essays in Honor of Paul Radin* (New York: Columbia University Press, 1960), 580–627.

3. Suggested readings about women creating themselves through storying: Carol Ascher, Louise DeSalvo, and Sara Ruddick, eds., *Between Women* (Boston: Beacon Press, 1984); Mary Catherine Bateson, *Composing a Life* (New York: Dutton, 1990); Mary Field Belenky et al., *Women's Ways of Knowing: The Development of Self, Voice, and Mind* (New York: Basic Books, 1986); Bella Brodzki and Celeste Schenck, eds., *Life/Lines: Theorizing Women's Autobiography* (Ithaca, N.Y.: Cornell University Press, 1989); Carol Christ, *Diving Deep and Surfacing: Women Writers on Spiritual Quest* (Boston: Beacon Press, 1980); Carolyn Heilbrun, *Writing a Woman's Life* (New York: Ballantine Books, 1988).

   Men also write profoundly about the importance of story. See, for instance, James Hillman, *Healing Fiction* (Barrytown, N.Y.: Station Hill Press, 1983).

4. Alexander Marshack writes that "the capacity to understand and communicate a 'story' was perhaps the basic, humanizing intellectual and social skill, the primary tool and technique of developing human culture." See *The Roots of Civilization*, 131. Frederick Turner agrees that "mythology is the ultimate technology." See his *Beyond Geography: The Western Spirit Against the Wilderness* (New Brunswick, N.J.: Rutgers University Press, 1990), 14.

5. The classic discussion of men as the norm and women as the Other appears in Simone de Beauvoir, *The Second Sex*, trans. by H. M. Parshley (1952; reprint ed., New York: Bantam Books, 1961).

6. Carol Christ calls herself a thealogian because *thea* means "goddess," and a Divine Female is the subject of her work. I quote here from her well-known article "Why Women Need the Goddess: Phenomenological, Psychological, and Political Reflections," reprinted in Charlene Spretnak, ed., *The Politics of Women's Spirituality* (New York: Anchor Books, 1982), 73.

7. Archaeologist Marija Gimbutas often says that the beginning of patriarchy—with its stratified societies, competition, hierarchies, and the wars that resulted from this tilted, unequal societal model—marks the end of the truly "civilized," cooperative behavior between people that characterized all foraging, Paleolithic cultures. Although it was formerly thought that early human beings were vicious, competitive "killer apes," it is now known that our kind is at base a cooperative, sharing species. We have no offensive sharp claws or fangs, we cannot easily climb or swing through trees, and we lack physical defenses like shells or quills. *We have survived only because of our*

VIRGIN

Mother ·

CRONE

Notes to pages 2–4

ability to help and nurture one another and because our ancestors understood the need for organizing themselves in a way that encouraged and effected that kind of behavior.

Information about the cooperative nature of the earliest human beings is found in the work of many scholars, including anthropologists, two of whom are Felicitas Goodman and Marvin Harris. On pages 17 and 18 of her *Ecstasy, Ritual, and Alternate Reality: Religion in a Pluralistic World* (Bloomington, Ind.: Indiana University Press, 1988), Goodman reports that at the "dawning" of human existence "life was as close to paradise as humans have ever been able to achieve. The men did the hunting and scavenging, working for about three hours a week, and the women took care of daily sustenance by gathering vegetal food and small animals. It was such a harmonious existence, such a successful adaptation that it did not materially alter for many thousands of years."

About more recent gatherer-hunters she writes, "Despite the unavoidable privations of human existence, despite occasional hunger, illness, and other trials, what makes their lifeway so enviable is the fact that knowing and loving every nook and cranny of their home territory and spending all their lives in it, the bands make regular rounds [through their land] and take only what they need. . . . *They live a life of total balance, because they do not aspire to controlling their habitat, [instead] they are a part of it."* The italics are Goodman's.

In his *Our Kind: The Evolution of Human Life and Culture* (New York: Harper & Row, 1989), Marvin Harris writes (on page 345) of humankind's ubiquitous trait of being able to "carry out a give-and-take . . . that is informal, uncalculating, and imbued with a spirit of generosity." And after giving much evidence, he concludes on page 351: "Then let me hear no more of our kind's natural necessity to form hierarchical groups. An observer viewing human life shortly after cultural takeoff would easily have concluded that our species was destined to be irredeemably egalitarian except for distinctions of sex and age. That someday the world would be divided into aristocrats and commoners, masters and slaves, billionaires and homeless beggars would have seemed wholly contrary to human nature as evidenced in the affairs of every human society then on earth."

8. The story of *The Iliad* comes from patriarchal times. The fact that Hera is the protectress of the Argive warriors in this story is a holdover from an earlier time and tradition when Hera's matristic religion was practiced in Argos. The Hera of *The Iliad,* however, is no longer a cognate of the Great Goddess. (See Chapter 2, "The Demotion of Hera.")

9. Riane Eisler, *The Chalice and the Blade* (San Francisco: Harper & Row, 1987), xviii.

10. The caduceus, two snakes twining around a winged staff, is the symbol of modern medicine's healing powers and a doctor's mission to serve others. But it is also a very ancient symbol of healing and of philosophical wholism (that is, a non-dualistic view of the world and reality). It was the defining image of Medea, the healing Mother Goddess of the Medes, whose chariot was propelled across the sky by two wings and guided by two snakes. Medea's name—like our word "medicine"—comes from *medha*, a Sanskrit word for knowledge or healing wisdom. Before classical times—before Medea and her story went through an Archetypal Reversal that changed her from a powerful, positive Force into the vixen murderer of her own children—Medea was revered as a Wisdom and Sun Goddess Who traversed the daytime sky in Her winged, snake-led chariot. This vehicle mimics the sun by going across the vaulted sky during the day from east to west (using its birdwing, flying powers) and traversing the underworld during the night from west to east (using its burrowing snake powers).

Complete, uninterrupted cycles are important to all female deities as well as to wholistic healing philosophies that practice service to others as a form of Self-interest, even Self-love.

This information can be found in many places, including Carl Kerenyi, *Goddesses of Sun and Moon,* trans. by Murray Stein (Dallas, Tex.: Spring Publications, 1979), in the section titled "Medea" (pages 20–40) and *passim.*

11. Stated on "Return of the Goddess," a series of four hour-long broadcasts produced and aired by the Canadian Broadcasting Company in 1986. Interview conducted by Merlin Stone. Available on audiocassettes from CBC Enterprises, P.O. Box 500, Station A, Toronto, M5W 1E6, Canada.

12. Turner, *Beyond Geography,* 8.

13. Michael Toms, "An Open Life: Conversations with Joseph Campbell," in *New Frontier,* January 1989, pp. 40, 41. My italics.

14. A famous Manhattan acting school, the Neighborhood Playhouse, has a motto displayed on big and little posters all over the school: *Act before you think.* The aim of much of the work of all performing artists—dancers, singers, actors, but even of many painters and writers too—is learning to let one's responses and impulses come out before they have been edited by one's cerebral cortex: they learn to act before they think.

15. The way of life of the Zuni, a peaceful tribe of people who have long lived in what is now New Mexico in the southwestern United States, is so steeped in myth and ritual that their language only has a present tense—no future, no past. That which endures in life and the landscape is of such abiding

282

value to them that other values and possibilities have no interest or reality for them.

16. Many scholars are rethinking our traditional notion of history and progress, seeing our western viewpoint as chauvinistic. Along with Frederick Turner (*Beyond Geography*), three such thinkers are the prolific Harvard paleontologist Stephen Jay Gould, Christopher Lasch, and Calvin Luther Martin. Gould's *Wonderful Life: The Burgess Shale and the Nature of History* (New York: W. W. Norton, 1989) proves that evolution on earth does not proceed in a straight line or according to any Plan but rather that its course is "utterly unpredictable and quite unrepeatable." Lasch asks "How does it happen that serious people continue to believe in Progress, in the face of massive evidence that might have been expected to refute the idea of Progress once and for all?" in *The True and Only Heaven: Progress and Its Critics* (New York: W. W. Norton, 1991), 13. Martin's *In the Spirit of the Earth: Rethinking History and Time* (Baltimore: Johns Hopkins University Press, 1992) is an extremely exciting and special contribution showing the flawed ideas at the base of western scholarship and civilization.

17. Charlene Spretnak, *States of Grace: Reclaiming the Core Teachings and Practices of the Great Wisdom Traditions for the Well-Being of the Earth Community* (San Francisco: Harper, 1991), 212.

18. I first learned about this "coming home" phenomenon from Margot Adler's documentation of it in her extraordinary book *Drawing Down the Moon: Witches, Druids, Goddess-Worshippers, and Other Pagans in America Today* (Boston: Beacon Press, 1979), *passim*.

19. For a more thorough discussion of dualisms and the gendered prejudices that are innate to them, see my article, "The Uses of Myth, Image, and the Female Body in Re-Visioning Knowledge," in Alison Jaggar and Susan Bordo, eds., *Gender/Body/Knowledge: Feminist Reconstructions of Being and Knowing* (New Brunswick, N.J.: Rutgers University Press, 1989), 92–114.

20. Mary Midgley, *Beast and Man: The Roots of Human Nature* (Ithaca, New York: Cornell University Press, 1978), 196–197.

21. Theologian Catherine Keller's brilliant, scholarly, poetic treatise on the Goddess and the Self as an ever-growing conglomerate is *From a Broken Web: Separation, Sexism, and Self* (Boston: Beacon Press, 1986).

My thanks to John Dewey, who felt that the smallest entity of human self that he could imagine was brain-in-body-in-environment *in flux*. This non-dualistic concept permeates his work, but the following passage is nicely succinct. "Many physiological

inquirers would doubtless feel enormously relieved if a specific portion of the cortex could be ascertained to be *the* seat of consciousness. . . . The world seems mad in pre-occupation with what is specific, particular, disconnected. . . . But recovery of sanity depends upon seeing and using these specifiable things *as* links functionally significant in a *process*. To see the organism *in* nature, the nervous system *in* the organism, the brain *in* the nervous system, the cortex *in* the brain is the answer to the problems which haunt philosophy. And when thus seen they will be seen to be *in*, not as marbles are in a box but as events are in history, in a moving, growing never finished process." In John Dewey, *Experience and Nature*, second ed. (New York: Dover Publications, 1958), 295. Dewey's italics.

22. A delightful essay that discourses on this awareness is Neil Douglas-Klotz's "The Skin Is the Surface of the Brain," in *Creation Spirituality Magazine*, May 1991, pp. 8–16, 48.

23. An excellent saying from Aristotle's *Nicomachean Ethics*: "It is the mark of an educated person to expect no more exactitude in a subject matter than the nature of the subject matter itself allows."

24. I found this quote from Mircea Eliade in Dolores LaChapelle, *Sacred Land, Sacred Sex, Rapture of the Deep: Concerning Deep Ecology and Celebrating Life* (Silverton, Colo.: Finn Hill Arts, 1988), 117. Italics his. It appears without documentation on a whole page of quotations heading a chapter entitled "The Sacred." I have been unable to locate it, although I suspect it comes from his essay "Methodological Remarks on the Study of Religious Symbolism," in M. Eliade and J. Kitagawa, eds., *The History of Religions: Essays in Methodology* (Chicago: University of Chicago Press, 1959).

25. James Hillman brilliantly discusses *anima mundi* as being "totally worldly," the spirit or essence of *the world*, not "a" disembodied or unworldly essence inside things of the world. *Archetypal Psychology* (Dallas, Tex.: Spring Publications, 1983), 18.

26. See James Hillman, "On the Necessity of Abnormal Psychology: Ananke and Athena" in an anthology he edited, *Facing the Gods* (Dallas, Tex.: Spring Publications, 1980), especially pages 5–7 and 14 where he calls the pathology of Necessity a "creating activity."

27. A midwife—from Old English *mid* ("with") and *wif*—is one who stays "with [the] woman [or wife]" during childbirth, responding empathically and co-operatively to her needs. *Wif* is also etymologically related to "weave," a wife being the one who weaves the cloth for her family's use as well as the fabric of family life.

28. Susun Weed, *Wise Woman Herbal: Healing Wise*

VIRGIN
Mother . . . .
CRONE

Notes to pages 12–16

(Woodstock, N.Y.: Ash Tree Publishing, 1989), 175 and *passim.*

29. Several Christian theologians posit this same theory nowadays, including Roman Catholics Thomas Berry and Matthew Fox, as does the Jewish mystic Martin Buber, whose *I and Thou* states that God is found when an *I*—each of us—is in right relationship with a *You,* be that You *any* Other—another human or tree or animal or whatever. The translation of *I and Thou* by Walter Kaufmann was published by Scribners, New York, in 1970.

30. Mary Daly, *Gyn/Ecology: The Metaethics of Radical Feminism* (Boston: Beacon Press, 1978), 27. In addition to Mary Daly, the women to whom I am most indebted for their scholarship, perseverance, and vision about the Goddess and another way of being in the world are given here, together with some of their books:

    • Marija Gimbutas, *The Civilization of the Goddess: The World of Old Europe* (San Francisco: Harper, 1991).

    • Elinor Gadon, *The Once and Future Goddess: A Symbol for Our Time* (San Francisco: Harper & Row, 1989).

    • Buffie Johnson, *Lady of the Beasts: Ancient Images of the Goddess and Her Sacred Animals* (San Francisco: Harper & Row, 1988).

    • Merlin Stone, *When God Was a Woman* (New York: Harcourt Brace Jovanovich, 1976).

    • Starhawk, *Dreaming the Dark* (Boston: Beacon Press, 1982) and *The Spiral Dance: A Rebirth of the Ancient Religion of the Great Goddess* (San Francisco: Harper & Row, 1979).

    • Monica Sjöö and Barbara Mor, *The Great Cosmic Mother: Rediscovering the Religion of the Earth* (San Francisco: Harper & Row, 1987).

    • Barbara Walker, *The Woman's Encyclopedia of Myths and Secrets* (San Francisco: Harper & Row, 1983) and *The Crone: Woman of Age, Wisdom, and Power* (San Francisco: Harper & Row, 1985).

    • Carol P. Christ, author of "Why Women Need the Goddess," *Laughter of Aphrodite: Reflections On A Journey To The Goddess* (San Francisco: Harper & Row, 1987), and other writings, including being co-editor with Judith Plaskow of *Womanspirit Rising: A Feminist Reader in Religion* (San Francisco: Harper & Row, 1979) and *Weaving the Visions: New Patterns in Feminist Spirituality*) (San Francisco: Harper & Row, 1989).

31. The noted authority on prehistoric Sumer, Samuel Noah Kramer, writes that the third millennium B.C.E. can be charcaterized by its "priestly piracy." It was a time when "male theologians manipulated the order of the deities in accordance with their chauvinistic predilections," abrogating the Goddess's characteristics or giving them wholesale to their gods, themselves, and their sons. Samuel Noah Kramer, *From the Poetry of Sumer* (Berkeley: University of California, 1979), 27, 29.

    Asphodel P. Long writes, "I see the bible as being in the forefront of gender politics. . . . My book seeks to show up facts and interpretations throughout the bible which demonstrate that the material is 'double faced.' . . . it seeks to deceive . . . to banish the female from divinity." Asphodel P. Long, *In a Chariot Drawn by Lions: The Search for the Female in Divinity* (London: The Women's Press, 1992), 12–13.

32. My sources specifically for pre-classical Hera include Jean Shinoda Bolen, M.D., *Goddesses in Everywoman* (New York: Harper & Row, 1984); Christine Downing, *The Goddess: Mythological Images of the Feminine* (New York: Crossroad, 1984); Marija Gimbutas, *The Goddesses and Gods of Old Europe* (Berkeley and Los Angeles: University of California Press, 1982); Robert Graves, *The White Goddess* (New York: Vintage Books, 1958); Jane Ellen Harrison, *Epilegomena to the Study of Greek Religion* (1921; reprint ed., New Hyde Park, N.Y.: University Books, 1962); Carl Kerenyi, *Zeus and Hera: Archetypal Image of Father, Husband, and Wife* (Princeton, N.J.: Princeton University Press, 1972); Charlene Spretnak, *Lost Goddesses of Early Greece: A Collection of Pre-Hellenic Myths* (Boston: Beacon Press, 1981); Merlin Stone, *Ancient Mirrors of Womanhood: A Treasury of Goddess and Heroine Lore from Around the World* (Boston: Beacon Press, 1979).

33. Diane Wolkstein and Samuel Noah Kramer, *Inanna, Queen of Heaven and Earth: Her Stories and Hymns from Sumer* (New York: Harper & Row, 1983), 30–49.

34. Maxwell Anderson wrote a scene into his play *Elizabeth the Queen* in which Elizabeth I and Mary, Queen of Scots, confronted each other face-to-face, although in actual life these two monarchs never met. Playwrights and other writers must sometimes take *dramatic license* in order to telescope and better communicate the truth or essence of historical facts and relationships for readers. I have upon occasion—as in the menstrual ritual performed in the Heraion—taken the same kind of dramatic license to bring an atmosphere and subtext to life, by combining authentic ingredients from many different sources—even from different eras—into one scene.

35. See Dolores LaChapelle's essay "Not Laws of Nature but *Li* (Pattern) of Nature," in Max Oelschlaeger, ed., *The Wilderness Condition: Essays on Environment and Civilization* (San Francisco: Sierra Club Books, 1992).

36. For example, Werner Heisenberg's theory of indeterminancy proposed in the 1920s. One of the most important scientists of the twentieth century, physicist Heisenberg made a vital point about the direction he felt science should take in the future by using the word "conversations" in the subtitle of one volume of his memoirs: *Physics and Beyond: Encounters and Conversations*, trans. by Arnold J. Pomerans (New York: Harper & Row, 1970). Heisenberg makes it explicit that knowledge of facts is not all that is important to scientific progress. He shows that it was *only through dialogue with other knowledgeable scientists*—that is, by practicing the Oral Tradition—that he and his colleagues came to understand what was happening in subatomic physics that eventually led them to figure out the deficiencies in Newtonian physics and describe quantum mechanics. He writes that only by inducing more and more constant face-to-face dialogue as an integral part of the scientific method of doing research can scientists of the future hope to understand problems sufficiently well to make the theoretical breakthroughs that will enable them to describe what is going on in Nature. His suggested method for science is: Talk and look and ponder together. And *then* go into the laboratory.

    He further quotes his colleague Niels Bohr as saying that the scientific method at some points is exactly like the artistic method: in order to make discoveries each field must at times *proceed by using image, parable, and metaphor*.

37. Many scientists are working in chaos theory today. James Gleick summarizes this popular new way of doing science in *Chaos: Making a New Science* (New York: Viking-Penguin, 1987).

38. An excellent introduction to this theory is Bart Kosko, *Fuzzy Thinking: The New Science of Fuzzy Logic* (New York: Hyperion, 1993).

ONE
The Triple Goddess

1. The Virgin personified the spring: the birth of baby animals, the rebirth of vegetation, the return of species that have spent the winter elsewhere. Water and water creatures are also ubiquitously associated with the Creating Virgin Mother. As far back as the late Ice Age (the Upper Paleolithic), carvings on a reindeer antler depict cavorting eels, salmon, seals, flower buds, and sprouting branches as "dramatic 'signs' of the coming of spring," according to Alexander Marshack, *The Roots of Civilization*, 172.

2. Pamela Berger, *The Goddess Obscured: Transformation of the Grain Protectress from Goddess to Saint* (Boston: Beacon Press, 1985), 1.

3. The oldest image of Her is a numinous palm-sized figurine carved in limestone approximately 29,000 B.C.E. Today this image, which was found near Willendorf, Austria, is called the Earth Mother of Willendorf. See Elinor Gadon, *The Once and Future Goddess*, 6.

4. The bas relief found near Laussel is 17 inches high (46 cm) and was carved high on a stone block. (Gravettian, Upper Perigordian, c. 25,000–20,000 B.C.E.)

    J. G. Lalanne, the physician who first discovered this carving, described it as "hovering," according to art historian S. Giedion, who writes, "The outward curve of the figure followed the natural curve of the surface of the block in which she was embedded, as if hovering." See Siegfried Giedion, *The Eternal Present: The Beginnings of Art* (New York: Pantheon Books, 1962), 469.

    Giedion later describes the female figures from the cave at La Magdeleine: "The sculptor saw the forms in the rock and had only to bring them forth" (478). This is, of course, the sacred tradition of the African or European wood carver or even of Michaelangelo. All such artists look carefully—meditatively—at the wood or marble before carving, "listening," allowing the material to tell them what is there to be released.

5. Traces of the original red ochre still remain on this figure after twenty thousand years. The tradition of painting sacred images or objects with red ochre has survived into the twentieth century. For many primal peoples this age-old ritual has specifically celebrated the life-giving, life-sustaining, and matrilineal kinship properties of women's blood.

6. Alexander Marshack pioneered the technique of looking at early carvings with a microscope to tell such things as the size of the point of the cutting instrument. He has shown that each line on Laussel's ibex horn was made by a different instrument. For this ethnologist-detective's fascinating methods and sensible ways of interpreting extant artifacts read his *The Roots of Civilization*.

    Marshack also provides extensive evidence that the earliest human notations, carvings, and paintings were concerned with the cycles of Nature, that all early art was in some way a calendric or a "time-factoring device" that accompanied stories or myths that helped people understand and share their lives with each other and generations to come.

7. Marshack, *The Roots of Civilization*, 333.

8. ibid., 333.

9. ibid., 339.

10. "Indeed what is striking is not the metamorphosis of the symbols over the millennia but rather the continuity from Paleolithic times on," writes Marija Gimbutas in *The Language of the Goddess: Unearth-*

ing the Hidden Symbols of Western Civilization (San Francisco: Harper & Row, 1989), xix.

"The practice of engraving the vulva as an abstract symbol upon almost naturalistic figures was the origin of a very long-lived tradition, which lasted from the Middle Magdalenian to the Cycladic age and was the forerunner of the Greek development. . . . That a tradition should persist through so many millenniums and occur in so many centers of culture surely indicates that these female figures were, from the outset, not intended as simple representations of the female body but were cult objects. . . . The earliest figures drawn in the damp clay of the caverns have a bond connecting them to Grecian civilization. . . . All were manifestations of fecundity, of the source of life, of the Great Earth Mother, bearing the vulva triangle as her sacred symbol." In Giedion, *The Eternal Present*, 178–179.

11. Many scholars now trace the continuity of the Goddess of pre-history into Christianity's Mother of God, including Marija Gimbutas, *The Civilization of the Goddess*.

    In this, her twenty-second book, Gimbutas "examines the way of life, religion, and social structure of the peoples who inhabited Europe from the seventh to the third millennia B.C.[E]." However, I know from personal conversations and from team teaching a course titled "The Goddess of Prehistory and Her Portrayals" with Gimbutas at Colorado College that she feels strongly that although the Divine Female tradition was modified, it remained in essence unbroken from earliest times to the present, from the Paleolithic depictions (those Goddesses found near Willendorf, Laussel, Lespugue, et al.) to and including the Virgin Mary of Christianity. See also: Berger, *The Goddess Obscured*, 3, 89, *passim*; Mary Condren, *The Serpent and the Goddess: Women, Power, and Religion in Celtic Ireland* (San Francisco: Harper & Row, 1989), 5, 74, 154–182, *passim*; and Gadon, *The Once and Future Goddess*, 189ff.

12. Among many sources for this information are: Gadon, *The Once and Future Goddess*, 12; Gimbutas, *The Language of the Goddess*, 265, 269, 280, 284–286; Buffie Johnson, *Lady of the Beasts*, "The Ewe and the Ram," 199–208 and "The Cow and the Bull," 269–320; Vincent Scully, *The Earth, the Temple, and the Gods,* rev. ed. (New Haven and London: Yale University Press, 1979), especially 13 and see figures 450–456 at end of book for Corinthian column capitals as Goddess's ram horns and simultaneously owl eyes.

13. When the wide assortment of Paleolithic figures of the Great Goddess were first found, they were called "venus figurines" or just "venuses." Some anthropologists at that time actually stated that a nude female image could only be a "fertility symbol" or "sexual stimulant" for men, as Venus, the Roman goddess of love, was. Today we are all learning to see females as more than sex objects, more than breeding opportunities for men. This recent expanded attitude is more akin to the way Paleolithic people regarded women than our traditional patriarchal, scholarly attitude has been toward women. In this case, progress has been made by going backward to see women and the world the way those who carved this immanent female figure near Laussel did. The name "venuses"—even "so-called venuses"— must be dropped. It is not accurate to call female figures who had cosmic and broad human significance "sexual stimulants" nor to label them mere "fertility symbols."

14. Some cosmologists and physicists, including Carl Sagan, now suggest that the whole universe unendingly cycles, that the cosmos expands and contracts endlessly, that there has been a Big Bang at the beginning of each of the universe's new expansions, and that matter was never created at all but just always has been. This theory fits the description of the Great Mother as the embodied eternal Cosmos and coincides with the Creation Myth I tell here.

    Among many interesting books on Earth Knowledge as a new way of knowing, see an anthology edited by William Irwin Thompson, *GAIA: A Way of Knowing—Political Implications of the New Biology* (Barrington, Mass.: Lindisfarne Press, 1987).

15. Marija Gimbutas, in a lecture given at Colorado College, March 1990.

16. Male trinity gods are a recent cultural invention, part of what one ancient Mesopotamian scholar, Samuel Noah Kramer, calls "priestly piracy," the common practice in which "male theologians manipulated the order of the deities in accordance with their chauvinistic predilections"; they stole the goddesses' prerogatives to give to their gods and stole priestess's prerogatives to pass on to their sons and priestly heirs. The threefold nature of the Great Mother Goddess is one of the traditional Female attributes that was transferred in time to male gods. See Samuel Noah Kramer, *From the Poetry of Sumer* (Berkeley and Los Angeles: University of California Press, 1979), 27, 29.

    Sometimes this piracy was merely the changing of the sex of the deity, creating unexplainable Great Mysteries like the male trinity, like the creation of matter out of spirit, like the conception of the divine son without sex, and so on. Of course, these Great Mysteries disappear when the sex of the deity is acknowledged as Female and sacred immanence is restored to Body and Matter.

17. "There are indeed pan-human systems of aesthetic creation, biogenetically imprinted upon us, whose

. . . . *Notes*

Notes to pages 22–25

basic rules we violate only at the risk of artistic ste-
rility. They include . . . certain fundamental mythical
stories, . . . basic rhythms and phases of performance
and ritual," writes Frederick Turner in "The Crisis
in Modern Aesthetics," *Performing Arts Journal 32,*
vol. 11, no. 2 (1988): 7–16.

18. One of the first people in modern times to propose
that the first human social groups consisted simply
of mothers and their children and that men and
women did not marry, nor cohabit all the time, was
the Swiss jurist J. J. Bachofen, who coined the term
"mother-right" in the title of his 1861 book, *Das
Mutterrecht.* Although Bachofen was correct in his
general thesis, a plethora of errors makes this Victo-
rian book of no value to the general public today;
for scholarly use it was translated into English by
Ralph Manheim as *Myth, Religion, and Mother-
Right* (Princeton, N.J.: Princeton University Press,
1967).

19. William Irwin Thompson, *The Time Falling Bodies
Take to Light: Mythology, Sexuality, and the Origins of Culture* (New York: St. Martin's Press,
1981), 137.

20. "Do humans have an unquenchable desire for power
that, in the absence of a strong ruler, inevitably leads
to a war of all against all? To judge from surviving
examples of bands and villages, for the greater part
of prehistory our kind got along quite well without
so much as a paramount chief, let alone the all-
powerful English leviathan King and Mortal God,
whom Hobbes believed was needed for maintaining
law and order among his fractious countrymen."
Marvin Harris, *Our Kind,* 344.

21. Eisler explains the term "gylany" this way: "*Gy* derives from the Greek root *gyne,* or 'woman.' *An* derives from *andros,* or 'man.' The letter 'l' between
the two has a double meaning." It *links* the two
halves of humanity in equal partnership and "stands
for the resolution of our problems" by freeing men
and women "from the stultifying and distorting ri-
gidity of roles imposed by the domination hierarchies inherent in androcratic systems." There was a
clear division of labor between the sexes in Paleolithic and Neolithic times, but the "stultifying" hierarchical valuing and delimiting of power within the
sex roles did not exist. See Riane Eisler, *The Chalice
and the Blade,* 105.

22. Dolores LaChapelle, *Sacred Land, Sacred Sex, Rapture of the Deep,* 157.

23. Thorkild Jacobsen, *The Treasures of Darkness: A
History of Mesopotamian Religion* (New Haven,
Conn.: Yale University Press, 1976), *passim,* especially Chapter 3: "Third Millennium Metaphors,"
77–92.

24. See Jacobsen's simple, clear description of the differ-

ence between a transcendent deity—like the Hebrew-
Christian God—and immanent deities like the Goddess. Although the Hebrew God is said to be immanent in some ways, Jacobsen shows there is a great
difference between him and truly immanent deities.
He mentions the Burning Bush in which God appeared to Moses, reminding us that there was a one-
time thing, that God would not like to be thought of
as a bush ordinarily, nor that his powers or nature
could be observed in a bush. Whereas for primal
peoples the bush itself *does* reveal the nature of divinity as well as Nature's powers.

Jacobsen notes that all deities prior to the fourth
millennium were immanent within Nature, not transcendent to it. *The Treasures of Darkness,* 6.

Of interest also is Jacobsen's chapter on the development of the notion of a Personal God and the inner contradictions within the concept. See Chapter 5,
"The Inner Gods As Parents: Rise of Personal Religion," 147–164.

Before humans could conceive of transcendence,
they first had to have the concept of hierarchies and
of rulers (whether on earth or in heaven). The concept of transcendence belongs to a dualistic way of
thinking and is therefore, in my opinion, not a sign
of progress, not an improvement in human reasoning
powers. For an analysis of dualisms and the sexism
inherent in their innate hierarchical structure see
Donna Wilshire, "The Uses of Myth, Image, and the
Female Body in Re-Visioning Knowledge," in Alison
Jaggar and Susan Bordo, eds., *Gender/Body/Knowl-
edge,* 92–114.

25. Huston Smith, *The World's Religions* (San Francisco: Harper, 1991), 367–368.

"Hunters don't worship gods at all; they don't
worship anything, for that matter. They converse
with local, earth- and sea-bound spirit persons without adoring them. They are animists, not theists."
From Calvin Luther Martin, *In the Spirit of the
Earth,* 41.

26. Quoted in Martin, *In the Spirit of the Earth,* 18.

27. ibid., 3.

28. Pamela Berger, *The Goddess Obscured: Transformation of the Grain Protectress from Goddess to Saint*
(Boston: Beacon Press, 1985).

29. The Roman Emperor Gallienus Augustus, having attached particular importance to his initiation at
Eleusis, issued coins in 265–266 C.E. on which he is
shown wearing a wreath of wheat on his head in
honor of Demeter. His name is inscribed:
GALLIENAE AUGUSTAE. I found this information
in Carl Kerenyi, *Eleusis: Archetypal Image of
Mother and Daughter,* trans. by Ralph Manheim
(Princeton, N.J.: Princeton University Press, 1967),
211, n.122.

30. We are now discovering, as Gimbutas writes in *The Civilization of the Goddess*, that "the path of 'progress' is extinguishing the very conditions for life on earth" (vii). "Civilization," she continues, "in the best sense of the word . . . lies in its degree of artistic creation, aesthetic achievements, nonmaterial values, and freedoms which make life meaningful and enjoyable for all its citizens" (viii).

TWO

The Demotion of Hera

1. Christine Downing, *The Goddess*, 71, 73. Downing took the final phrase (in quotes) from a song in praise of Hera: *The Orphic Hymns* translated by Apostolos N. Athanassakis (Missoula, Mont.: Scholars Press, 1977), 27.

2. Jane Ellen Harrison, *Prolegomena to the Study of Greek Religion* (New York: Meridian Books, 1957), 315ff. Quoted in Downing's *The Goddess*.

3. Sources for information on Hera as positive Goddess:

    Jane Ellen Harrison is essential reading for anyone who wants to understand that the first deities were animals and Mother Goddesses (she mentions archaic Hera as one of the last of these), but under ensuing patriarchal regimes these divinities lost favor, their numinous immanence, their sanctity. Her books include *Prolegomena to the Study of Greek Religion*, *Themis: A Study of the Social Origins of Greek Religion*, and *Epilegomena to the Study of Greek Religion*.

    Other excellent sources include: Downing, *The Goddess*, especially Chapter 1 ("The Goddess") and Chapter 4 ("Coming to Terms with Hera"); Robert Graves, *The Greek Myths*, vol. 1 (Middlesex, England: Penguin Books, 1955); Carl Kerenyi, *Zeus and Hera*; Philip Slater, *The Glory of Hera: Greek Mythology and the Greek Family* (Boston: Beacon Press, 1968); and Charlene Spretnak, *Lost Goddesses of Early Greece*.

    Kerenyi's book has much detailed archaeological information specifically about Hera. Kerenyi, moreover, was an excellent guide in pinpointing praiseworthy things about Hera that usually go unnoticed or unmentioned in old texts like *The Iliad*, the *Orphic Hymns*, or our other usual mythic and archaeological sources. Kerenyi follows his own advice of reading all that is available with an eye and ear trying "to detect a more complex figure than that which [Hera] later became by sublimation and reduction" (114). Kerenyi analyzes sites sacred to Hera, noting their settings in the landscape and the layout of ritual spaces, explaining, "Only from her sanctuaries can we learn more about Hera." (115).

4. Marija Gimbutas, *The Goddesses and Gods of Old Europe*, 149–150.

5. Kerenyi, *Zeus and Hera*, 114.

6. Harrison, *Prolegomena to the Study of Greek Religion*, 316.

7. Marija Gimbutas, *The Civilization of the Goddess*, 351–401.

8. Catherine Keller, *From a Broken Web*, 71–118.

9. Pamela Berger, *The Goddess Obscured*.

10. Mary Condren, *The Serpent and the Goddess*.

11. Mary Daly, *Gyn/Ecology*, 79.

12. Jean Markale, *Women of the Celts* (Rochester, Vt.: Inner Traditions International, 1986), 14.

13. For a full, moving treatment of the archetypal reversal of Herakles into Hercules, and the enormous consequences men today still pay for the loss of the early Herakles—loving co-creator and green bough on the Tree of Life—as a Model for maleness, read the extraordinary book by Glen Mazis, *The Trickster, Magician, and Grieving Man: Reconnecting Men with Earth* (Santa Fe: Bear & Co., 1994).

14. Jane Ellen Harrison calls Hercules a "half-barbarian" hero on page 365 in her discussion of Heracles as a fertility *daimon* who was depicted with a bough from a living tree: *Epilegomena to the Study of Greek Religion*, 364–373.

15. Many of the ideas in this paragraph as well as the quote come from Downing, *The Goddess*, "Coming to Terms with Hera," 91.

16. E. O. James, *The Cult of the Mother Goddess* (London: Thames and Hudson, 1959), 144.

17. Mount Olympus and Olympia are two different places with which Hera is associated. Zeus ruled from Mount Olympus near the northeastern shore of Greece overlooking the Aegean Sea; after Hera married Zeus, She went to sit on a throne there at his side. But for a millennia prior to that marriage—and long after—She had Her own temple and devoted followers at Olympia, the site of the first Olympic Games, a town located in the western part of the Peloponnesian peninsula, on the other side of Greece from Mount Olympus.

18. John C. Wilson's italics, from his preface to the first American edition of Jane Ellen Harrison, *Epilegomena to the Study of Greek Religion* and *Themis*, ix.

    The Mysteries Harrison mentions by name are the Dionysian and Orphic, but as Arthur Evans explains, Dionysos "assimilated many of the beliefs and practices of the agrarian lower classes . . . [and] the Minoan [Goddess] world-view" as well as many of the Goddess's rites, including titles and epithets that had earlier been "applied to the Great Mother of the Gods." More "priestly piracy." Arthur Evans, *The God of Ecstasy: Sex-Roles and the Madness of*

Dionysos (New York: St. Martin's Press, 1988), 42, 107.

19. According to Pindar, Zeus raped Metis and was, as well, responsible for Her death.

   Catherine Keller uses the incident of Metis's death and Athena's birth to make a fascinating observation about patriarchal usurpation. Warrior Athena, loyal daughter of Zeus, denies she has a mother, denies any relationship to Metis, but through an accomplice kills Medusa and thereafter wears the image of that monster's severed snake-haired head like a trophy on her armor-breastplate. It is telling, Keller writes, that "the name Medusa, a feminine form for *ruler*, stems from the same Sanskrit root *medha* meaning 'wisdom,' from which comes the Greek *metis*, 'prudent counsel.' . . . Metis and Medusa are one."

   Athena does more than deny her female lineage to please her father; she—the patriarchs' goddess of knowledge and military strategy—commits matricide. But then Athena is the judge who exonerated Orestes for killing his mother in Aeschylus's *Oresteia*. So Zeus kills Athena's mother, Metis, Goddess of Dark Wisdom, and then Athena kills the Wise Old Crone, the many-snaked one, the age-old symbol of Female Wisdom. And it is all forgivable if those deaths advance the cause of the father-archy. *From a Broken Web*, 57.

20. Evans, *The God of Ecstasy*, 42.

21. James, *The Cult of the Mother Goddess*, 145.

22. W. K. C. Guthrie, *The Greeks and Their Gods* (Boston: Beacon Press, 1950), 95, 99. I found this information in Jean Graybeal, *Language and the Feminine in Nietzsche and Heidegger* (Bloomington, Ind.: Indiana University Press, 1990), 164–165 n.7.

23. Several commentators suggest that while the matristic people of the central mainland endured a *harsh conquering* experience at the hands of the horse-riding worshipers of the sky-god, the coming of the new religion to the island of Samos most likely was a *benevolent arrival* of the northern tribes by sea, followed by an amicable, happy blending of new male arrivals with local women. The different versions of Hera's myths would indicate different histories of the tellers, different beginnings to the colonization of the agrarian peoples by the northerners.

24. Although the books that record classical Greek history and art tend to claim the highest standards of civilization for that era, that version of events is being demolished these days. One historian, Eva C. Keuls, writes, "In the case of a society dominated by men who sequester their wives and daughters, denigrate the female role in reproduction, erect monuments to the male genitalia, have sex with the sons of their peers, sponsor public whorehouses, create a mythology of rape, and engage in rampant saber-rattling, it is not inappropriate to refer to a reign of the phallus. Classical Athens was such a society." *The Reign of the Phallus* (Berkeley and Los Angeles: University of California Press, 1993), 1.

   Martin Bernal is another scholar who is reanalyzing the scholarship that has claimed ancient Aryan, patriarchal Greece to be the primary origin of all highly civilized culture. Bernal's own scholarship shows this version of history to be biased, deliberately fabricated by the racism of European scholars over many centuries. See *Black Athena: The Afroasiatic Roots of Classical Civilization, Volume 1, The Fabrication of Ancient Greece 1785–1985* (New Brunswick, N.J.: Rutgers University Press, 1987).

25. An interesting remnant of early matristic Spartan culture turns up in this story. It was not necessarily Helen's beauty that motivated her husband, Menaleus, to go as far away as Troy to get her back. Sparta was an ancient Goddess-revering mother-right nation-state, and so a man could rule there *only* by being chosen king by the queen—by Helen, in this case, whose inheritance rights, handed down to her from her mother, included giving the kingship to whomever she pleased by means of the rite of *hieros gamos*. Menaleus would have been keenly aware that as long as Helen cohabited with Paris, that Trojan prince was legally the proper king of Sparta. So it is likely that King Menaleus of Sparta was fighting less for his wife herself than for the throne of Sparta, which he could retain only if he retrieved Helen and her sexual favors.

26. Historically, the heroes of *The Iliad* are Hera's men, but the two words are also etymologically related. "The basic sense of both *Hera* and *hero*" [from Gr. heros] is "protector." Eric Partridge, *Origins: A Short Etymological Dictionary of Modern English* (New York: Greenwich House, 1983), 287.

27. Although the Great Mother Goddess is frequently pictured and storied with one or more lions, Maarten Vermaseren and other scholars now say that the two great felines at Mycenae are lionesses. As anyone can see, they have no manes. See Vermaseren, *Cybele and Attis: The Myth and Cult*, trans. by A. M. H. Lemmers (London: Thames and Hudson, 1977), 14.

   After dealing with ancient artifacts for a while one will notice that the first assumption an anthropologist or historian usually makes about an important find is that it is male or had something to do with a man's life. The deities may all obviously have breasts, as a line of them do in a beautiful Egyptian pyramid artifact now in Cincinnati, yet the caption underneath reads: "Gods."

28. Quite likely the Goddess-as-Pillar represents Her in an early version of World Tree, an important fact,

VIRGIN
Mother ·
CRONE

Notes to pages 36–39

for as Tree She has the capacity to hold together all three realms—heaven, earth, and the underworld—into Oneness. The use of columns around typical Greek temples stems from the age-old practice in pre-history of representing the Goddess-as-Tree as a simple, unadorned wooden or stone pillar or column. The Goddess can be represented by one or by many columns, for She is simultaneously the One-and-the-Many, both the single tree and the grove or forest.

Caryatids are columns that are unambiguously carved into women's bodies, for example, those that border the porch of the Erechthyon, a temple on the Acropolis in Athens (see illustration 96 in Chapter 10). The capitals of caryatid columns sometimes explicitly show tree tops, fronds, or branches. Obviously, the distinctive, leafy design atop Corinthian columns depicts tree foliage.

29. Keller, *From a Broken Web*, 26, 55.

30. This marble frieze is now in the British Museum.

Another fierce struggle by women is depicted in the marble frieze from the Temple of Zeus at Olympia. Here Lapithan women and men are seen fighting the centaurs, creatures who have four-legged horse bodies but at their broad necks spring men's bodies from the hips up. It is interesting that when Cortez and his men came on horseback to conquer the Aztecs, those incredulous, overpowered Native Americans thought at first that the horse and man were one animal. It seems entirely understandable to me that the Lapithan women would also perceive man and horse as one brutal animal and that mythic stories of raping centaurs—horse-men—proliferated over time, because pre-Greek agrarian people *had never ridden horses* and their entire region was overrun for hundreds of years by invaders on horseback from the north who raped and pillaged as they went.

31. Jean Shinoda Bolen, *Goddesses in Everywoman*, 132–167, especially 146.

32. Sylvia Brinton Perera, *Descent to the Goddess: A Way of Initiation for Women* (Toronto, Ontario: Inner City Books, 1981), 11, 29–30, 39–40, 51–54.

33. Jean Baker Miller, *Toward a New Psychology of Women* (Boston: Beacon Press, 1986), throughout.

34. *Webster's First New Intergalactic Wickedary of the English Language,* Conjured by Mary Daly in cahoots with Jane Caputi (Boston: Beacon Press, 1987), 92–93.

35. Merlin Stone details the coincidence in Indo-European cultures between demotion of the Goddess and women with the demonizing of the Powers of Darkness and the corresponding growth of fear of dark-skinned peoples: Merlin Stone, *Three Thousand Years of Racism* (New York: New Sybylline Books, 1981).

36. One can find this information in many places, including Monica Sjoo and Barbara Mor, *The Great Cosmic Mother*, 21.

37. Ean Begg, *The Cult of the Black Virgin* (London: Routledge & Kegan Paul, Arkana, 1985).

On the main floor of Chartres Cathedral is a Goddess maze—the spiral of Birth-Death-ReBirth—a marker reminding worshipers that underneath that floor is a cave where the Black Mother Goddess Chartres (Car) was revered before Christianity became the state religion on that site.

Every Gothic cathedral in France is built on the site of a Mother Goddess shrine; every Gothic cathedral has a Lady Chapel dedicated to Mary, because the followers of the Mother Goddess were not easy converts to Christianity and had to be mollified by some way of continuing their Virgin Mother Goddess veneration in the new edifice.

38. Daniel F. McCall, "West Africa and the Eurasian Ecumene: Mother Earth, the Great Goddess of West Africa," unpublished manuscript, cited in Mickey Hart, *Drumming at the Edge of Magic* (San Francisco: Harper, 1990), 206–210; Judith Gleason, *Oya: In Praise of the Goddess* (Boston: Shambhala, 1987); and Luisa Teish, *Jambalaya* (San Francisco: Harper & Row, 1985).

39. See Ajit Mookerjee, *Kali: The Feminine Force* (Rochester, Vt.: Destiny Books, 1988); and David R. Kinsley, *The Sword and the Flute: Kali and Krishna, Dark Visions of the Terrible and the Sublime* (Berkeley and Los Angeles: University of California Press, 1975).

40. Paula Gunn Allen, *Grandmothers of the Light: A Medicine Woman's Sourcebook* (Boston: Beacon Press, 1991) and *The Sacred Hoop* (Boston: Beacon Press, 1986); Sheila Moon, *Changing Woman and Her Sisters* (San Francisco: Guild for Psychological Studies, 1984).

41. Resit Ergener, *Anatolia: Land of Mother Goddess* (Ankara, Turkey: Hitit Publication, 1988).

42. Among the many discourses that have been written on the meaning of the Rainbow Snake, anthropologist Chris Knight's is the most meaningful to me, the one that best understands metaphor, symbol, and women's lives in Aboriginal life. Chris Knight, *Blood Relations: Menstruation and the Origins of Culture* (New Haven, Conn.: Yale University Press, 1991), Chapter 13, "The Rainbow Snake," 449–479.

43. *Burnum Burnum's Aboriginal Australia* (North Ryde, Australia: Angus & Robertson, 1988), 168. Details of this discussion also stem from my personal knowledge from visiting the site.

THREE

Always Female, Never Feminine

1. Charlene Spretnak, "Problems with Jungian Uses of Greek Goddess Mythology," in *Anima: The Journal of Human Experience* 6, no. 1 (Fall 1979): 30.

2. This distinction is the subject matter of many feminist (or womanist) theorists today. This theorizing comprises a new discipline within philosophy and social science called Gender Studies. The French feminists Luce Irigaray, Julia Kristeva, and Monique Wittig have written at length on why the word "feminine" gives us a socially constructed model, without touching at all on what a female actually is or might be. Many other philosophers have written on this subject also, too many to list here, but Alison Jaggar, Susan Bordo, and Elizabeth Potter are among them.

3. Emily James Putnam writes in the introduction to her book *The Lady: Studies of Certain Significant Phases of Her History* (New York: G. P. Putnam's Sons, 1921), vii-xx: "Every discussion of the status of woman is complicated by the existence of the lady. . . . Her history is distinct from that of woman. . . . Economically [the lady] is supported by the toil of others . . . [so] her fortunes do not rise and fall with those of women but with those of men. . . . Where he set her, there she stays."

   After reading the chapters in this book about the restrictions imposed on ladies in ancient Greece, ladies in ancient Rome, ladies in the Confederate States of America, and so on throughout history, no woman would ever again want to be treated like a lady and have to suffer the many true deprivations of Self that go with that so-called elevated station. This brilliant, close analysis shows that the perks and homage a lady receives in no way make up for the opportunities and fullness of life she loses when she accepts the appellation.

4. Catherine Keller discusses such "women in waiting" in this fashion: "Kierkegaard perceptively links woman's weakened sense of self to her self-loss in service to others, that is, to her devotion. He recognizes that the traditional feminine devotion is a sin, not a virtue, because it is a form of despair and self-abnegation: 'by devotion (the word literally means giving away) she has lost herself.'" *From a Broken Web*, 12. Keller quotes S. A. Kierkegaard, *The Sickness Unto Death*, trans. by Walter Lowrie (Princeton, N.J.: Princeton University Press, 1968), 183.

5. Chromosomally there are exceptions to a child's being born either male or female. Basic maleness is determined by having one X sex chromosome and one Y sex chromosome. Basic femaleness is determined

by having two X sex chromosomes. But there are people born with only one sex chromosome, an X; some are born with two or more X sex chromosomes (up to seven) along with one Y. These variations—and the other variations that are biological and temperamental but not chromosomal, as in the case of homosexuality—cause social problems *only* when cultural preferences about masculinity and femininity are applied rigidly to all, not allowing for individual variations.

6. David D. Gilmore, *Manhood in the Making: Cultural Concepts of Masculinity* (New Haven, Conn.: Yale University Press, 1990), 11.

7. To get a feeling for yourself about whether anima is a positive notion of womanhood, read a summary of Jung's description in Robert A. Johnson, *She: Understanding Feminine Psychology* (New York: Harper & Row, 1977). Jung did not make up this description of femininity; he merely wrote down the rules that the conventions of his time prescribed for "ladies"—and then wrongly considered its preferences and prescriptions to be the innate, universal, inviolable traits of all females in all times.

   Johnson also perpetuates our tradition's destructive gender constructs of masculinity in *He: Understanding Masculine Psychology* (New York: Harper & Row, 1986). There is an equally offensive summary of traditional, unequal relationships between the sexes in his book *We: Understanding the Psychology of Romantic Love* (San Francisco: Harper, 1985).

8. Naomi Goldenberg, "Jungian Psychology and Religion," Chapter 5 of *Changing of the Gods: Feminism and the End of Traditional Religions* (Boston: Beacon Press, 1979), 46–71.

9. For a whole book on the subject of *femaleness*, not *femininity*, as the basic archetype of womanhood, read Estella Lauter and Carol Rupprecht, eds., *Feminist Archetypal Theory: Interdisciplinary Re-Visions of Jungian Thought* (Knoxville, Tenn.: University of Tennessee Press, 1985).

10. Jane Ellen Harrison, *Epilegomena to the Study of Greek Religion*, 364–367.

11. Jean Shinoda Bolen, *Goddesses in Everywoman*, 20–22. Unfortunately, this extraordinary healer and scholar retains throughout her writing the Jungian dualism that sees the Goddess as divided into two aspects: She is said to have a Good Mother (or positive) side that is in constant opposition to a Terrible Mother (or negative) side.

12. See: Christine Downing, *The Goddess*; Sylvia Brinton Perera, *Descent to the Goddess*; and Ginette Paris, *Pagan Meditations: The Worlds of Aphrodite, Artemis, and Hestia*, trans. by Gwendolyn Moore (Dallas, Tex.: Spring Publications, 1986).

13. Samuel Noah Kramer, *From the Poetry of Sumer,* 27ff.

14. Perera, *Descent to the Goddess,* 12.

15. In an interesting essay on the political implications inherent in our western notion of gardening, Eleanor Perényi writes: "It may come as a surprise that sexism should play any part in horticulture but the more you read of gardening history the more convincing the case for it becomes." This is excerpted from "Woman's Place," a chapter in Eleanor Perényi, *Green Thoughts: A Writer in the Garden* (New York: Random House, 1981). I found it in Bonnie Marranca, ed., *American Garden Writing: Gleanings from Garden Lives Then and Now* (New York: PAJ Publications, 1988), 306–317.

16. A provocative essay examining the origins of this word and its meaning to industrialized peoples today is Jay H. Vest, "Will-of-the-Land: Wilderness Among Early Indo-Europeans," in Dolores LaChapelle, *Sacred Land, Sacred Sex, Rapture of the Deep,* 310–311.

17. Lynn Margulis and Dorion Sagan, *Microcosmos: Four Billion Years of Microbial Evolution* (New York: Summit Books, 1986), 14–15.

18. Robert Augros and George Stanciu, *The New Biology: Discovering the Wisdom in Nature* (Boston and London: Shambhala, 1988), *passim,* but in particular Chapter 4, "Cooperation," 89–129, especially 116–117 and 24–25.

19. Lewis Thomas, "On the Uncertainty of Science," in Phi Beta Kappa *Key Reporter,* no. 6, 1980, 1.

20. Augros and Stanciu, *The New Biology,* 138–139.

21. ibid., 129.

FOUR

Virgin Consciousness

1. In classical times, "The word 'Virgin' described a woman who was free, not at the beck and call of any man. . . . Pindar and *The Iliad* use *parthenos* to mean an unmarried young girl, not necessarily a 'virgin' in the modern sense of the word." Hans Peter Duerr, *Dreamtime: Concerning the Boundary between Wilderness and Civilization,* trans. by Felicitas Goodman (Oxford, England: Basil Blackwell, 1985), 16, 174, n.1.

"Concubines, that is, unmarried women, were called the same [*parthenia* or "virgins"] in Sparta, and their children were designated as *partheniai* [or virgin-born]." C. Seltman, *The Twelve Olympians and Their Guests* (London, 1956), 127.

Accounts of Greek goddesses who were Virgins, meaning "belonging to themselves," can be found in Jean Shinoda Bolen, *Goddesses in Everywoman,* especially 35–130, and M. Esther Harding, *Women's Mysteries* (New York: Harper & Row, 1971).

Primal peoples rarely if ever value abstaining from sexual activity. Most tribal societies permit children to begin to learn to do all the things they will be expected to do well as adults. So as soon as they are interested, youngsters will play at sexual touching just as they play at shooting arrows with bows, at preparing animal hides for leather, at making pots, and so on.

2. I am indebted to Merlin Stone for first putting me in touch with this simple but transforming way of recognizing and honoring my femaleness—that it comes unbidden and without effort.

3. Menarche (men-AR-kee) is a girl's first menstrual period. The word is made up of two Greek words: *men,* meaning "month," and *arche,* meaning "rule of" or "PATTERN of."

These celebrations are most powerful when they do not focus only on "the arrival" of menstrual periods—that theme is too *fait accompli,* too finished and completed for the Virgin. Virgin consciousness is non-goal-oriented, not focused on having arrived at a mature state as if it were an achievement reached at last, once and for all. Menarche rituals appropriately have Potential and Expectation as their theme: flowing, budding, unfolding, Mystery-full gifts that are on the way and that will keep arriving over many years to come. . . .

4. What I describe here as "the essence of maidenhood"—a lifeway of *allowing, being, and becoming*—is essentially the Way of Taoism, which was the Goddess-Nature religion of Neolithic China. See Ellen Marie Chen, "Tao as the Great Mother and the Influence of Motherly Love in the Shaping of Chinese Philosophy" in *History of Religions* 14, no. 1 (1974–1975): 51–63, and Joseph Needham, *Science and Civilization in China,* vol. 2 (Cambridge, England: Cambridge University Press, 1961), Chapter 10 on Taoism, 33–164.

There are several books that offer relatively simple but good explanations of Taoism. I recommend most highly: Greg Johanson and Ron Kurtz, *Grace Unfolding* (New York: Bell Tower, 1991) and Dolores LaChapelle, *Sacred Land, Sacred Sex, Rapture of the Deep.* And of course, *The Way of Life According to Lao Tzu* itself; but be careful which translation you use. Some can be very dualistic and patriarchal, the translator reading into the original what he expects and wants to find. Stephen Mitchell's translation is good; he uses both female and male pronouns for the Sage, which honors the original intent of the Tao more than most other translations do. *Tao Te Ching* (New York: Harper Perennial, 1991).

5. Catherine Keller, *From a Broken Web,* 83.

6. Barbara Walker, *The Woman's Encyclopedia of Myths and Secrets,* under "Eve," 289.

7. Gia-fu Feng and Jane English, trans., *Tao-te Ching* (New York; Vintage Books, 1989), Chapter 8.

8. Making a distinction between what is natural and what is unnatural bothers many great minds. And it is proper that all the best thinkers concern themselves with this distinction, because Earth is in great peril today. We must all keep in mind, however, that there is no clear line between nature and culture. There may be no demarcation at all between "good and natural" and "good technology." Birds use technology to make their nests, but one wouldn't say they "go against nature." Beavers make dams, but do they go against nature by stopping the flow of a stream? To me, Nature would be accurately described not as the opposite-of-culture, but as full-of-culture. Nature is lots of things working together in communities—the water and wind work together to modify stone mountains to make sand, thereby modifying Nature . . . and so forth. Animal, bird, and fish communities abound in Nature, and many of these species modify their home-place considerably. Very small—even microscopic—creatures have built the imposing Great Barrier Reef! Humans can modify without harm, and humans can modify in very harmful ways. It is not the modification that is wrong, it is the harm that is wrong.

   To my way of perceiving this issue, it is one that must be constantly measured and considered. Let's remember Aristotle's advice when we try to draw our conclusions: "It is the mark of an educated person to expect no more exactitude in the subject matter than the nature of the subject matter itself allows" (from *Nicomachean Ethics*). When one is doing mathematical problems, one must be very precise. When one is dealing with Nature-as-culture there are no precise answers or distinctions. One can aspire to being relatively certain of one's values and of the meaning Nature has in one's scheme of things, but then one proceeds to evaluate or experience one case or one instance at a time.

9. Many details on the carved vulvas of pre-history are shown and explained exactingly by Alexander Marshack in his heavily illustrated book *The Roots of Civilization.*

10. Among other sources: Elise Boulding, *The Underside of History* (Boulder, Colo.: Westview Press, 1976); and Elizabeth Fisher, *Woman's Creation: Sexual Evolution and the Shaping of Society* (New York: McGraw-Hill, 1979).

    Of interest from Fisher's book is this passage: "Cave art shows that the woman was more important than the male [in the formation of human culture] and that her body was connected with fullness and plenty. . . . Aggressive syndromes . . . that are evidence for male domination . . . [only] appear later in the human story," 152.

11. Evelyn Reed, *Women's Evolution from Matriarchal Clan to Patriarchal Family* (New York: Pathfinder Press, 1975), 48. This quote also appears in Grace Shinell, "Women's Collective Spirit," in Charlene Spretnak, ed., *The Politics of Women's Spirituality,* 513.

12. Only when family crop-farming and horticulture developed into big business were cultivation efforts called agriculture. And only then did men step in and take it over from its originators and reassign them— the women—*only* to the home.

13. A few of the many books that speak about women as the major creators of human culture are: Fisher, *Woman's Creation;* Marilyn French, *Beyond Power: Of Women, Men, and Morals* (New York: Summit Books, 1985); Chris Knight, *Blood Relations;* and William Irwin Thompson, *The Time Falling Bodies Take to Light.*

14. Linguist-anthropologist Roger W. Wescott writes that the name Easter, as well as the archetypal "goddess of dawn and springtime" that the name identifies, both derive from far back in pre-history. The name has a long continuity "in the sacred terminology of the ancestral Indo-Europeans." Although Easter comes to us directly through Old English, the root word (its proto–Indo-European reconstructed form being [a]usos) can be traced through many diverse cultures and languages, including Sanskrit, Avestic, and Greek. See "Proto-Aryan Hieronyms: Names of the Sacred in Reconstructed Indo-European" from *Names of the Sacred,* (Pittsburgh, Pa.: University of Pittsburgh Press, 1986) vol. 2, no. 1. (This information is from a reprinted version of the article that the author gave me; Easter appears on page 2 and in note 5.)

15. Tiamat was originally Great Cosmic Mother Sea Serpent, the Creatrix Who was Herself the agent of creation, but whose myth evolved until She was demoted, eventually overthrown as Creating One, by Her son, the Hero Marduk, who killed Her and cut Her Body into pieces out of which *he* created the world, mythically robbing Her of her initiatory, Self-creating powers. Historically, at the same time, women were being robbed of their powers of self-naming, of self-determination, of belonging to themselves. Tiamat's name remains in the Bible as Tehom, the Darkness and the Deep. See Keller, *From a Broken Web,* 73, 82.

16. Marija Gimbutas, *The Goddesses and Gods of Old Europe,* 149–150.

17. Knight, *Blood Relations,* 480–483, 506–508.

18. Deena Metzger, *The Woman Who Slept with Men to Take the War out of Them* (Berkeley, Calif.: Wingbow Press, 1983).

VIRGIN
Mother ·
CRONE

Notes to pages 60–114

19. Miriam Robbins Dexter explains this "tripartite" theory of French mythologist George Dumézil in *Whence the Goddesses: A Source Book* (New York and London: Teachers College Press, 1990), 35 ff.

20. ibid., 35.

21. ibid., 30. Dexter's italics.

22. ibid., 31.

23. Morris Berman, *Coming to Our Senses* (New York: Simon and Schuster, 1989), 71. Also see Riane Eisler, *The Chalice and the Blade*; French, *Beyond Power*; Marija Gimbutas, *The Civilization of the Goddess*; Marvin Harris, *Our Kind*; Calvin Luther Martin, *In the Spirit of the Earth*; and any other books in the reading list in this volume that explain Paleolithic gathering-hunting societies.

24. This information about the recent advent of war and the archetype of warrior—even of spiritual warriors!—can be found in many places: Eisler, *The Chalice and the Blade*; Gimbutas, *The Civilization of the Goddess*; and Martin, *In the Spirit of the Earth*. A summary of much of the scholarly data on this can be found in Frederick Turner, *Beyond Geography*.

    If a non-hostile archetype is desirous, then the word "warrior," which has *war* as part of its very being—even when modified by the sweetness of the word "spiritual"—would seem to be an inappropriate word to use as a guide and Model.

FIVE

The Myth of Creation

1. *Ohm* or *Om* is a mantra, actually a *matrikamantra*, or the Mother of Mantras, because it is the sound made by Kali Ma, the most ancient Hindu Mother Creatrix, as She gave birth to the universe. *Om* is an "invocation of Her own pregnant belly," a sound any woman might make as she gives birth.

    See Barbara Walker, *The Woman's Encyclopedia of Myths and Secrets,* under the listings "Kali Ma," "Mantra," and "Om."

    For Hindus *Om* must be entoned in a precisely correct way. I wish to join in any timeless woman-honoring tradition but do not wish to be limited to one usage. I use the word as an opportunity to carry the laughter, sighs, groans, exultation, moans—whatever vocalization is needed to communicate the particular emotional quality of a particular moment in the story. For me it is a sacred vowel, because it affords so much opportunity and potential for sharing with others.

    Om has a symbolic shape too: perfectly round and whole. And when sounded, the throat and breathing tubes are open, the whole upper body is open, the mouth round. Her breath, your breath, our breath is the same breath, so *Ohm* can be a vehicle of One-ness, of the Much-at-Once.

    Have fun with it. Play with the sound, let the air of the breath make the sound as it comes in as well as when it goes out; let it be vocal and aspirate, that is, sometimes use the voice box, but sometimes let a sound be made only with air coming in without voice. Put in one or two *Oms* whenever you feel the need of them to express your own unique interpretation.

2. This is usually sung, "Oh, Tannenbaum," but "tannen" is the male fir tree. The female fir tree is "*tanna*-baum." Since this is a song that comes out of Teutonic pre-history, times when the Celts had a Mother Goddess and trees were sacred, I sing it this way to harken back and honor Her.

    I have also borrowed or adapted other familiar "Christmas carols" that were once, many centuries ago, age-old Pagan songs of winter, like "The Holly and the Ivy" and "Deck the Halls." Traditions like bringing in the evergreen tree, lighting the Yule log, making wreaths of evergreens, and so forth are also age-old festive Pagan rites. "Carol" is one of the words we get from the Goddess Car, Kar, or Ker of the Carians, a "carol" being a song sung to honor Car (in France Her name became Chartres). The Greek word *kardia* means "heart"; the "germ or core of life in the wheat" was the Goddess *Kore,* from which we get "core" and Latin *cor* for "heart."

    The religion of the Goddess Car (or Kore) also gives us the words "charm," and "carmen"; Our Lady of Chartres is one of the Black Madonnas, and Mount Carmel of Israel is named for Her. Kore is not just the Greek's daughter of Mother Demeter, She is the daughter of the pre-Islamic Arabian Mother Goddess Ah-Lat, and Their Mother-Daughter "Sacred Teachings" give us the "Koran" and "Allah" along with an archetypal reversal from Goddess sensibility into a patriarchal sensibility. See Resit Ergener, *Anatolia*, 50, 52, 96.

    Also see Walker, *The Woman's Encyclopedia of Myths and Secrets,* under "Koran" and "Kore." Joseph Campbell and E. A. Wallis Budge are sources for this information also.

    When one becomes familiar with pre-Christian European Goddess myths and rituals, one begins to see that the whole Christian calendar is based on the natural cycle of the seasons and ancient Pagan customs that have commemorated the Cycle of the Year from time immemorial. This is most evident in Christmas customs, which so obviously are only slight modifications of Pagan Winter Solstice symbols and rituals, although few people seem to be cognizant of this fact. The theme of Marian Zimmer Bradley's popular novel *The Mists of Avalon* is the slow confiscation of the Goddess religion by Christianity.

3. This is one of Isis's titles according to Sir E. A. Budge

in *Dwellers on the Nile* (New York: Dover, 1977), 265. In *Larousse Encyclopedia of Mythology* (London: Hamlyn Publishing Group, 1968), 37, one finds that these words were carved over the entrance to Neith-Isis's temple at Sais. This information can also be found in Budge's *Gods of the Egyptians* (New York: Dover, 1969), vol. 1, 93, 213–214, 459, 463; and in Gaston Maspero's *Popular Stories of Ancient Egypt* (New York: University Books, 1967), 286–287.

And of course I learned about it first in Walker, *The Woman's Encyclopedia of Myths and Secrets*, under various entries.

SIX

Mother Consciousness

1. The recent work of many therapists and scholars indicates that as long as *only* women do the nurturing, care-taking, parenting work that we call "mothering," women will be regarded with the benign contempt habitually given to lowly menial-service providers, to all excrement-handling others. It has become clear that assigning "mothering" only to females in our system is one cause of the inequality we suffer between the sexes, one structural reason for the common occurrence of dysfunction in our families. As our literature and lives attest, care-taker women are loved and tolerated, but at the same time belittled and despised by those in power—who are their own sons and husbands.

Three important, pioneering works on this aspect of sexism are: Nancy Chodorow, *The Reproduction of Mothering: Psychoanalysis and the Sociology of Gender* (Berkeley and Los Angeles: University of California Press, 1978); Dorothy Dinnerstein, *The Mermaid and the Minotaur: Sexual Arrangements and Human Nature* (New York: Harper & Row, 1977); and Carol Gilligan, *In a Different Voice: Psychological Theory and Women's Development* (Cambridge, Mass.: Harvard University Press, 1982).

2. R. L. Cann, M. Stoneking, and A. C. Wilson, "Mitochondrial DNA and Human Evolution" in *Nature* 325 (1987): 31–36.

My son, Gil Wilshire, M.D., whose specialty is reproductive endocrinology, has helped me understand at least the basics of this phenomenon. I am also grateful to Sharon Flynn for sharing her research with me.

Let me summarize in slightly greater detail for those who are interested. Twenty-three pairs of chromosomal DNA—half derived from her father and half from her mother—reside on a special scaffolding in the nucleus—or yolk—of a woman's eggs. When a child is conceived, these chromosome pairs will be halved, the woman's offspring receiving only half of her chromosomal DNA. On the other hand, mitochondria, with their own special kind of bacterial-type DNA, are carried in the cytoplasm, the material which surrounds the nucleus (or yolk) of the egg (and which might roughly be called "the white") and are *passed on whole to offspring, unmodified by any male contributor.* This non-yolk or non-nuclear contribution of the egg is called our "cytoplasmic inheritance" and comes only from our mothers. This cytoplasmic material contributes *all* the extra-nuclear machinery—that is, all the miniature organization—of every cell in all human bodies. The cells of a woman's sons, as well as the cells of her daughters, require this extra-nuclear DNA to function, but males do not have the means to pass it on. Therefore, essentially, all the cellular machinery in our bodies is inherited from our mothers, coming from the cytoplasmic nourishment, from the mitochondrial material that is passed on whole *to* all of a woman's children but which is passed on only *by* her daughters.

Mitochondrial DNA happens to be pared down to a small, basic amount—the minimum needed to control its life-maintaining functions. Therefore, almost any change or mutation can be lethal. As a result, this kind of DNA has changed very little within our species—generation after generation—and very little even *between species.*

3. Luce Irigaray, *This Sex Which Is Not One*, trans. by Catherine Porter (Ithaca, N.Y.: Cornell University Press, 1985).

4. Carl Kerenyi, *Eleusis*, xxxi. Italics mine.

5. A thorough discussion of this concept in primal thought PATTERNS can be found in Jean Gebser, *The Ever-Present Origin*, trans. by Noel Barstad with Algis Mickunas (Athens, Ohio: Ohio University Press, 1985).

6. The Eternal present is not the same as immortality. See the discussion in Chapter 9, "Crone Consciousness," of why the concept of immortality has no place in the Goddess Model.

7. Gary Snyder, *The Old Ways* (San Francisco, Calif.: City Lights Books, 1977), 38.

Matristic social PATTERNS and the Inner Wisdom tradition can also be found in the ancient and recent Ways of the natives of Hawaii and many Polynesian islands, in the ancient and recent Ways of many indigenous peoples of North America like the Hopi and Pueblo peoples, in Paleolithic and Neolithic Europe and Asia from Ireland in the West to Siberia in the East, from Scandinavia in the North to the islands of the Mediterranean in the South. Basic elements of this Wisdom tradition are also found all through the Middle East at the lowest level of archaeological digs, in pre-dynastic Egypt, Africa (especially well-evidenced among the Yoruba people of Nigeria), in pre-Islamic Arabia, in pre-Vedic Asia, as well as places in contemporary India still.

See Joseph Needham, *Science and Civilization in China*, vol. 2, 33–164.

8. I am deeply indebted to the scholarship and perceptions of Grace Shinnell. She briefly but succinctly elucidates what early women's lives and ways were like in her article "Women's Collective Spirit," in Charlene Spretnak, ed., *The Politics of Women's Spirituality*, 514.

9. Quoted and called "The Ancient Way" by Kendrick Frazier in *People of Chaco: A Canyon and Its Culture* (New York: W. W. Norton, 1986), 15.

10. It is said that we (of the species Cro-Magnon or *homo sapiens sapiens*) survived and thrived while Neanderthal, our close cousins, died out, because our kind practiced closer, more cooperative, more resourceful clan kinship PATTERNS. These close bonds and shared responsibilities—helping one another systematically and regularly—kept us alive in times of dire consequence when those species whose members remained opportunistic, more on their own, died out. The close kinship ties responsible for our survival were, of course, the cooperative, sharing, mutually supportive *matristic* PATTERNS developed and kept in good working order by our foremothers.

Among other sources for this information, see: Chris Knight, *Blood Relations*.

11. "I reject the assumption that civilization refers only to androcratic warrior societies," asserts Marija Gimbutas. The "generative basis" of a civilization lies in the substantive quality of life valued and enjoyed by all its citizens, which includes a balance of powers between the sexes, she says, concluding: "It is a gross misunderstanding to imagine warfare as endemic to the human condition." Marija Gimbutas, *The Civilization of the Goddess*, viii.

12. One finds a rich discussion of many of the ways in which women typically represent non-linear time—for example, cyclical or spiraling time and the enduring or "Eternal Present"—in: Dorothy Emmet, *The Passage of Nature* (Philadelphia: Temple University Press, 1991); and Frieda Johles Forman with Caoran Sowton, eds., *Taking Our Time: Feminist Perspectives on Temporality* (Oxford and New York: Pergamon Press, 1989).

Mary Morse summarizes medical research on the emotional and health advantages of understanding and honoring the cyclicalness of our male and female lives in "We've Got Rhythm: Humans' Internal Body Clocks Keep Track of Health and Happiness," in *The Utne Reader*, September/October 1991, pp. 24–26.

13. Catherine Keller writes beautifully and with impeccable scholarship about the making of a Self in *From a Broken Web*—demonstrating how our patriarchal culture keeps telling us we become a Self by separating from everyone else, especially from our mothers. She shows that this is a fallacious model for Selfhood, that the process actually happens another way: *by adding on*. By constantly throughout life adding onto the basic core of ourself little bits or big hunks of others we become our fullest, richest selves.

Another feminist scholar, the sociologist Suzanna D. Walters, also decries the false "ideology" that claims separation from mother is normal or desirable for sons or daughters. This dogma, she writes, robs us all of a wonderful closeness, of friendship, of opportunities for bonding that add strength and invaluable resources to our lives: Suzanna D. Walters, *Lives Together, Worlds Apart: Mother and Daughter in Popular Culture* (Berkeley and Los Angeles: University of California Press, 1992).

14. In *Themis* Jane Ellen Harrison cites the names variously by themselves but also as Pandora-Anesidora (295) as well as Demeter Anesidora. On hearing Pandora called "she of the pithos," (295) one immediately suspects a lack of goodwill in the archetypal reversal that this Goddess underwent in the overthrow of early matristic myth-culture and its transmogrification into patriarchal myth-culture. From being Mother Earth, the boundless Vessel of All Creation, the Giver of All Good Things whose seed and oil treasures were stored in large underground clay vessels shaped like wombs or teardrops (the *pithos*), Pandora became a naughty girl who unleashed all kinds of mayhem on the world from a small square box. If nothing else, one cannot consider the translation of *pithos* into "square box" to be an innocent mistake.

15. Paula Gunn Allen, *Grandmothers of the Light*, xiv.

16. Grace Shinell, "Women's Collective Spirit," in Charlene Spretnak, ed., *Politics of Women's Spirituality*, 521.

17. ibid., 521, 522.

18. ibid., 523, 524.

19. Elise Boulding, *The Underside of History*, 246. Shinnell has a note on page 528 in *Politics of Women's Spirituality* that includes this interesting information: "According to myth, Theseus observed Cretan women doing the *Geranos*, or crane dance; . . . flocks of cranes actually perform a circling dance, the outer ring moving to the right, the core group to the left."

20. Marija Gimbutas, *The Language of the Goddess*, 60–67, *passim*.

21. This wording comes from a suggestion I first heard from Kristina Berggren, a scholar of Etruscan and Minoan Goddess imagery and culture. In describing early Artemis-like images in which the Divine Female holds up a bird in either hand, Berggren writes that She seems to exclaim: "I am these!" Berggren's research on these figures appeared in *Journal of Prehistoric Religion 5* (1991), published in Sweden and difficult to obtain in America.

22. Yahweh is said to have "nursed" Israel from his "breast," and indeed his name, El Shaddai, literally translates as "he, the breasted one." But it should be noted that he fed *only* his own people while calling for the obliteration of other peoples (in Deuteronomy), so he cannot count as a universal model of nurturance and comfort.

23. Annette Hamilton, *Nature and Nurture: Aboriginal Child-Rearing in North-Central Arnhem Land* (Canberra, Australia: Australian Institute of Aboriginal Studies, 1981), 15. This book specifically describes the Anbarra society of Australia, but it seems also to characterize all gathering cultures I have studied.

24. I first heard about gathering societies nursing their children into their fourth and fifth years in a lecture given by Ashley Montagu at Omega Institute. This information can be found in many places, including in Marjorie Shostak, *Nisa, the Life and Words of a !Kung Woman* (Cambridge, Mass.: Harvard University Press, 1981).

25. Hamilton, *Nature and Nurture*, 31, 32.

26. Shostak, *Nisa, The Life and Words of a !Kung Woman*.

27. Hamilton, *Nature and Nurture*, 31, 97–98.

28. Oedipal complexes are absent in gathering-hunting families. On hearing about the long nursing period, contemporary men are liable to think that such a son would be even more attached to his mother, would have even more sexual fantasies about her. But it doesn't happen that way. Perhaps in the west a feeling of possession or ownership of the mother by the father does something to promote the competitive Oedipal phenomenon; perhaps this problem is also abetted by the feeling a child gets that he is owned and some helplessness results that fosters dependency.

In order to understand the lack of the Oedipal syndrome among matristic sons, it is useful to factor into the equation psychiatrist Martha Welch's research into the emotional stability that results in children *and* in their mothers from protracted holding: Martha Welch, *Holding Time: The Breakthrough Program for Happy Mothers and Loving, Self-Confident Children Without Tantrums, Tugs-of War, or Sibling Rivalry* (New York: Simon & Schuster, 1988).

29. This phenomenon is reported by many anthropologists, including Shostak in *Nisa, the Life and Words of a !Kung Woman.*

30. Nor Hall's conclusion in this last sentence was delivered in a talk at Rowe Conference Center and in personal correspondence with me. But see also Nor Hall and Warren Dawson, *Broodmales: A Psychological Essay on Men in Childbirth—Introducing "The Custom of Couvade"* (Dallas, Tex.: Spring Publications, 1989).

Hall's conclusion that male initiation has long been a secret ceremony in which men ritually become like women is bolstered by the widespread practice of "male menstruation" or sub-incision, in which male penises are lifted and given a vertical surface wound that produces "genital bleeding" and which is encouraged to heal in an open scar that resembles a vulva. The scar can be opened again when another menstrual bleeding is desired; that is, when men too want some of the *blood power* and *blood magic* that women are seen to have a monopoly on—unless men perform this ritual. This information is available in many places; see: G. Gillison, "Images of Nature in Gimi Thought," in C. P. MacCormack and M. Strathern, eds., *Nature, Culture and Gender* (Cambridge, England: Cambridge University Press, 1980), 143–173; I. A. Hogbin, *The Island of Menstruating Men* (Scranton, London & Toronto: Chandler, 1970), a study of Wogeo Islanders; and Knight, *Blood Relations*, 428–435 and her bibliography.

It seems relevant to mention here Elinor Gadon's observation that the word "ritual" actually comes from *rtu*, the Sanskrit word for menses, which is evidence that the first rituals of any kind were women's monthly blood-flows. Elinor Gadon, *The Once and Future Goddess*, 2.

31. Robert Lawlor, *Earth Honoring: The New Male Sexuality* (Rochester, Vt.: Park Street Press, 1989), 27.

32. Sylvia Brinton Perera, *Descent to the Goddess*, 13–14.

33. Kristina Berggren, scholar of Neolithic Etruscan and Minoan symbolism, explains in a personal communication to me that nets or woven patches are womb symbols or signs of new life or of transformation, because nettles, flax, wool, and the likes are transformed by spinning and weaving from their natural state into another state, creating a new form, new life, as a mother's womb changes her body's ingredients into another body, another life form.

Marija Gimbutas has labeled woven patches or net motifs as womb symbols for decades. See her rich explanation in Chapter 10, "Net Motif," in her *Language of the Goddess*, 81–87.

VIRGIN
Mother . . . .
CRONE

Notes to pages 134–140

SEVEN

Attributes of Fullness

1. Samuel Noah Kramer, *From the Poetry of Sumer.* This hymn has been made somewhat more accessible in Diane Wolkstein's collaboration with Samuel Noah Kramer, *Inanna, Queen of Heaven and Earth: Her Stories and Hymns from Sumer.*

2. Although this poem describes the rites of Inanna in a wholesome, non-objectifying way, Inanna was a reduced form of the Great Goddess in the pantheon of a patriarchal state. But it was early patriarchy, and obviously, everything about the Great Goddess had not been irretrievably lost.

   The use of others—especially women—as sex objects is new in the course of human events. The objectification of others began with the first experiences of private property: the development of pastoralism and animal husbandry around 9000 B.C.E. It expanded when a settled agrarian community's crops were only available part of the year and they were forced to maintain a surplus for consumption at a later time. The evolution from males' owning animals, to owning land, to owning wives, children, and slaves is traced by historian Gerda Lerner, *The Creation of Patriarchy* (New York: Oxford University Press, 1986), 50ff.

3. One source that details quite a few such celebrations is Hans Peter Duerr, *Dreamtime*, 24–35.

   Celebrations that equated the fecundity of the fields with female sexuality, menses blood, and specific rituals continued in Europe through medieval times. For details of folk festivals that involved young women's dancing and singing lusty songs as they circled the fields to ensure their own and the fields' fertility see Pamela Berger, *The Goddess Obscured*, especially 78–81.

   Note, of course, that while women's sexual acts and nature's fecundity were experienced as having a correspondence, women's sexuality was not limited to making themselves and the fields fecund, and women's importance to themselves and society in matristic times was *not limited to their sexuality and fecundity*!

4. For a short history of the ecstatic drumming cults of the Great Mother—Kybele and others—that were repressed—actually forbidden—by patriarchy by classical times, read Mickey Hart, *Drumming at the Edge of Magic*, 206–210.

   For detailed archaeological "evidence of the intimate relation between the drum and the Goddess" see Marija Gimbutas, *The Language of the Goddess*, 71–73; also Maarten J. Vermaseren, *Cybele and Attis, passim.*

5. Arthur Evans, *The God of Ecstasy*, 72–74, *passim.*

6. Grace Shinell, "Women's Collective Spirit," in Charlene Spretnak, ed., *Politics of Women's Spirituality*, 515.

7. Arthur Evans, *The God of Ecstasy*, 73, quoting Claude Calame, *Les choeurs des jeunes filles en Grèce archaïque*, 1977.

8. This quotation is from an untitled book in progress by Betty Meador about the Sumerian high priestess Enheduanna, who wrote poetry to Inanna around 2300 B.C.E. and was the first writer who signed a piece of literature.

9. Mircea Eliade, *A History of Religious Ideas*, vol. 1 (Chicago: University of Chicago Press, 1978), 23.

10. Among the many studies written on the subject of the Goddess as pillar, column, and tree is an often-cited article by Arthur J. Evans, "Mycenean Tree and Pillar Cult," in *Journal of Hellenic Studies* (London: Richard Clay and Sons, 1901), 99–204.

11. Mary B. Kelly, *Goddess Embroideries of Eastern Europe* (Winona, Minn.: Northland Press, 1989), 55–56. Here Mary Kelly is summarizing the documentation of art historian Douglas Fraser in his article "The Heraldic Woman: A Study in Diffusion" in *The Many Faces of Primitive Art* (Englewood Cliffs, N.J.: Prentice Hall, 1966).

12. ibid., 67–68.

13. ibid., 51–68, *passim.*

14. Thomas L. Markey, "The Language of Stonehenge," in *LSA Magazine,* vol. 10, #3, a publication of the University of Michigan, spring 1987, p. 8. In discussing the non–Indo-European origins of the word for apple, Markey is drawing on the research and insights of the linguist Eric Hamp. Some of Hamp's findings on this intriguing subject can be found in a letter entitled "Big Apple" in *Comments on Etymology* 18, no. 5 (Feb. 1989): 9–10. And see "The Pre-Indo-European Language of Northern (Central) Europe" in *When Worlds Collide: Indo-Europeans and Pre-Indo-Europeans, the Bellagio Papers*, eds. T. L. Markey and John A. C. Greppin (Ann Arbor, Mich.: Karona, 1990), 291–305.

15. I used to think that "the cow jumped over the moon" was a fanciful, ridiculous juxtaposition, but as I learn about the Goddess Hathor as Mother Cow, Hathor as Mother Goose (Great Bird Goddess who created the universe out of Her Golden Egg), and Hera as the Great White Cow, Hera as Goddess of Women-who-cycle-with-the-Moon, I feel that the association between moon and cow in this traditional "Mother Goose" rhyme is likely a prehistoric one, that it probably had some sacred meaning in the matri-lineal traditions.

16. There are many different attitudes about using the

animal epiphanies of beloved deities as food. Some peoples have taboos that prohibit eating totemic animals, as in India where cows cannot be eaten. But early gathering-hunting peoples daily ate their animal totems, calling them Brothers and Sisters, even Mothers.

Some peoples, like the Goddess-revering Canaanites and Philistines, were prohibited from eating their most revered Sow Goddess except on Holy Days, when they ate and greatly enjoyed pork. Archaeologists no longer equivocate that "pork was part of the diet" of the Philistines. At Ekron, a recently excavated site in Israel, several "strata from the twelfth century B.C.[E.] contain a profusion of pig bones." So pork was not at all unhealthy or harmful to eat in Biblical times. See Sharon Begley, "The Hunt for a Lost Holy Past—Archaeologists Search for Biblical History," in *Newsweek*, June 22, 1987, p. 60.

17. Kerenyi, *Zeus and Hera*, 139.
18. Thorkild Jacobsen, *The Treasures of Darkness*, 6, 75ff.
19. Gimbutas, *Language of the Goddess,* 134.
20. ibid., 318.

EIGHT

The Myth of the Triple Goddess

1. Some people think that "my sweet honey man" must be a modernism that I put into this song, but no, the words are right there in the original Sumerian Hymn to Inanna recorded around 1900 B.C.E., as translated from that ancient language by Samuel Noah Kramer. The text is published and commented on in two of his books: *From the Poetry of Sumer* and *The Sacred Marriage Rite* (Bloomington, Ind.: University of Indiana Press, 1969).
2. The Rose Window is a year sign, standing for the sun's continuous cycling through the seasons. This variation of the once-sacred swastika says "the Wheel is ever turning." The four seasonal cusps that divide the year into four equal seasons (the two equinoxes and two solstices) are represented by the four cardinal positions on the circumference (top, bottom, left, right) that form a cross when they meet in the center; the four cross-quarter days of the agricultural calendar (that fall halfway between each cusp) form an *X* when they meet in the center. The cross and *X* together form an eight-pointed star, the basic form of all Rose Windows, often called Saint Catherine's Wheel of Fire (because the Fires of Transformation are said to power the constantly transforming Year Wheel). The stages of a woman's life, symbolized by the Triple Goddess, are also a

metaphor for the passage of a year: spring being the Virgin, summer the Mother, fall-winter the Crone.

3. A good book about the history of menstruation with ancient lore, hut rituals, dances, trance journeys, and a listing of many resources is: Luisa Francia, *Dragontime: Magic of Menstruation* (Woodstock, NY: Ash Tree Publishing, 1988). Another is Lara Owen, *Her Blood is Gold: Celebrating the Power of Menstruation* (San Francisco: Harper, 1993).
4. I took these three lines from some poetry I admired. My note says: "From Barbary My Own Ritual," p. 85, n.19. I now cannot relocate it. Obviously this is an incomplete notation—I have recorded no author. If anyone recognizes it, please let me know so I can acknowledge the poet with a proper credit in a reprint.
5. This final speech for Evangelis was inspired by the famous passage in Monique Wittig's novel *Les Guérillères*: "You say you have lost all recollection of it? Remember! . . . I say, remember! Make an effort to remember! . . . And failing that invent!" Monique Wittig, *Les Guérillères* (Boston: Beacon Press, 1985).

NINE

Crone Consciousness

1. One important book on this archetype is Barbara Walker, *The Crone: Woman of Age, Wisdom, and Power* (San Francisco: Harper & Row, 1985).
2. Hans Peter Duerr, *Dreamtime*, 46, 243 n. 14.
3. From a poem called "Warning" by Jenny Joseph, printed in Fleur Adcock, ed., *The Faber Book of 20th Century Women's Poetry* (London: Faber and Faber, 1987), 229.

   I first heard this poem read by Deborah Light in her charming, inimitable way. Deborah has put together a dazzling collection of poetry written by women; she advised me as to where this one was first published.
4. David R. Kinsley, *The Sword and the Flute: Kali and Krishna, Dark Visions of the Terrible and the Sublime* (Berkeley, Calif.: University of California Press, 1975).
5. Calvin Luther Martin, *In the Spirit of the Earth*, 46–47.
6. Duerr, *Dreamtime*, quoted by Dolores LaChapelle in *Sacred Land, Sacred Sex, Rapture of the Deep*, 71.
7. Robert Graves relies on this metaphor for the Goddess of Death in his *The White Goddess*.
8. The idea of rebirth that I describe here—that matter decays and changes from one form into completely different forms without retaining its original form or

Self—is different from the theory that one's disembodied soul is continually reborn in different bodies, allowing the Self, the "I" or ego of each person to continue throughout eternity in different housings. Some theories of rebirth insist that the human soul is always reborn in a human body, because in the Great Chain of Being more lowly creatures have no souls. Other somewhat less hierarchical, less purist theories allow the soul to survive reborn in other animals' bodies, even in the bodies of insects, but they strive to be eventually reborn as privileged humans and then as pure spirit. One thing that all "soul" theories have in common is the ultimate end of all the rebirthing: the desire to arrive eventually at the highest state of existence, that is, to become so "good" that one can leave one's body behind forever and reside eternally—fixed—as spirit. The goal: get rid of matter and change.

9. Personal communications. But see also Monica Sjöö and Barbara Mor, *The Great Cosmic Mother.*

10. In Taoism the concept of *wu* is, according to Ellen Marie Chen, "non-being . . . the most dynamic and fertile life force" while *yu* is "this dark nothingness which is the fountain of all being." Ellen Marie Chen, "Tao as the Great Mother," 52–53.

   To me, "the most dynamic life force" is automatically the core of Being itself, and therefore cannot be "non-being." With apologies to the long tradition of Taoism and its countless wise men, calling Life Force "non-being" sounds like cerebral gobbledegook to me. Unless by "non-being" is meant "not-one-particular-being"; unless it means that the Life Force generates Life in a myriad number of forms while it itself is formless (is not-one-particular-thing).

   If by *yu*, or "dark nothingness," is meant "dark no-one-thing," then *yu* can mean "the fountain of all being." Otherwise, it seems to me that "the fountain of all being," although it may be formless and not-one-thing, is "something very special indeed" and that to call it "nothingness" is unnecessarily vague, even wrong. It denies the Body as the core of human Being; it denies the embodied state as the ultimate, only, and best Way of Being. Since the Great Mother Goddess is the personification of "the Fountain of All Being" in my Model, I have a hard time letting the concept get reduced to "nothingness." Seeking nothingness, emptiness, and non-being as the "highest" or "purest" forms of being strikes me as the ultimate demotion or denial of the Body as sacred. When we live fully as Bodies-in-the-World, meaning will return to us with full force.

   When I hear the Taoist conundrum "emptiness is fullness" and "the life force is non-being" spoken as if these paradoxes were profoundly true rather than profoundly contradictory, I remember my years as a girl in a Roman Catholic convent school when the

nuns and priests explained that the Trinity was so profound a truth that it was not understandable by human beings, that it was a Mystery known only to and by God. I remember briefly wondering to myself how anyone could know enough under those circumstances even to formulate a statement about what the Mystery was and give it the name "Trinity." But I didn't want to appear more ignorant than everybody else, and I feared committing a sin of doubt, so I never formulated the question seriously even to myself—until my blind faith was long gone.

11. Huston Smith writes that in primal religions there is "nothing like the notion of creation *ex nihilo,*" because primal peoples are too immersed in the flow of "a single cosmos," too committed to Being even to consider *nihilo* or non-Being as the ascetic religions of east and west do. *The World's Religions* (San Francisco: Harper, 1991), 377.

12. Leo Steinberg, "The Eye is Part of the Mind," in Joseph Frank, ed., *Modern Essays in English* (Boston: Little, Brown, and Company, 1966), 380.

13. Sylvia Brinton Perera, *Descent to the Goddess,* 37.

14. The Goddess Ishtar (a cognate of Inanna) and Her son Tammuz (a cognate of Damuzi and Adonis) are mentioned frequently in the Hebrew Bible. Tammuz is the name of a month in the Jewish calendar.

15. See Karen Malpede's sensitive discussion of the transforming, renewing power of the single weeping-birthing sound as it was used in the dramatic, matristic ritual forms that antedated ancient Greek theater in her introduction to Karen Malpede, ed., *Women in Theatre: Compassion and Hope* (New York: Drama Book Specialists, 1983).

   This cry—a sound of wholeness from ancient women's traditions—is discussed at greater length in an article I coauthored with Bruce Wilshire, "Theatre and the Retrieval of the Pregnant Goddess as a Paradigm of What is Human," *Performing Arts Journal* 33/34 (June 1989): 22–35.

16. Duerr, *Dreamtime,* 33.

17. Some classical linguists point out that the name Persephone contains the root word "to destroy" as does the name of the hero Perseus, "the Destroyer." Professor Marcia Dobson, classicist at Colorado College, first pointed this out to me.

TEN

The Mysteries of Death and Transformation

1. There are many versions of the Goddess Kybele's name—sometimes spelled Cybele and pronounced with the soft *C,* including her namesake the Sybil,

and sometimes with the hard *K* sound, as in the old Female version of Allah, "Alli-Kubaba," meaning "Kubaba is the Lady [Goddess]." The black meteorite stone in Mecca is the Kaaba, of course—which is too close a similarity to the black meteorite Goddess Kubaba to be accidental. Sili-Kubabat means "[The Goddess] Kubabat is my Protection." All of this information can be found in many places, among them Maarten J. Vermaseren, *Cybele and Attis*, 24. He also gives references and sources.

2. The detailed description of this artifact from the Archive for Research in Archetypal Symbolism at the Jungian Institute in Manhattan helps us understand its symbolism. I summarize here. "Three pair of boldly arching, crescent ibex horns" rise from the nipple at the center of the lid. The entire cover is ringed by a dark circle at the rim. The six angular shapes within the arch of each pair of horns and above the tips of each are abstract frogs.

The description says that such lids are meant to rest rim down, since they were used as covers for libations, that is, sacred offerings of food, placed directly on the ground. As the life-giving and life-sustaining milk of the Earth Mother flows from deep within Her breast, so any produce of the earth that is placed on the earth and covered by this evocative lid would symbolically well up from the earth to fill this breast and thence the Great Breast (Mother Sky), where it would stand ready to fortify and nourish us.

The curved horns of the ibex are a symbol of the moon and the great arch of heaven, beneath which all life is born, flourishes, and dies, each life being one small cycle within the greater, eternal circuit of heaven. The bodies of the ibex, whose forms are unimportant, are subsumed into the dense, whirling center of the cosmos and the nipple from which comes the milk of life)--the flow constantly going in and out. Between the horns are stylized frogs, symbols of the newly awakening life forms which emerge in multitudes from the earth with the first nourishing rains and warmth of spring.

ELEVEN

Male and Female Deities Who Create the Universe

1. Marta Weigle, *Creation and Procreation: Feminist Reflections on Mythologies of Cosmogony and Parturition* (Philadelphia, Pa.: University of Pennsylvania Press, 1989). Publication of the American Folklore Society. From the jacket.
2. Joseph Campbell, *The Inner Reaches of Outer Space: Metaphor as Myth and as Religion* (New York: Alkfred van der Marck, 1986).

3. Among many others who are saying that the Bible's values and its patriarchal deity are not good enough as a Model for us today are: Thomas Berry, *The Dream of the Earth* (San Francisco: Sierra Books, 1989); and Frederick Turner, *Beyond Geography*.

Calvin Luther Martin, writes that the Jewish and Christian tradition is no longer a valid value system, for it is based completely on "Neolithic" needs and perceptions. See Martin, *In the Spirit of the Earth*; William Irwin Thompson, *The Time Falling Bodies Take to Light*; and Robert Lawlor, *Earth Honoring*.

4. Elaine Pagels, *Adam, Eve, and the Serpent* (New York: Random House, 1988), xxviii.

For another statement of this same point read Mary Condren, *The Serpent and the Goddess*, 8–10, but especially 11.

5. Catherine Keller, *From a Broken Web*, 36.
6. ibid.
7. Cultural historian and Roman Catholic priest Thomas Berry discusses at length the ways in which the Christian doctrine of personal salvation contributes greatly to worldwide ecological problems in *Dream of the Earth,* especially his chapter on "Christian Spirituality and the American Experience."

See also Turner, *Beyond Geography*.

8. For a more thorough discussion of dualisms and the gendered prejudices that are innate to them, see my article, "The Uses of Myth, Image, and the Female Body in Re-Visioning Knowledge," in Allison Jaggar and Susan Bordo, eds., *Gender/Body/Knowledge*.
9. For a brilliant analysis of the possibilities the Goddess as Spider Woman models for us, see Keller, *From a Broken Web*, Chapter 5, "The Spider's Genius," 216–252.
10. Sonia Johnson calls the attempt to re-gender the Bible by using female pronouns and throwing in a "Mother" here and there: "God in drag."
11. Yahweh is said to have "nursed" Israel from his "breast," and his name, El Shaddai, literally translates as "he, the breasted one." But not only is this an unnatural image for a man (it sounds like another case of "priestly piracy" to me), it should be noted that Yahweh fed *only* his own people while calling (in Deuteronomy) for the obliteration of other peoples, so he cannot count as a universal Model of nurturance and comfort.

There is much evidence in the Bible of priestly piracy. One example is giving the female name Shaddai, meaning "breasted one," to the male deity, and another is giving the female name Elohim to the Creator in Genesis. Elohim does not mean "Father God" in the original language but instead is the plural of Eloah, the name of a Semitic Mother Goddess. Elohim, the Creating Deity, then, is feminine plural. See Jann Aldredge Clanton, *In Whose Image? God* and Gender (New York: Crossroad, 1990), 21–22.

Of course, to describe womanly things as "base" is a compliment to those who hear this word as meaning *basic, or that on which everything else rests and depends.*

12. Calvin Luther Martin offers a succinct discussion of the development of priests as part of the ruling elite of a stratified society in Neolithic times, whereas no such roles existed before in gathering-hunting societies. See *In the Spirit of the Earth,* 40, 56.

13. Condren, *The Serpent and the Goddess,* 97, 144–53.

14. Condren gives marvelous examples of attempts by early Christians to explain the physical conception and birth of Jesus as a non-physical phenomenon in her *The Serpent and the Goddess,* 154–182.

15. *In a Chariot Drawn by Lions* is a full-length treatise by Asphodel P. Long on biblical Hokhmah as "the wisdom of God from the beginning" (the Greeks called Her Sophia). The author describes Wisdom's early many-faceted divine nature—akin to all other All-Mother Goddesses—and then details how She was slowly recast and diminished—the PATTERN we have come to recognize as typical—until eventually She was divided into two polar opposite personae: The Good Wisdom who dwells in heaven, the Bad Folly woman who tempts men on earth. The scholarship and choice of details in this book are extremely edifying.

Another book on this subject is Joan Chamberlain

Engelsman, *The Feminine Dimension of the Divine* (Philadelphia: Westminster Press, 1979), especially 74–120.

16. All information in this paragraph and its quotes come from Barbara Walker, *The Woman's Encyclopedia of Myths and Secrets,* 973, 929.

17. ibid., 495–496.

18. Julia Kristeva, *About Chinese Women,* trans. Anita Barrows (New York: Urizen Press, 1977). I learned about this phrase from Jean Graybeal, *Language and the Feminine in Nietzsche and Heidegger* (Bloomington, Ind.: Indiana University Press, 1990), 15–20, *passim.*

19. Graybeal, *Language and the Feminine in Nietzsche and Heidegger,* 15, 17.

20. Jane Gallop, *"Quand nos lèvres s'écrivent*: Irigaray's Body Politic," in *Romantic Review* 74 (1983): 30–31. Quoted in Arleen Dallery, "The Politics of Writing (The) Body: Écriture Féminine," in Jaggar and Bordo, eds., *Gender/Body/Knowledge,* 56.

21. Many feminists are suspicious of the concept of androgyny. Naomi Goldenberg writes in *The Changing of the Gods* that it is difficult to know what people mean when they speak about androgyny. "Carolyn Heilbrun uses the term in her book *Toward a Recognition of Androgyny* [but she] never really defines it at all." Goldenberg herself calls it "a tricky image which needs to be considered very carefully," for it subsumes all behavior into its non-specific amor-

phous area. She finds that its use is often an avoidance tactic and that it denies women their specific, unique experience as women.

Goldenberg continues by noting that Christians use it to mean what happens in the hereafter when there will be neither female nor male, but for now in this world she writes that "androgyny appears insubstantial—veiled in heavenly fluff—a rather impotent label to put on two sexes alive in this world." Naomi Goldenberg, *The Changing of the Gods,* 81.

Mary Daly, always forthright, writes that the word androgyny is a "vacuous term," a "trap" which expresses "pseudo-wholeness in its combination of distorted gender descriptions," and she disappointedly accuses those who foster the term as "misrepresenting" and "betraying" feminist thought about female oppression. Mary Daly, *Gyn/Ecology,* xi, 387.

Catherine Keller points out that "although androgyny has proved a valuable ideal for many feminists pointing beyond the restrictions of gender stereotype to the cultivation of the full range of human capacities by both sexes, . . . the very metaphor presupposes the recapitulation of stereotypical sex distinctions." Keller, *From a Broken Web,* 253 n.3.

John Rowan in *The Horned God,* a book on maleness, is also impatient with the goals of those who would promote androgyny; "I believe that men can cry and cry [feminize themselves] and still pull the trigger . . . [and] drop the bomb . . . just as women can become strong and fearless [masculinize themselves] and still let a man walk all over them. . . . None of this [androgyny] makes any difference to the patriarchal structure of our society," which is the real culprit. John Rowan, *The Horned God: Feminism and Men as Wounding and Healing* (London: Routledge and Kegan Paul, 1987), 64.

22. C. P. Mountford, *Ayers Rock* (Sydney, Australia: Angus & Robertson, 1965), 24.

23. From Merlin Stone's recounting of this story in her compilation of Goddess myths and stories from all over the world: *Ancient Mirrors of Womanhood,* 291–292.

24. N. M. Williams, *The Yolngu and Their Land* (Canberra, Australia: Australian Institute of Aboriginal Studies, 1986), 30.

25. N. Scott Momaday made this statement in an interview I heard on National Public Radio in December of 1989. I took down his words, but I don't remember any other details of the broadcast.

26. Gary Snyder, *The Old Ways,* 35.

Epilogue

1. Barry Lopez, *Crow and Weasel* (San Francisco: North Point Press, 1990), 48.

2. Huston Smith, *The World's Religions,* 369.

SUGGESTED READINGS

· · · · · · · · · ·

Adler, Margot. *Drawing Down the Moon: Witches, Druids, Goddess-Worshippers, and Other Pagans in America Today.* Boston: Beacon Press, 1979.

Allen, Paula Gunn. *Grandmothers of the Light: A Medicine Woman's Sourcebook.* Boston: Beacon Press, 1991.

———. *The Sacred Hoop.* Boston: Beacon Press, 1986.

Begg, Ean. *The Cult of the Black Virgin.* London: Routledge & Kegan Paul, Arkana, 1985.

Berger, Pamela. *The Goddess Obscured: Transformation of the Grain Protectress from Goddess to Saint.* Boston: Beacon Press, 1985.

Bolen, Jean Shinoda. *Goddesses in Every Woman: A New Psychology of Women.* New York: Harper & Row, 1984.

Chen, Ellen Marie. "Tao as the Great Mother and the Influence of Motherly Love in the Shaping of Chinese Philosophy" in *History of Religions,* Vol. XIV, #1, 1974–75: 51–63.

Christ, Carol. *Laughter of Aphrodite: Reflections on a Journey to the Goddess.* San Francisco: Harper & Row, 1987.

———. "Why Women Need the Goddess: Phenomenological, Psychological, and Political Reflections," in Charlene Spretnak, ed., *The Politics of Women's Spirituality.* New York: Anchor Books, 1982.

Christ, Carol, and Judith Plaskow, eds. *Womanspirit Rising: A Feminist Reader in Religion.* San Francisco: Harper & Row, 1979.

Clanton, Jann Aldredge. *In Whose Image? God and Gender.* New York: Crossroad, 1990.

Condren, Mary. *The Serpent and the Goddess: Women, Power, and Religion in Ancient Ireland.* San Francisco: Harper & Row, 1989.

Daly, Mary. *Gyn/Ecology: The Metaethics of Radical Feminism.* Boston: Beacon Press, 1978.

———. *Webster's First New Intergalactic Wickedary of the English Language,* Conjured by Mary Daly in Cahoots with Jane Caputi. Boston: Beacon Press, 1987.

Dexter, Miriam Robbins. *Whence the Goddesses: A Source Book.* New York and London: Teachers College Press, 1990.

Downing, Christine. *The Goddess: Mythological Images of the Feminine.* New York: Crossroad, 1984.

Eisler, Riane. *The Chalice and the Blade.* San Francisco: Harper & Row, 1987.

Ergener, Resit. *Anatolia: Land of Mother Goddess.* Ankara, Turkey: Hitit Publication, 1988.

Evans, Arthur. *The God of Ecstasy: Sex-Roles and the Madness of Dionysos.* New York: St. Martin's Press, 1988.

Forman, Frieda Johles, with Caoran Sowton, eds. *Taking Our Time: Feminist Perspectives on Temporality.* Oxford and New York: Pergamon Press, 1989.

Francia, Luisa. *Dragontime: Magic of Menstruation.* Woodstock, N.Y.: Ash Tree Publishing, 1988.

Gadon, Elinor. *The Once and Future Goddess: A Symbol for Our Time.* San Francisco: Harper & Row, 1989.

Gimbutas, Marija. *The Civilization of the Goddess: The World of Old Europe.* San Francisco: Harper, 1991.

———. *The Language of the Goddess: Unearthing the Hidden Symbols of Western Civilization.* San Francisco: Harper & Row, 1989.

Goldenberg, Naomi. *Changing of the Gods: Feminism and the End of Traditional Religions.* Boston: Beacon Press, 1979.

Hall, Nor, and Warren Dawson. *Broodmales: A Psychological Essay on Men in Childbirth—Introducing "The Custom of Couvade".* Dallas, Tex.: Spring Publications, 1989.

Hamilton, Annette. *Nature and Nurture: Aboriginal Child-Rearing in North-Central Arnhem Land.* Canberra: Australian Institute of Aboriginal Studies, 1981.

Harris, Marvin. *Our Kind: The Evolution of Human Life and Culture.* New York: Harper & Row, 1989.

Harrison, Jane Ellen. *Prolegomena to the Study of Greek Religion; Themis: A Study of the Social Origins of Greek Religion; and Epilegomena to the Study of Greek Religion.* Originally published in England by Cambridge University Press, 1911–1921.

Hart, Mickey. *Drumming at the Edge of Magic.* San Francisco: Harper, 1990.

Hillman, James. *Archetypal Psychology.* Dallas, Tex.: Spring Publications, 1983.

Jacobsen, Thorkild. *The Treasures of Darkness: A History of Mesopotamian Religion.* New Haven, Conn.: Yale University Press, 1976.

Jaggar, Alison, and Susan Bordo, eds. *Gender/Body/Knowledge: Feminist Reconstructions of Being and Knowing.* New Brunswick, N.J.: Rutgers University Press, 1989.

Johanson, Greg, and Ron Kurtz. *Grace Unfolding.* New York: Bell Tower, 1991.

Johnson, Buffie. *Lady of the Beasts: Ancient Images of the Goddess and Her Sacred Animals.* San Francisco: Harper & Row, 1988.

Johnson, Sonia. *Out of This World.* Estancia, N.M.: Wildfire Books, 1993.

Keller, Catherine. *From a Broken Web: Separation, Sexism, and Self.* Boston: Beacon Press, 1986.

Kelly, Mary B. *Goddess Embroideries of Eastern Europe* (Winona, Minn.: Northland Press, 1989).

Keuls, Eva C. *The Reign of the Phallus.* Berkeley, Los Angeles, London: University of California Press, 1993.

Knight, Chris. *Blood Relations: Menstruation and the Origins of Culture.* New Haven, Conn: Yale University Press, 1991.

LaChapelle, Dolores. *Sacred Land, Sacred Sex, Rapture of the Deep: Concerning Deep Ecology and Celebrating Life.* Silverton, Colo.: Finn Hill Arts, 1988.

Lauter, Estella, and Carol Rupprecht, eds. *Feminist Archetypal Theory: Interdisciplinary Re-Visions of Jungian Thought.* Knoxville: University of Tennessee Press, 1985.

Lawlor, Robert. *Earth Honoring: The New Male Sexuality.* Rochester, Vt.: Park Street Press, 1989.

Long, Asphodel P. *In a Chariot Drawn by Lions: The Search for the Female in Divinity.* London: The Women's Press, 1992.

Margulis, Lynn, and Dorion Sagan. *Microcosmos: Four Billion Years of Microbial Evolution.* New York: Summit Books, 1986.

Markale, Jean. Women of the Celts. Rochester, Vt.: Inner Traditions, 1986.

Marshack, Alexander. *The Roots of Civilization: The Cognitive Beginnings of Man's First Art, Symbol and Notation.* New York: McGraw-Hill, 1972.

Martin, Calvin Luther. *In the Spirit of the Earth: Rethinking History and Time.* Baltimore: Johns Hopkins University Press, 1992.

Mazis, Glen. *The Trickster, Magician, and Grieving Man: Reconnecting Men with Earth.* Santa Fe, N.M.: Bear & Co., 1993.

Mookerjee, Ajit. *Kali: The Feminine Force.* Rochester, Vt.: Destiny Books, 1988.

Nobel, Vicki. *Shakti Woman: Feeling Our Fire, Healing Our World—The New Female Shamanism.* San Francisco: Harper, 1993.

Oelschlaeger, Max, ed. *The Wilderness Condition: Essays on Environment and Civilization.* San Francisco: Sierra Club Books, 1992.

Owen, Lara. *Her Blood is Gold: Celebrating the Power of Menstruation.* San Francisco: Harper, 1993.

Paris, Ginette. *Pagan Meditations: The Worlds of Aphrodite, Artemis, and Hestia,* translated from the French by Gwendolyn Moore. Dallas, Tex.: Spring Publications, 1986.

Perera, Sylvia. *Descent to the Goddess: A Way of Initiation for Women.* Toronto: Inner City Books, 1981.

Shinell, Grace. "Women's Collective Spirit" in Charlene Spretnak, ed. *The Politics of Women's Spirituality.* New York: Anchor Books, 1982.

Shostak, Marjorie. *Nisa, The Life and Words of a !Kung Woman.* Cambridge, Mass.: Harvard University Press, 1981.

Sjöö, Monica, and Barbara Mor. *The Great Cosmic Mother: Rediscovering the Religion of the Earth.* San Francisco: Harper & Row, l987.

Snyder, Gary. *Old Ways.* San Francisco: City Lights Books, 1977.

Spretnak, Charlene. *Lost Goddesses of Early Greece: A Collection of Pre-Hellenic Myths.* Boston: Beacon Press, 1984.

———. *States of Grace: Reclaiming the Core Teachings and Practices of the Great Wisdom Traditions for the Well-Being of the Earth Community.* San Francisco: Harper, 1991.

———, ed. *The Politics of Women's Spirituality: Essays on the Rise of Spiritual Power Within the Feminist Movement.* New York: Anchor Books, 1982.

Starhawk. *Dreaming the Dark.*Boston: Beacon Press, 1982).

———. *The Spiral Dance: A Rebirth of the Ancient Religion of the Great Goddess.* San Francisco: Harper & Row, 1979.

Stone, Merlin. *When God Was a Woman.* New York: Harcourt Brace Jovanovich, 1976.

Vest, Jay H. "Will-of-the-Land: Wilderness Among Early Indo-Europeans" in Dolores LaChapelle, *Sacred Land, Sacred Sex, Rapture of the Deep: Concerning Deep Ecology and Celebrating Life.* Silverton, Colo.: Finn Hill Arts, 1988.

Walker, Barbara. *The Woman's Encyclopedia of Myths and Secrets.* San Francisco: Harper & Row, 1983.

———. *The Crone: Woman of Age, Wisdom, and Power.* San Francisco: Harper & Row, 1985.

Walters, Suzanna D. *Lives Together, Worlds Apart: Mother and Daughter in Popular Culture.* Berkeley and Los Angeles: University of California Press, l992.

Weed, Susun. *Wise Woman Herbal: Healing Wise.* Woodstock, N.Y.: Ash Tree Publishing, 1989.

———. *Menopausal Years.* Woodstock, N.Y.: Ash Tree Publishing, 1992.

Welch, Martha, M.D. *Holding Time: The Breakthrough Program for Happy Mothers and Loving, Self-Confident Children Without Tantrums, Tugs-of-War, or Sibling Rivalry.* New York: Simon & Schuster, 1988.

Wolkstein, Diane and Samuel Noah Kramer, *Inanna, Queen of Heaven and Earth: Her Stories and Hymns from Sumer.* New York: Harper & Row, l983.

INDEX

· · · · · · · · · ·